VERSATILE OPTIONS

Ceramic and natural stone tile surfaces add both functionality and beauty and can be used effectively both inside and outside a home. Whether you're looking for something as simple as tile for a kitchen floor, bathroom shower stall, or a patio, tile options range from basic choices to fully customized and handmade decorative pieces that are works of art in and of themselves.

At first glance setting tile may seem like a big job, and some installations are, but success with most tile jobs is a matter of common sense, getting good advice, practicing techniques unfamiliar, and following the instructions. Guiding you through the tiling process from design to execution is what *Tiling 1-2-3®* is all about. On the following pages you'll find more than 80 step-by-step installation, repair, and maintenance projects for your home. Each project has been reviewed by the experts at **The Home Depot®** to ensure that it's accurate and easy to follow so you can get the job done right the

tiling tips and good advice that will sa

every job easier.

Of course, some tiling jobs are be

to understand that you should not att

and experience until you're ready.

There's a great deal of personal s

the surfaces in your home. You'll add

sit on your patio or work at your kitc

something that the whole family can

Tiling 1-2-3

Meredith® Books Development Team
Project Editors: John P. Holms, Catherine M. Staub
Art Director: John Eric Seid
Writer: Charlie Wing
Illustrator: Jim Swanson
Copy Chief: Terri Fredrickson
Managers, Book Production: Pam Kvitne, Marjorie J. Schenkelberg
Contributing Designer: Tim Abramowitz
Contributing Copy Editor: Margaret Smith
Contributing Proofreaders: Steve Hallam, Gretchen Kauffman,
   Debra Morris Smith
Indexer: Kathleen Poole
Electronic Production Coordinator: Paula Forest
Editorial Assistants: Renee E. McAtee, Karen Schirm

Meredith® Books
Editor in Chief: James D. Blume
Design Director: Matt Strelecki
Managing Editor: Gregory H. Kayko
Executive Editor; Home Improvement and Garden: Benjamin W. Allen

Director, Retail Sales and Marketing: Terry Unsworth
Director, Sales, Special Markets: Rita McMullen
Director, Sales, Premiums: Michael A. Peterson
Director, Sales, Retail: Tom Wierzbicki
Director, Book Marketing: Brad Elmitt
Director, Operations: George A. Susral
Director, Production: Douglas M. Johnston

Vice President, General Manager: Jamie L. Martin

Meredith Publishing Group
President, Publishing Group: Stephen M. Lacy
Vice President, Finance & Administration: Max Runciman

Meredith Corporation
Chairman and Chief Executive Officer: William T. Kerr

Chairman of the Executive Committee: E. T. Meredith III

The Home Depot®
Senior Vice President, Marketing and Communications: Dick Sullivan
Marketing Manager: Nathan Ehrlich

Image Studios / Image I.T.
Account Executive: Lisa Egan
Set Building: Rick Nadke
Primary Photography: Bill Rein
Contributing Photography: John von Dorn
Assistant: Max Hermans
Production Manager: Jill Ellsworth
Account Representative: Cher King
Design Tile Consultant: Christine Myers,
   The Stem of Things, Appleton, WI

Note to the Reader: Due to differing conditions, tools, and individual skills, Meredith Corporation and The Home Depot® assume no responsibility for any damages, injuries suffered, or losses incurred as a result of following the information published in this book. Before beginning any project, review the instructions carefully, and if any doubts or questions remain, consult local experts or authorities. Because codes and regulations vary greatly, you always should check with authorities to ensure that your project complies with all applicable local codes and regulations. Always read and observe all of the safety precautions provided by any tool or equipment manufacturer, and follow all accepted safety procedures.

The editors of *Tiling 1-2-3®* are dedicated to providing accurate and helpful do-it-yourself information. We welcome your comments about improving this book and ideas for other books we might offer to home improvement enthusiasts. *Contact us by any of these methods:*

1 Leave a voice message at **800/678-2093**

2 Write to **Meredith Books, Home Depot Books, 1716 Locust Street, Des Moines, IA 50309–3023**

3 Send e-mail to **hi123@mdp.com**. Visit The Home Depot website at **homedepot.com**

Tiling 1-2-3

Floors

Walls

Countertops

Fireplaces

Decorating Ideas

Custom Design

Meredith
BOOKS

Tiling 1-2-3. TABLE OF CONTENTS

HOW TO USE THIS BOOK   PAGE 4

Chapter 1
DESIGNING WITH TILE
PAGE 6

8 Tile Grades	15 Pattern Gallery
9 Tile Size	17 Border Gallery
10 Color	18 Decorative Tile
12 Texture and Shape	20 Decorative Tile Gallery
14 Patterns	

Chapter 2
FLOORS
PAGE 24

26 Choosing Floor Tile	43 Evaluating a Concrete Slab
28 Tile Ratings	44 Leveling a Concrete Slab
30 Tools for Tiling Floors	45 Preparing Other Floors
31 Tools for Measuring and Laying Out	48 Laying Backerboard
32 Tools for Cutting and Shaping	50 Tile Layout
36 Tools for Setting and Grouting	51 Laying Out a Kitchen Floor
37 Tools for Cleanup	53 Laying Out Diagonal Patterns
37 Tools for Removal	55 More Layouts
38 Floor Tiling Materials	57 Marking Tile for Cutting
40 Project Planning	59 Cutting the Tile
41 Evaluating Wood Floors and Subfloors	61 Setting Tile
42 Reinforcing an Existing Framed Floor	63 Grouting and Sealing
	65 The Rustic Look of Tumbled Stone
	66 Building a Custom Shower Pan

Chapter 3
WALLS
PAGE 72

74 Choosing Wall Tile	84 Installing Backerboard
75 Tile Ratings	86 Tile Layout Lines
76 Tools for Tiling Walls	88 Marking and Cutting the Tiles
80 Wall Tiling Materials	90 Setting and Grouting
81 Project Planning	94 Tiling a Tub or Shower Surround
82 Preparing the Base	

Chapter 4
COUNTERTOPS
PAGE 98

100 Tile for Countertops	108 Laying Backerboard
102 Tools for Tiling Countertops	112 Marking and Cutting Tile
104 Countertop Tiling Materials	113 Setting the Tile
105 Project Planning	114 Grouting the Joints
106 Preparing the Base	115 Sealing the Joints
107 Tile Layout Lines	

Chapter 5

PATIOS

PAGE 116

118	Tile for Patios	
119	Choosing Patio Tile	
120	Tools for Tiling Patios	
122	Patio Tiling Materials	
122	Project Planning	
123	Evaluating the Slab	
124	Establishing Layout Lines	
126	Marking and Cutting Tile	
127	Mixing the Mortar	
128	Setting the Tile	
130	Grouting the Joints	
132	Using Cleft Stone Instead of Tile	

Chapter 6

MORE TILING PROJECTS

PAGE 134

136	Selecting Tile for Projects	
137	Tools	
138	Planning and Materials	
139	Techniques	
141	Coasters with Felt Backs	
142	Tiling a Tabletop	
144	Mural Backsplash	
146	Window Treatment	
148	Door Casing Rosettes	
149	Chair Rail	
150	Framed Mirror	
151	Staircase Risers	
152	Fireplace Surround	
156	Fireplace Hearth	
156	Stove Base	
158	Gas Stove Alcove	
160	Stove Heat Shield	
162	Plant Pot	
164	Bird Bath	
166	Garden Bench	
168	Tile Name Sign	
170	Wind Chimes	
172	Outdoor Checkerboard	

Chapter 7

MAINTENANCE AND REPAIR

PAGE 174

176	Maintenance	
178	Replacing Grout	
180	Replacing Expansion Joint Materials	
181	Diagnosing Cracks	
181	Isolating Cracks	
182	Removing Ceramic Tiles	
183	Replacing a Tile	

GLOSSARY PAGE 184

INDEX PAGE 188

ACKNOWLEDGMENTS

PAGE 192

HOW TO USE THIS BOOK

Professional tilesetters and store associates from The Home Depot® stores across the country created *Tiling 1-2-3*® to give homeowners a comprehensive and easy-to-follow guide to the most common tiling applications. Their expertise and years of experience guarantee successful completion of every job, from simple craft projects to tiling a shower stall. Clear instructions and step-by-step photography make every project accessible and easy to understand.

Chapter 1: Designing with Tile gets you started by introducing the dual functions of tile: as timeless building material and as a creative design element. The chapter begins by describing the physical properties of tile and introducing a rating system that helps you select the right tile for the job. Next it discusses the design elements of size, shape, texture, and color, as well as the myriad of patterns available for layout. The chapter ends with a gallery of design ideas illustrated by a range of decorative tiles.

Chapter 2: Floors tells you how to evaluate an existing floor as a base for

tile, how to upgrade the floor if necessary, and how to select a quality floor tile. It lists the tools required for cutting and setting tile and how to use each one. It takes you through tiling a kitchen floor, from establishment of layout lines to grouting and sealing. Finally it shows, step by step, how to tile a custom shower pan.

Chapter 3: Walls covers every step of tiling a wall, from selection, preparation, and laying out the design to final grouting and sealing. The process is illustrated by step-by-step photos of the tiling of a tub/shower surround.

Chapter 4: Countertops deals with the application of tile to kitchen and bathroom countertops. While typically smaller than a floor or wall application, a tiled countertop involves more attention to layout and requires trimming around sinks, backsplashes, and counter edges.

Chapter 5: Patios treats setting tile in outdoor areas differently from indoor applications due to their possible exposure to freeze/thaw conditions. The chapter shows how to apply conventional tile to an exterior concrete slab, as well as irregularly-

shaped (cleft) stone.

Chapter 6: More Tiling Projects offers additional useful and decorative applications ranging from simply cutting a large floor tile into coasters to tiling a fireplace surround. No matter what your skill level, you will find a fun project here.

Chapter 7: Maintenance and Repair shows you how to keep your installation in tip-top shape. And we've included a **Glossary** of tile terminology at the end of the book.

Finally: Even if you end up hiring a professional tilesetter this book will provide an overview that will be useful when negotiating contracts and giving final approval to a project.

UP TO CODE

Building codes are guidelines required by local authorities to make sure installations in your home are safe and will work properly. Do your research before you start actual work to make sure you're meeting code. A failed inspection can mean expensive alterations. When applying for permits, present precise drawings of your plans that are easy to read. Include a complete list of materials to be used in the project.

TRICKS OF THE TRADE

Tips from the pros at The Home Depot® are scattered throughout this book.
Their expert advice will help you successfully complete the projects in *Tiling 1-2-3*®.

 **WORK SMARTER**
Make smart work choices.

 **TIME SAVER**
Save time and money.

 TOOL TIP
Use specialty tools to their best advantage.

 **CLOSER LOOK**
Understand all the details.

 **UP TO CODE**
Make sure your work is legal.

 **GOOD IDEA**
Info you need to know <u>before</u> you begin.

 SAFETY ALERT!
Prevent unsafe situations.

 *Homer's Hindsight*
Avoid common mistakes.

 OOPS!
Fix common mistakes.
(Not that you'll make any.)

 **BUYER'S GUIDE**
Select the best materials.

GENERAL TILING SAFETY

If you use common sense and follow the instructions, you can do any tiling project safely and with confidence. But even tiling involves safety issues to consider, such as the fine, abrasive dust and sharp edges left when cutting a glass-like vitreous tile. It's essential to have a proper working environment.

Remember that safety is always your number one priority.

MORTAR IS CAUSTIC

The lime in mortar is alkaline and therefore caustic. We are all familiar with the dangers of working with acid. Alkalines are the chemical opposites of acids, but they are nearly as harmful to bare skin, as you will quickly discover if you neglect to wear gloves when handling mortar.

WORKING SAFELY

■ **Wear eye protection.** Safety goggles are an absolute must whenever cutting, drilling, hammering, or working above your head. They protect against flying chips, airborne particles, and splashing liquids. Get used to wearing them when you're working.

■ **Wear a respirator.** Airborne particles can damage your lungs. Use a dust respirator when cutting and shaping tile or stone and a respirator specified by the manufacturer when working with chemical solvents.

■ **Wear gloves.** Sturdy gloves are essential when working with mortar, chemical cleaners, sharp-edged objects, or heavy, awkward loads. Special gloves are designed for different types of protection. Wear rubber or plastic gloves resistant to chemicals. Wear heavy canvas or leather gloves when handling cutting tools and sharp objects.

■ **Wear good-quality work clothes.** Protect yourself from injury by wearing heavy clothing—especially long sleeves and long pants. Wear knee pads when working on the floor.

■ **Use the right tool.** Use the right tool for the job—a screwdriver isn't a cold chisel and an adjustable wrench isn't a hammer. Improper tool use can cause injuries and damage fixtures and equipment.

■ **Heed all Safety Alerts.** Safety alerts are placed in the book to remind you to work with care and caution.

TRUST THE EXPERTS

The experts at home centers and hardware stores are great resources for advice on projects and problems. Take advantage of their experience and skills.

QUALIFYING YOURSELF

Store associates at The Home Depot® qualify customers for tiling projects by asking some basic questions to get a sense of their abilities and interests.

QUALIFYING QUIZ

■ **Do you mind getting your hands and clothes dirty?** Tiling projects can get messy and always require a lot of cleanup; it's why the pros call mortar "mud."

■ **How about heavy lifting?** Individual tiles are not heavy, but cartons of tile and bags of mortar are. Enjoying physical labor is part of being a tilesetter.

■ **Do you like working with tools?** Most tiling projects involve a variety of basic tools. **Chapter Two** covers the basic tiling tools, but you will find more tool details in every chapter.

■ **How about a little geometry?** Thinking in terms of level, vertical, and dimensions (including fractions) will be a real asset when you are laying out projects.

■ **Are you willing to research projects and make a plan?** Doing your homework to develop an understanding of the process and scope of a project is essential. Learn the skills you'll need and explore all the safety issues before you start.

■ **Do you enjoy working on your house?** If you don't enjoy maintaining and improving your home, you may not want to get involved in tiling a floor or tub/shower surround.

■ **Do you know your limitations?** It's OK to admit that a particular project is a little beyond your current skill level. It's better to pay a professional to do a job you're not comfortable with rather than paying extra for one to fix your mistake.

DESIGNING WITH TILE

Tile is a perfect combination of functionality and artistic expression—it not only protects surfaces but adds beauty and color wherever it is used. In this chapter, as well as throughout the book, we will introduce you to a wide spectrum of design possibilities.

QUALITY IS THE KEY

Just as artists must consider quality of paint and paper or canvas to create lasting results, you should consider quality in selecting tile for a particular application. Strength and durability are not as important when tile is serving a decorative function, such as in a wall mural, but they are all-important where the tile will be exposed to heavy traffic or repeated freeze-thaw cycling. We will show you how to interpret tile ratings and provide selection guidelines for various applications.

CREATING YOUR DESIGN

Then on to the fun part—creating your design.

Designing in tile involves the variables of size, shape, color, and texture. We will show you the possibilities for each and provide some simple principles to help you create a pleasing design.

Most tile designs are mosaics (combinations) of individual tiles. The way in which tiles are arranged—the pattern—thus becomes a key design element. We've provided a gallery of patterns which you can use to spark your imagination.

TILE AS ART

Next, we'll show you how tile can be used as art. Thousands of artisans around the world offer thematic tiles of stunning creativity and beauty. Some of these tiles are of such beauty that, like pottery or sculpture, they can stand alone as works of art. Art tiles within a field of plain wall or floor tile are like gems in a jeweler's setting. We've included a gallery of examples to inspire you. Chapter Six, "Other Applications," will help you incorporate art tiles in an overall design.

CHAPTER ONE CONTENTS

8	Tile Grades		17	Border Gallery
9	Tile Size		18	Decorative Tile
10	Color		20	Decorative Tile Gallery
12	Texture and Shape			20 Murals
14	Patterns			21 Listellos
15	Pattern Gallery			22 Animals and Birds
				23 Aquatic Motifs

TILE GRADES

Tile consists of a body (the bisque) of clay and, most often, a surface coating of silicates and pigment (the glaze). The quality of the tile depends somewhat on the quality of the clay, but more on the temperature at which it has been fired. Low-temperature firing (as low as 1,000 degrees F) results in a porous bisque that absorbs water and a soft glaze that is easily abraded. High temperature firing (as high as 2,500 degrees F) produces a dense, impervious bisque and a hard glaze that will stand up to years of heavy traffic.

SIMPLIFYING THE RATINGS GAME

As an aid to do-it-yourselfers, Home Depot requires its suppliers to label floor tile cartons with the comprehensive grade label (above right). If you need help with interpreting the ratings or determining whether a tile can be used in your application, ask the tile salesperson for help.

WEAR AND WATER

The quality of tile used to be judged only by two ratings:

- Permeability to Water
- PEI (Porcelain Enamel Institute) Wear Rating

Permeability to Water is measured by a procedure specified by the American National Standards Institute (ANSI) and is expressed as a percentage by weight. The test consists of boiling the tile in water for 5 hours and dividing its gain in weight by its original dry weight. From most permeable to least permeable, the ratings are:

- nonvitreous, more than 7%
- semivitreous, 3–7%
- vitreous, 0.5–3%
- impervious, less than 0.5%

The PEI Wear Rating measures a tile's resistance to abrasion and its suitability for degrees of foot traffic:

1. no traffic, walls only (interior)
2. residential low traffic (interior)
3. all residential/medium commercial (interior)
4. heavy commercial (interior)
5. extra-heavy commercial (interior/exterior)

GRADING ART AND IMPORTED TILES

Art tile and many imported tiles are ungraded. That doesn't mean they can't be used, but it does mean that you should discuss your application with your tile supplier to make sure your choice is appropriate.

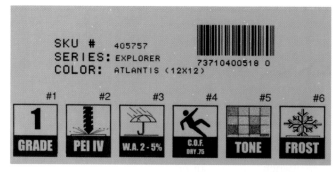

1 **GRADE:** #1 Standard—suitable for most applications; #2 Second—structurally similar to Standard, but with minor glaze or size imperfections; #3 Decorative—thin wall tile, suitable only for wall applications.

2 **PEI WEAR RATING:** 1,2—not suitable for floors (walls only); 3—all residential; 4—residential and light commercial (restaurants, etc.); 4+—commercial and heavy traffic (airports, public buildings, etc.).

3 **WATER ABSORPTION:** Percentage by weight: nonvitreous, more than 7%; semivitreous, 3–7%; vitreous, 0.5–3%; impervious, less than 0.5%. Only vitreous and impervious tiles should be used in wet and freeze/thaw applications.

4 **COEFFICIENT OF FRICTION:** The resistance to slip, expressed as horizontal force required to move an object across the tile, divided by its weight. The Americans with Disabilities Act (ADA) requires a minimum of 0.6 for dry floors.

5 **TONE:** The multishaded icon shows the tile has variations in tone. This is true of most tile, except for those of pure color, such as white or black. No tone variation is indicated if all squares are the same shade.

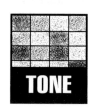

6 **FROST RESISTANCE:** A snowflake shows the tile is suitable for use in exterior freeze/thaw applications. It does not guarantee the tile won't lift, however, as that is also a function of the adhesive and the conditions when set.

TILE SIZE

The Tile Council of America lists standard sizes for modular tile (see the "Buyer's Guide" at right), but many imported tiles don't conform to these guidelines. American tile is sized in inches, while most imported tile is sized in centimeters (1 inch = 2.54 centimeters). Size can be nominal, with "8-inch" tile measuring anywhere from $7\frac{1}{2}$ inches to $8\frac{1}{2}$ inches. So the rule is "Let the buyer beware."

DETERMINING SIZE

Because of the variability and uncertainty of size, the first step in planning any installation is to measure an actual tile. This will help provide a rough estimate of the number of tiles needed.

Before establishing the final design you should lay out a row of 10 tiles, including spacers if you plan to use them, to determine the average dimension of the tile.

If the joints will be tightly spaced (which will magnify any alignment issues), make sure the size printed on the cartons is all the same. If the joint size will be $\frac{1}{4}$ inch or more, a small variation in size will not be apparent.

DESIGN GUIDELINES

The size of the tile is your choice, but a general rule is that it should be proportional to the space: large tile for a large space, small tile for a small space. Also, small tiles separated by contrasting grout can create a dynamic effect but might seem busy. You need to lay out enough tile to get a clear idea of how the pattern will work in your room. When the tile has to conform to a curved surface, you must use mosaic (2"×2" maximum) tile.

BUYER'S GUIDE

MODULAR SIZES OF CERAMIC TILE

Type	Shape	Height (in.)	Length × Width (in.)
Glazed Wall	Rectangle	$\frac{5}{16}$	3×6, $4\frac{1}{4}$×$4\frac{1}{4}$, 6×$4\frac{1}{4}$, 6×6, 6×8, 8×10
Mosaic	Rectangle	$\frac{1}{4}$	1×1, 2×1, 2×2
	Hexagon	$\frac{1}{4}$	1×1, 2×2
Paver	Rectangle	$\frac{3}{8}$	4×4, 6×6, 8×4
		$\frac{1}{2}$	4×4, 6×6, 8×4
Porcelain or Ceramic Floor	Rectangle	$\frac{3}{8}$	6×6, 6×12, 12×12, 13×13, 16×16
Quarry	Rectangle	$\frac{1}{2}$	3×3, 4×4, 6×3, 6×6, 8×4, 8×8
		$\frac{3}{4}$	6×6, 8×4

1 SMALL ROOM/SMALL TILE. Bathrooms and shower enclosures are two small spaces often tiled in mosaic (2"×2" or smaller) tile.

2 LARGE ROOM/LARGE TILE. The larger the room, the larger the tile. Tiles up to 24"×24" are available, but 12"×12" is the most common.

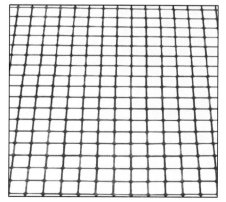

3 SMALL TILE WITH CONTRASTING GROUT accentuates the tile. Do this if the small size of the tile is an element of the design.

4 MOSAICS CAN CONFORM TO CURVES such as in tubs. Cut the mesh backing only as necessary to allow the tile to conform to the surface.

COLOR

olor affects your perception of space, alters your mood, hides a problem, or accentuates a feature. Using color effectively is a powerful design tool.

COORDINATING WALLS AND FLOORS

When creating a design, think of the floor as a fifth wall. Generally, a light floor makes a room seem larger, and a dark floor makes the same room smaller. If the floor contrasts with the walls, the floor will stand out. If it is similar in color, it will seem to disappear.

Remember, however, that changing the color of a wall is simply a matter of a new can of paint, but ripping up and replacing tile is much more involved. Considering the expense of installation, you may want to install a neutral color for the floor and leave the bold colors and accents to the furnishings and walls.

A few warnings:

- If your tile is uniform in color, make sure it is all from the same dye lot as printed on the carton.
- White may differ between manufacturers.
- Use white mortar under natural stone and under light-colored grout.

Do not damp cure tinted grout. Damp curing can dissolve the tint and leave an inconsistent color.

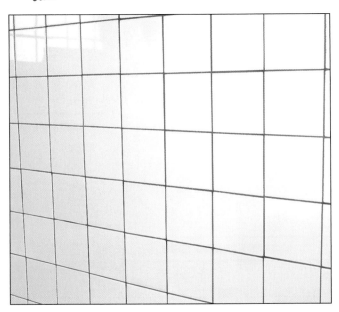

GROUT CAN BE A DESIGNER COLOR. Contrasting grout can make small tile seem busy, but designers sometimes use grout colors as a design element. If you use a colored grout, dry-mix all of the grout and dye before preparing the mortar to avoid color variation, or buy premixed, colored grout.

GROUT CAN BE THE SAME COLOR AS THE TILE. Most tile dealers can provide samples to help you match the color of the grout to the color of your tile. When the grout matches the tile, the individual tiles seem to disappear, and the floor becomes a uniform field. This is a useful technique when the floor is not a major design element.

GROUT CAN CONTRAST WITH THE TILE. When the color of the grout strongly contrasts with the color of the tile, the individual tiles stand out, making the floor a strong element in the room design. This is a useful technique when you wish to emphasize pattern. Other ways to emphasize pattern are to use two or more tile colors, sizes, or shapes.

LIGHT COLORS MAKE A ROOM SEEM COOL. Perhaps the reason is that snow and ice are white, perhaps that light colors reflect heat, but no matter what the reason, light and pastel colors are favored in hot climates. Many designers also feel light colors make a room seem larger.

DARK COLORS MAKE A ROOM WARM AND INTIMATE. Here the floor is light, but the dark walls are more visually present, making the room seem cozy. The darker table also seems to draw us to it, inviting us to sit down.

CONTRASTING COLORS MAKE THE FLOOR STAND OUT. With a strong contrast between floor and walls, especially with the vibrant hue of the floor, the floor becomes a strong element in the design of the space.

SIMILAR COLORS MAKE THE FLOOR RECEDE. The lilac floor is potentially a strong visual element, but when the walls are painted the same color, the floor nearly disappears. However, the room certainly conveys a mood.

TEXTURE AND SHAPE

Texture and shape are as important as color in the overall effect of a tile design. Glossy glazed tile invokes a cold, bright, clean feeling. Matte-finish glazed tile looks more natural. Roughly-textured tile, especially when not sealed with a surface-type coating, has a totally natural feel. And handmade Saltillo tiles from Mexico evoke a human and earthy feeling, often preserving fingerprints and animal tracks.

Texture has added ramifications. Gloss tiles are often used on the walls in kitchens and baths because they are easily cleaned. A gloss finish is not desirable for floor tiles—because it can be slippery when wet.

Shape is a purely visual element. An isolated irregular shape within a regulated pattern jumps out and grabs your attention. Different shapes, set into a field of regular tile, can form a pattern themselves, draw attention to a direction or feature, or form a border.

Tiles can be purchased as squares, rectangles, hexagons (six sides), or octagons (eight sides). Triangles are easily made by cutting squares on the diagonal.

ROUGH TILES FOR TRACTION. A wet tile floor can be dangerous if too glossy. Be sure to check the Coefficient of Friction on the tile's grade label (see page 8) for kitchen and bathroom floors. A static coefficient of at least 0.6 is recommended.

GLOSSY TILES HIDE COLORS AND CAUSE GLARE. Light reflected from the tile surface masks the tile's own colors, no matter how vibrant. Gloss tiles are excellent for kitchen and bath walls, however, because they are easy to clean.

MATTE GLAZED TILE LOOKS MORE NATURAL. A tile cast with a matte finish reduces glare, allowing the tile to show its true colors. The texture of the finish also increases traction, so matte finish tiles are perfect for floors.

HONED, POLISHED, AND TUMBLED STONE. Granite can be polished as smooth and hard as glass with sharp edges, while tumbled marble has a water-worn and rounded look. Polished stone is formal; honed and tumbled is informal.

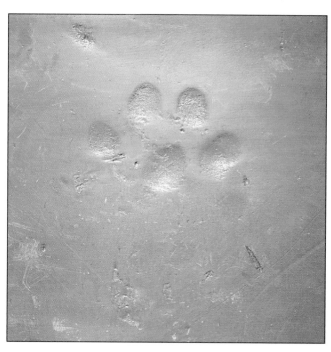

HANDMADE TILES LOOK MORE RUSTIC. If you want a warm, earthy, country look, consider terra-cotta tiles. If you're lucky, Saltillo tiles from Mexico will often contain animal tracks, invoking a feeling of the American Southwest.

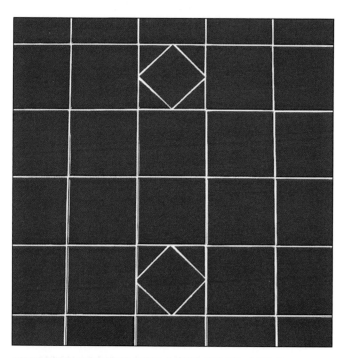

DIFFERENT SHAPE MAKES A TILE STAND OUT. The most common trick is to set a smaller square tile diagonally within a regular tile space. Another way is to use a full-size diagonal tile with notches cut out of the four surrounding tiles.

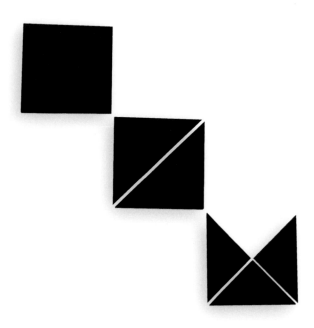

CUT TILE IN TWO TO MAKE TRIANGLES. Making triangles is easy if you have a wet saw. Simply cut a square tile into two or four pieces. You can also use a snap cutter, but the edges will probably require smoothing.

PATTERNS

If you want the tile to have design interest of its own, set it in a pattern instead of a plain grid.

CREATING PATTERNS

Patterns are created using one or more of the variables of **shape**, **size**, **color**, or **texture**. Modular tile of differing sizes may be set in any of dozens of repetitive patterns, and tile of identical size and shape but different color may be set in the same patterns with even more dramatic effect. An alternative is a plain field of tiles, framed by a decorative border.

EXPERIMENT WITH JOINT ALIGNMENT

Rectangular tiles set end-to-end create a linear pattern. Running the lines lengthwise adds depth to a room; running the lines crosswise makes a room seem shorter and wider. Using tiles of different color enhances both effects.

Tiles run diagonally create a tension which can be contained by a border.

MAKE A TILE BORDER

Borders can either frame a field of tiles, making it more interesting, or divide the tiled surface into different areas.

As with patterns, a border can be created with ordinary tiles of contrasting shape, size, color, or texture. Below, a plain floor of light-colored tile is simply and effectively framed with a border of darker tile.

LISTELLOS PROVIDE RELIEF

A whole category of tile termed "listellos" is designed specifically for the creation of borders. Listellos for floors are typically long mesh-backed strips of mosaic tile designed to lie flush with the surface. Listellos for walls are generally thicker than wall tile so the border stands out in relief as well as design and/or color.

ADD MOSAICS OR MEDALLIONS

Decorative tiles in the form of ready-made mosaics or medallions add interest and a personal touch to walls, floors, and countertops. You can also create your own mosaics or medallions from stock tile.

LENGTHWISE TILES add depth to a room in the direction of the tiles.

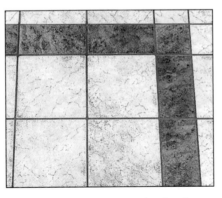

FRAMING PLAIN TILE with a border adds elegance to any floor.

LISTELLOS separate this wall into upper and lower areas, like a chair rail.

CROSSWISE TILES make a room seem shorter and wider.

LISTELLOS AND DECORATIVE TILE lend elegance to this bathroom wall.

COLORFUL LISTELLOS add warmth and charm to a kitchen wall.

PATTERN GALLERY

When buying tile for patterns, first determine the **repeat**, which is the smallest arrangement of tiles that, when combined, create the pattern. Then, determine the percentage area covered by each type of tile and multiply that percentage by the entire area of the room. The result is the area each of those types of tiles covers. Sample patterns and the percentages of each kind of tile are shown on the following pages. Percentages are rounded to the nearest whole number. Look on the boxes the tile comes in to see how much area the tile in each box covers. Buy enough to cover the area of the room for each kind of tile, and get 10 percent more in case the tiles break during installation or if you need to cut tiles for the edge of a pattern. If you have some left over, store them so you can replace tiles that crack with exact matches to the originals.

Dark: 50%   Light: 50%

Dark: 50%   Light: 50%

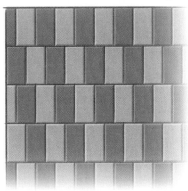

Dark: 50%   Light: 50%

Dark: 50%   Light: 50%

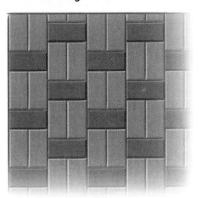

Dark: 33%   Light: 67%

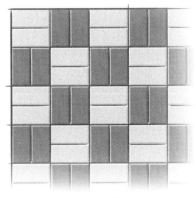

Dark: 50%   Light: 50%

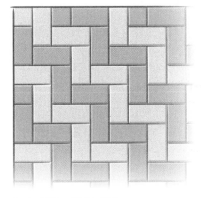

Dark: 50%   Light: 50%

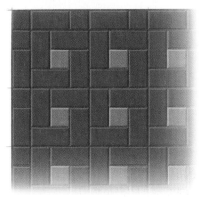

Dark: 89%   Light: 11%

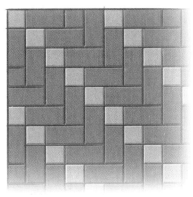

Dark: 80%   Light: 20%

Dark Square: 58%   Light Square: 12%
Dark Rectangle: 22%   Light Rectangle: 8%

PATTERN GALLERY *(CONTINUED)*

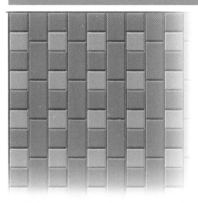

Dark Square: 25% **Light Square: 25%**
Rectangle: 50%

Rectangle: 67% **Square: 33%**

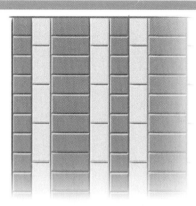

Dark Square: 20% **Dark Rectangle: 40%**
Light Rectangle: 40%

Large Square: 80% **Small Square: 20%**

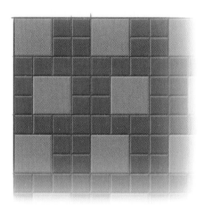

Large Square: 33% **Small Square: 67%**

Large Square: 50% **Small Square: 50%**

Small Square: 25% **Large Square: 50%**
Rectangle: 25%

Small Square: 20% **Large Square: 40%**
Rectangle: 40%

Small Square: 4% **Large Square: 64%**
Rectangle: 32%

Small Square: 10% **Large Square: 40%**
Rectangle: 50%

Small Dark Square: 17%
Large Dark Square: 33%
Large Light Square: 33%
Rectangle: 17%

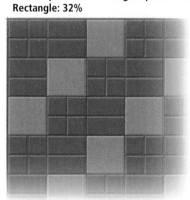

Small Dark Square: 17%
Small Light Square: 17%
Large Dark Square: 33%
Rectangle: 33%

16

BORDER GALLERY

Whether on a wall or floor, borders help define space and create visual boundaries. Borders offer a variety of opportunities to add color and style to a room.

BORDER OPTIONS

Border tiles can match the texture and color of the field tiles

GET PROFESSIONAL HELP

Measuring a room for tile can be confusing. Use the experts at your home center or tile store to help you come up with a realistic estimate of what you will need.

that make up the body of the installation or can be comprised of a contrasting color scheme and a different textural feeling. More complex variations can include adding occasional accent tiles or creating a border made entirely of decorative, highly glazed, or hand-painted, custom-made variations.

Borders with complex patterns and mosaics can be also be purchased preassembled and attached to a net backing that makes installation a breeze.

CALCULATE YOUR NEEDS

Borders that run around the edge of an installation are often easier to plan and install than some of the intricate combinations required for complex floor patterns.

To calculate the amount of tiles you'll need for the border, measure each tile that will make up the border pattern; then measure the perimeter of the room. Multiply the number of tiles needed for each foot of the perimeter by the total perimeter feet. Add in a 10% overage. Calculate the area for the field tiles as explained on page 15.

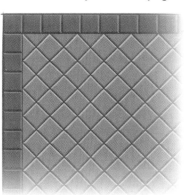

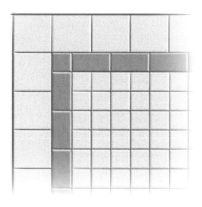

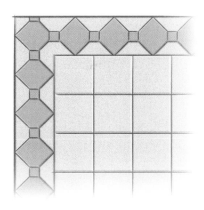

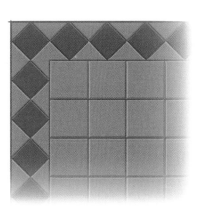

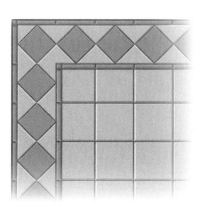

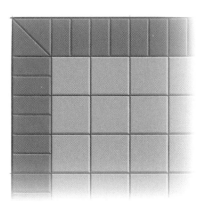

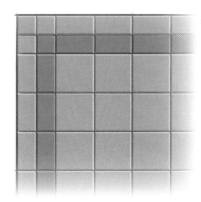

DECORATIVE TILE

Tiles fall into two categories: field and decorative. Field tiles are the basic, mass-produced tiles purchased by the carton to cover walls and floors. Decorative art tiles are produced in smaller quantity, often by individual artisans, and are usually either painted or embossed with a design.

Decorative tile allows you to personalize your design. It can tell a story, express an interest or hobby, be funny, or serve as a stand-alone work of art.

WHERE TO FIND DECORATIVE TILE

Home centers and carpet and tile stores carry a wide array of field tile and a limited variety of decorative tile. Specialty tile stores carry more decorative tile and can order more through their suppliers' catalogs. Most also display samples from local tile makers and may be able to arrange a visit to a studio. Finally, search the Internet for "tile," as many artisans have their own websites displaying photographs of their work. See page 192 for information on contacting manufacturers of the tiles pictured.

SOME TILES ARE SO BEAUTIFUL they can stand alone as pieces of art. Collect individual tiles that remind you of places you have lived, places you have visited, and places in your heart.

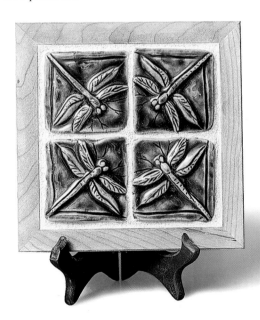

MAKE A TRIVET, OR HOT PLATE, of either a single 8"×8" tile, or set a group of smaller tiles into a frame. This trivet serves both as a hot plate and as a dining room table decoration.

A LARGER TRIVET, or a piece of art to be hung on the wall or set on a table. This design consists of sixteen leaf-motif 2"×2" tiles.

A CONCEPT BOARD can give you a good idea of the finished design. If done neatly you can later hang it as a piece of art.

ART TILES ADD FLAIR even to plain concrete. Here small tiles are cast into a birdbath and a large tile decorates the base. The project on pages 164–165 shows how to set art tile into an ordinary concrete birdbath purchased at a home and garden center.

A COLLECTION of dinosaur-motif tiles rings this lap pool. Clearly, the owner has a special interest in dinosaurs.

THIS CUSTOM RANGE-BACK MURAL, with its wheat stalks, pussy willows, and cattails, integrates its owner's interests in food and nature. The rustic and timeless look in the field tiles and the mural comes from the use of tumbled marble.

19

DECORATIVE TILE GALLERY

MURALS

Murals are scenes displayed on walls. The scene can be painted and baked on a set of tiles, rather than painted directly on a wall. While most murals are intended as decoration for walls, much like hanging pictures, the realistic "oriental rug" at bottom right is set on a floor.

Some artisans will create a mural from a photograph or sketch that you provide. See page 192 for information on contacting manufacturers of the tiles pictured.

▼ **SCREEN PRINTED LITHOGRAPHY MURAL**

LISTELLOS

Listellos form borders. Those intended for floors are usually flush, net-backed mosaics with repeating patterns. The repeating pattern and modular widths and lengths simplify installation, allowing creation in a few hours of a design that would otherwise take days or weeks.

Listellos for walls often have raised relief and are used for cornice moldings, mural frames, chair rails, to break a wall into sections or add visual interest. See page 192 for information on contacting manufacturers of the tiles pictured.

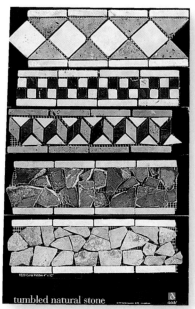

tumbled natural stone

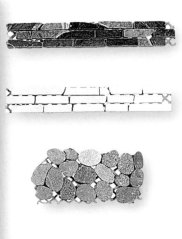

▼ PHOTO TRANSFER LISTELLOS AND FIELD TILE

▼ DECORATIVE LISTELLOS

▼ MOLDED LIMESTONE LISTELLOS

ANIMALS AND BIRDS

Animals and birds are favorite themes of decorative tile makers. Birds and other forms of wildlife indigenous to an area are timeless. Use these to bring nature into your kitchen or bathroom year-round. Some are intended for children's bathrooms (see Noah's Ark below and the cow jumping over the moon on page 20). However, a tile motif that is perfect for younger children may not work as well as they become teenagers. A fourteen-year old is probably not going to appreciate nursery rhyme tiles. Better to set the tiles on a hanging backing so they can be taken down and brought out again for your grandchildren.

The alphabet tiles at right can be set into concrete or on plywood to display names and addresses. (See the name project on pages 168–169.) See page 192 for information on contacting manufacturers of the tiles pictured.

▼ **HAND-PAINTED CERAMIC TILES** ▶

▼ **HAND-PAINTED RELIEF CERAMIC TILES**

AQUATIC MOTIFS

Aquatic motifs are popular in bathrooms, especially in tub and shower surrounds.

Designs can be expressed in several ways. All of the tiles in the top three groups use raised relief but a single color; the four at bottom left use color only; while the four at bottom right use both color and raised outlines. See page 192 for information on contacting manufacturers of the tiles pictured.

▼ HANDMADE LISTELLOS AND ▶ FIELD TILES

▼ GLASS TILES

▼ HAND-PAINTED CERAMIC TILES

2 FLOORS

Tile is elegant, versatile, permanent, easy to clean, and timeless in appearance. Vinyl floors can provide the look of tile and are typically less expensive, but you might be surprised at how close tile and a high-quality vinyl floor are in cost—particularly if you install the tile yourself. Before the development of modern thin-set mortars and cement backerboards, setting tile required specialized knowledge and skills. Today, however, setting tile requires only that you choose a type appropriate to the purpose and that you follow manufacturer's directions explicitly.

Designing and setting your own tile floor is truly a creative experience. There are hundreds of tiles from which to choose and limitless patterns into which they can be arranged. To get you off to the right start, attend a tile-setting workshop at a home center and then go to work.

CHAPTER TWO CONTENTS

26   **Choosing Floor Tile**

28   **Tile Ratings**

30   **Tools for Tiling Floors**

31   **Tools for Measuring and Laying Out**

32   **Tools for Cutting and Shaping**

     33   Using a Wet Saw

     35   Using a Snap Cutter

     35   Using Tile Nippers

     35   Using a Carbide Bit or Hole Saw

36   **Tools for Setting and Grouting**

37   **Tools for Cleanup**

37   **Tools for Removal**

38   **Floor Tiling Materials**

     38   Backerboard and Fasteners

     38   Membranes

     39   Adhesives

     39   Grouts

     39   Sealers

40   **Project Planning**

     40   Special Height Considerations

41   **Evaluating Wood Floors and Subfloors**

42   **Reinforcing an Existing Framed Floor**

43   **Evaluating a Concrete Slab**

44   **Leveling a Concrete Slab**

45   **Preparing Other Floors**

46   **Laying Backerboard**

50   **Tile Layout**

51   **Laying Out a Kitchen Floor**

53   **Laying Out Diagonal Patterns**

55   **More Layouts**

     55   Small Room

     55   Combination Room

     56   Connected Rooms

57   **Marking Tile for Cutting**

     57   Marking Holes

     58   Marking Straight & L-Cuts

     58   Marking Notches

     58   Marking Complex Cuts

59   **Cutting the Tile**

     59   Straight & L-Cuts

     59   Cutting Notches

     60   Curved Cuts

     60   Cutting Holes

     60   Smoothing Edges

61   **Setting Tile**

63   **Grouting and Sealing**

65   **The Rustic Look of Tumbled Stone**

66   **Building a Custom Shower Pan**

CHOOSING FLOOR TILE

Floor tiles come in many varieties. The thing to remember is that not all floor tile is equal. This information is intended to expose you to the variety of tile available for possible consideration. It's also meant to keep you from selecting tile that is unsuited to your particular application.

Your first task is to determine the look you wish to achieve. Look in design magazines and books, look at your friends' and neighbors' tile floors, and look in public buildings and restaurants. Read the materials to learn the names of the types and the specifications. Visit tile outlets to see what is available and at what price. Finally, ask. A knowledgeable salesperson, especially one who has set tile for a living, can save you money, much labor, and possible disappointment.

FLOORS

▶ **GLAZED TILES** are generally machine-made of clay, pressed in a die, and fired in a kiln. The glaze, a mixture of ground glass and metal oxides, adds color and a hard surface.

Many glazed tiles are intended for wall installation, so check the grade ratings carefully before using on a floor. The rule is, "You can use a floor tile on a wall, but not a wall tile on a floor." Before you purchase floor tile for use on a wall, however, be aware that there are generally no trim pieces for floor tile.

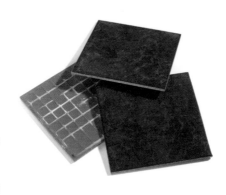

◀ **PORCELAIN TILES** are made of highly refined clay and fired at very high temperatures. As a result they are dense and hard, so they wear well, even under heavy traffic. They are also among the most water-resistant tiles, so they can be used in constantly wet and exterior freezing conditions. Most ceramic mosaic tile (2"×2" and smaller) is porcelain.

Through-body porcelain tiles are uniform in color throughout, so there is no danger of their colors wearing off.

▶ **QUARRY TILE** gets its name from originally being quarried stone, but today most quarry tile is clay extruded through a die, cut to size, and fired in a kiln. The result is an extremely hard, unglazed, low-cost tile ideal for flooring. Most quarry tile can be used outdoors, even in freeze/thaw areas. Check the "Frost Resistance" rating (see pages 8 and 28).

TERRA-COTTA TILES are made of unrefined natural clay fired at very low temperatures. Because they require little equipment or energy to produce, most is produced in Mexico.

Their appeal lies in their low cost and their rustic hand-made charm. Low density and high water absorption, however, dictate frequent sealing to prevent staining and prohibit use in freeze/thaw situations.

If you want to see a good example, visit any chain Mexican restaurant.

NATURAL STONE includes granite, marble, and slate. Granite and marble are available in polished (very shiny but slippery) and honed (dull and less slippery) finishes. Tumbled marble tiles have an antique, rustic look and are the least slippery. Slate has a natural cleft surface and provides good traction.

Stone, except for some granite, is porous and requires periodic sealing. Get specific advice on cleaners and grouts since many stones can be stained or etched by the common products.

CEMENT-BODIED TILES are made of mortar, not clay, and are cured, not fired. They can be made to resemble brick, glazed tile, or stone and are very durable. Since the color is added to the mortar, it runs through the tile and cannot wear off.

Cement-bodied brick, a variety of cement-bodied tile made to look like real brick, comes in two sizes: that of the face of a common brick, and that of its side. They can be used to "brick" concrete patios and concrete block fireplaces.

27

TILE RATINGS

Any tile that strikes your fancy may be used on walls in dry locations, but floor tiles require special consideration. Four qualities need to be considered:

- **PEI WEAR RATING:** The tile's resistance to abrasion and, therefore, its suitability for foot traffic.

- **WATER ABSORPTION:** The percentage of water the tile can absorb, a measure of its suitability for wet areas such as shower stall floors.

- **COEFFICIENT OF FRICTION:** Slip resistance of a tile (scale of 0 to 1.0), measuring safety for steps, walks, and wet areas such as kitchen and bathroom floors.

- **FROST RESISTANCE:** Whether a tile is warranted against damage by freezing and thawing.

All floor tiles carried by Home Depot display a rating label on their cartons such as that on the right. Use the label to determine—with the sales associate—a tile's suitability for your application.

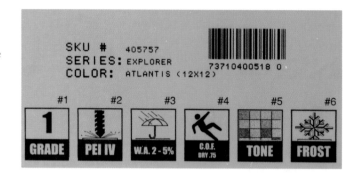

GRADE: #1 Standard—suitable for most applications; #2 Second—structurally similar to #1, but with minor glaze or size imperfections; #3 Decorative—thin wall tile, suitable only for wall applications.

PEI WEAR RATING: 1,2—not suitable for floors (walls only); 3—all residential; 4—residential and light commercial (restaurants, etc.); 4+—commercial and heavy traffic (airports, public buildings, etc.).

WATER ABSORPTION: Percentage by weight: nonvitreous, more than 7%; semivitreous, 3–7%; vitreous, 0.5–3%; impervious, less than 0.5%. Only vitreous and impervious tiles should be used in wet and freeze/thaw applications.

COEFFICIENT OF FRICTION: The resistance to slip, expressed as horizontal force required to move an object across the tile, divided by its weight. The Americans with Disabilities Act (ADA) requires a minimum of 0.6 for dry floors.

TONE: The multishaded icon shows the tile has variations in tone. This is true of most tile, except for those of pure color, such as white or black. No tone variation is indicated if all squares are the same shade.

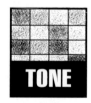

FROST RESISTANCE: A snowflake shows the tile is frost-resistant and is suitable for use in exterior freeze/thaw applications. It does not guarantee the tile won't lift, however, as that is also a function of the adhesive and the conditions when set.

CLOSER LOOK

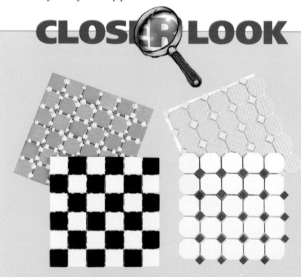

CERAMIC MOSAIC TILE

Small porcelain tiles, measuring from ¼"×¼" to 2"×2", that are squares, hexagons, and octagons are known as "ceramic mosaic tile." They are extremely hard, dense, and impervious to water, and are thus well suited for both wet and exterior freeze/thaw applications.

The tiles come in sheets, held together with a mesh backing or a paper face. Each has an advantage and a disadvantage. The mesh backing makes it easy to see the design and to grout, but weakens the mortar adhesion. The paper face makes it difficult to see the design, but is easily removed with water after the tile is set.

FLOORS

RATING GUIDELINES FOR RESIDENTIAL FLOORS

CONDITIONS/ TYPICAL AREAS	GRADE	PEI	WATER ABSORPTION	COEFFICIENT OF FRICTION	TONE	FROST PROOF YES/NO
Interior, light traffic (sunspace, living, dining)	1or 2	3+	any	any	any	No
Interior, heavy traffic (entrance, stairs, hall)	1or 2	3+	any	0.6 minimum	any	No
Interior, occasionally wet (bathroom, kitchen)	1or 2	3+	less than 7%	0.6 minimum	any	No
Interior, constantly wet (tub, shower, pool)	1or 2	3+	less than 3%	0.6 minimum	any	No
Exterior, warm climate (patio, walkway, stairs)	1or 2	3+	any	0.6 minimum	any	No
Exterior, freeze/thaw (patio, walkway, stairs)	1or 2	3+	less than 0.5%	0.6 minimum	any	Yes

A+ WORK SMARTER

BACK-BUTTERING FOR AN EXTRA GOOD BOND

A thin, combed adhesive bed requires that the back side of the tile is flat and fairly smooth. If the tile is warped or uneven, as is often the case with terra-cotta or rough stone, you should back-butter the tile. Comb the adhesive on the setting surface with a square notched trowel as usual. Then spread and press a small amount of adhesive on the back of each tile with the flat side of the notched trowel. This accomplishes two things: First, it ensures maximum adhesion because both of the surfaces are wet completely. Second, it creates a thicker bed to fill in the irregularities.

TOOLS FOR TILING FLOORS

Tools come in a wide range of quality and durability. Professional tools can last a lifetime if properly cared for; they are quite expensive. Many home centers carry **good, better,** and **best** tools for most jobs. **Good** tools are for small one-time jobs; **better** tools are often those carrying the store label; and **best** are the ones the professionals use.

BUY OR RENT?

Some people collect tools and derive great satisfaction from having a complete workshop. They feel that, no matter what happens, they have the knowledge and equipment to deal with it.

If you are not that type, realize that nearly any tool can be rented. Your question should be, "How many times will I ever have need for this tool?" If the purchase cost divided by the rental cost is greater than the number of times you will use the tool, then rent it.

TOOL MAINTENANCE

How long a tool will last depends on two things: the quality of the tool and how well you care for it. The best tool in the world will be rendered useless in short order if you leave it exposed to the elements. This is especially true of tiling tools, such as trowels and mortar mixing paddles, which come into contact with wet mortar. Acrylic-modified thin-set mortar and epoxy adhesives are so tenacious, you will damage a tool trying to remove them once they have set or cured. Remember: the job is not finished until your tools are clean.

BUYER'S GUIDE

TOOL	USE FOR	RELATIVE PRICE, $	HOW IMPORTANT
MEASURING AND LAYING OUT			
Chalk line	layout, cut lines	$	must have
Framing square	establishing square	$$	must have
China marker	marking tile cuts	$	can use felt tip or pencil
Tape measure	measuring	$	must have
Combination square	marking tile cuts	$$	nice to have
4-foot level	establishing level, vertical	$$	can use smaller level
CUTTING AND SHAPING			
Carbide (glass) bit	small holes in tile	$$	only for small holes
Carbide hole saw	large holes in tile	$$	by size of hole
Carbide-grit rod saw	curved tile cuts	$$	nice to have
Rotary grinding tool	smoothing cut edges	$$$	nice to have
Snap cutter	straight tile cuts	$$$	must, or wet saw
Tile nippers	intricate tile cuts	$$	must have
Wet saw	straight tile cuts	$$$	nice to have
SETTING AND GROUTING			
Caulking gun	caulking joints	$	must have
½-inch drill	mixing adhesives	$$$	must have
Foam paintbrushes	applying sealer	$	must have
Grout bag	grouting more than ½" joints	$	must for large joints
Grout float	spreading grout	$$	must have
Margin trowel	mixing/spreading grout	$	nice to have
Notched trowel	applying mortar	$$	must have
Mortar mixing paddle	mixing grout	$$	must have
CLEANUP			
Clean, soft cloth	removing haze	$	must have
Round-corner sponge	removing excess grout	$	must have
Nonabrasive pad	removing excess grout	$	must have
REMOVAL			
Bricklayer's chisel	removing tile, old adhesive	$$	nice to have
Claw hammer	striking chisels, punch	$$	must have
Cold chisel	breaking tile	$	must have
Grout saw	removing old grout	$	must have
Point punch	breaking tile	$	nice to have
PROTECTION			
Chemical Respirator	respiratory protection	$$	must have
Dust Respirator	respiratory protection	$	must have
Ear plugs	hearing protection	$	must have
Knee pads	knee protection	$	nice to have
Rubber gloves	hand protection	$	must have
Safety glasses	eye protection	$	must have

TOOLS FOR MEASURING AND LAYING OUT

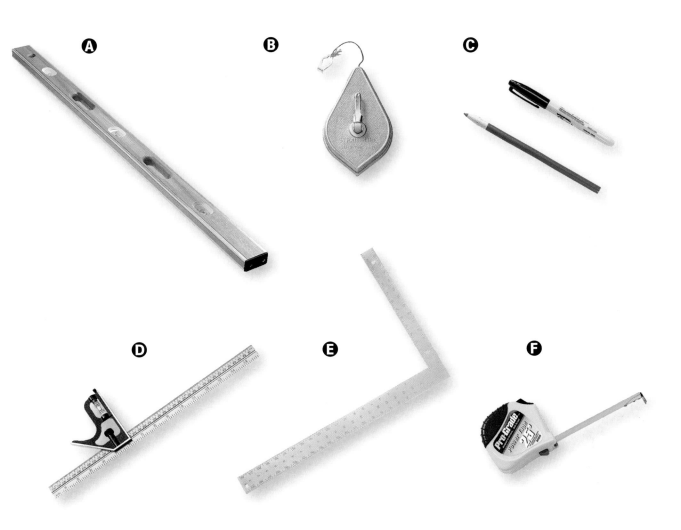

Ⓐ 4-FOOT LEVEL
Used primarily to establish level and vertical. Can also be used as a straightedge in marking and determining evenness of a floor.

Ⓑ CHALK LINE
Used to snap tile and backerboard layout lines on floors and walls. Powdered chalk comes in red, orange, and blue, so a second set of lines can be snapped without removing the first.

Ⓒ CHINA MARKER (WAX PENCIL)
Used to make temporary cut marks on the face of a tile. Better than permanent felt-tip marker because it's easily removed.

Ⓓ COMBINATION SQUARE
Used primarily as a guide for marking straight, notch, and L-shaped cuts on tiles.

Ⓔ FRAMING SQUARE
Can be used as a straightedge for cutting, for establishing perpendicular, for measuring and laying out, and for aligning small tiles in a rectangular pattern.

Ⓕ TAPE MEASURE
For all measurement tasks, from the width of a joint, to the dimensions of a tile, to the dimensions of the whole floor.

TOOLS FOR CUTTING AND SHAPING

A

B

C

D

E

F

G

H

I

J

K

FLOORS

A CARBIDE HOLE SAW
Drills larger holes through tiles, such as for water pipes. Available in a variety of sizes.

B CARBIDE (GLASS) BIT
Drills small holes through tiles, such as for telephone wires, and for starting larger holes to be cut with rod saw.

C CARBIDE-GRIT ROD SAW
Used for intricate cuts in soft tile only. The rod can be removed and fed through a hole made by a carbide bit to make large, enclosed holes.

D DUST RESPIRATOR
Wear respirators when working with mortar and chemical powders.

E EAR PLUGS
Protect hearing from damaging sounds such as power tools.

F ROTARY CUTTING AND GRINDING TOOL
Smooths and bevels sharp tile edges. Cuts tile with special attachments.

G SAFETY GLASSES
Wear safety glasses when working with hand and power tools.

H SNAP CUTTER
Used for scoring and snapping tiles in straight lines.

I SPIRAL SAW
Quickly and easily cuts soft wall tile.

J TILE NIPPERS
Make curved or intricate cuts by nibbling tile away.

K WET SAW
The fastest, cleanest way to make straight, notched, and L-shaped cuts. With practice, can be used to make intricate cuts.

USING A WET SAW

STRAIGHT CUTS

1 **WEAR SAFETY GLASSES,** because floor tile is brittle and shatters like glass; wear ear plugs for repetitive cuts. Don't wear gloves because they may be pulled into the blade.

2 **HOLD TILE FIRMLY WITH BOTH HANDS.** Advance the tile steadily into the blade, using the fence as a guide. Slow toward the end to avoid chipping the tile.

NOTCHES

1 **MAKE BOTH SIDE CUTS** like straight cuts, but stop exactly at the intersection of marks. Don't worry about the undercuts on the bottom side.

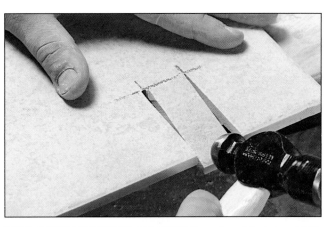

2 **IF THE NOTCH IS NARROW** (less than 1 inch in width) tap the tongue with a hammer to break it off.

3 **IF THE NOTCH IS WIDER,** make a series of parallel cuts spaced ¼ inch apart.

4 **BREAK OFF THE SLIVERS,** then trim the jagged edge with sideways pressure on the tip of the abrasive blade.

USING A WET SAW (CONTINUED)

L-CUTS

1 **MAKE THE FIRST CUT** like a straight cut, but stop exactly at the intersection of the marks.

2 **MAKE THE SECOND CUT** also like a straight cut, but slow as you approach the first cut so the tile doesn't break prematurely and leave material.

CURVES AND COMPLEX CUTS

1 **MAKE A SERIES OF STRAIGHT CUTS** from the edge to the cut mark. Space the parallel cuts ¼ inch.

2 **BREAK OFF THE SLIVERS,** then trim the jagged edge with sideways pressure on the tip of the abrasive blade.

SQUARE HOLES

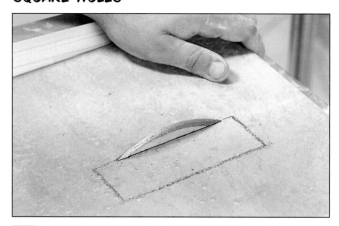

1 **REST ONE TILE EDGE ON THE TABLE** and lower the tile body onto the wheel until the entire visible line is cut.

2 **REPEAT PREVIOUS STEP** with the other three cuts, and the center rectangle will simply drop out.

USING A SNAP CUTTER

1 PLACE THE TILE so that the cutting wheel lies on top of the cut line, then move the wheel back to the far edge of the tile.

2 PULL THE CUTTING WHEEL toward you, exerting light pressure on the handle. If the tile is thick (more than ¼ inch), repeat to deepen the score.

3 LIFT THE CUTTING WHEEL, lower the pressing tee, and strike the handle quickly to snap the tile along the scored line.

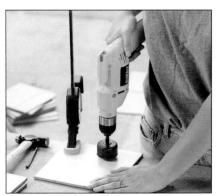

USING TILE NIPPERS

1 START AT ONE END of the cut line, using no more than half of the jaws to make the bite.

2 WORK FROM BOTH ENDS toward the middle. If the nipping is difficult, take smaller bites.

3 TRIM THE EDGES with a wet saw if you have one and if the appearance of the cut is important.

USING A CARBIDE BIT OR HOLE SAW

1 BREAK THROUGH the surface glaze with a center punch to create a dimple to keep the drill bit from wandering.

2 CLAMP THE TILE firmly to the table of a drill press or workbench. Even better, fasten wood cleats around the tile to keep it from moving.

3 GO SLOWLY and exert light pressure to avoid breaking the tile. Some vitreous and impervious tile is just too hard for even a carbide bit or saw.

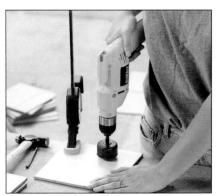

FLOORS

35

TOOLS FOR SETTING AND GROUTING

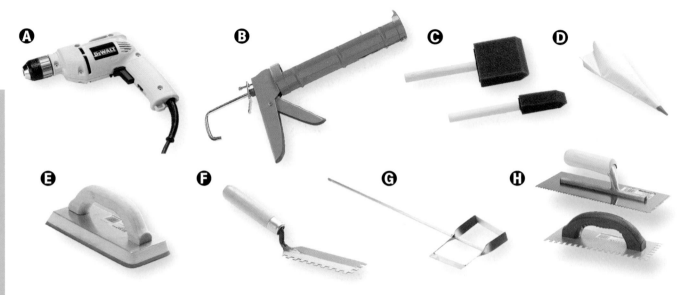

Ⓐ ½-INCH ELECTRIC DRILL
For mixing large amounts of mortar and grout.

Ⓑ CAULKING GUN
Used for caulking and filling grout joints over ½ inch wide.

Ⓒ FOAM PAINTBRUSHES
For applying sealer: ½-inch brush for grout joints, 3-inch brush for tile.

Ⓓ GROUT BAG
For filling wide (more than ½-inch) joints and joints between rough tile.

Ⓔ GROUT FLOAT
For filling grout joints.

Ⓕ MARGIN TROWEL
For mixing and applying small amounts of mortar and grout.

Ⓖ MORTAR MIXING PADDLE
For mixing large amounts of mortar and grout.

Ⓗ NOTCHED TROWEL(S)
For spreading adhesive to setting bed.

TOOL TIP

TROWEL SIZE GUIDE FOR THESE TILES	NOTCH	TROWEL	MORTAR PATTERN
Mosaic and smaller tile (less than 2"×2")	$^3/_{16}$"×$^5/_{32}$" V-notch		
4$^1/_4$"×4$^1/_4$" wall tile	$^1/_4$"×$^3/_{16}$" V-notch		
Flat-backed floor tile to 8"×8" Marble and granite	$^1/_4$"×$^1/_4$" Square-notch		
Lug-backed tile Flat-backed floor tile over 8"×8"	$^1/_4$"×$^3/_8$" Square-notch		
Saltillo tile Cleft stone	$^1/_2$"×$^1/_2$" Square-notch		

TOOLS FOR CLEANUP

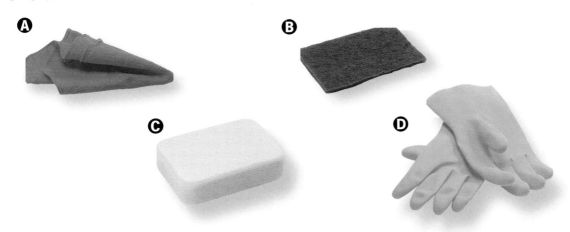

Ⓐ CLEAN, SOFT CLOTH
For removing grout haze.

Ⓑ NONABRASIVE SCOURING PAD
For removing stubborn grout residue.

Ⓒ ROUND-CORNERED SPONGE
For removing grout residue and applying sealer.

Ⓓ RUBBER GLOVES
For protecting hands from grout and other caustic materials.

TOOLS FOR REMOVAL

Ⓐ BRICKLAYER'S CHISEL
For removing broken tile and old adhesive.

Ⓑ CHISEL HOLDER
To protect hands while striking chisel.

Ⓒ CLAW HAMMER
For striking chisels and punches.

Ⓓ COLD CHISEL
For breaking up tile to be removed.

Ⓔ DUST RESPIRATOR
To protect lungs against harmful dust particles.

Ⓕ FACE SHIELD
To protect face from flying debris.

Ⓖ GROUT SAW
For removing old grout from tile joints.

Ⓗ LEATHER GLOVES
To protect hands from tile shards and to cushion against missed hammer blows.

Ⓘ POINT PUNCH
To puncture tile before breaking up to remove.

Ⓙ SAFETY GLASSES
To protect your eyes from flying debris when removing tile.

FLOOR TILING MATERIALS

BACKERBOARD AND FASTENERS

CEMENT BACKERBOARD, a rigid, water-resistant, glass-fiber reinforced cement panel, is a perfect base for setting tile. It comes in two thicknesses (¼ inch and ½ inch) and three sizes (3'×5', 4'×4', and 4'×8').

SPECIAL FASTENERS for cement backerboard are 1¼ inch (1½ inch for ½-inch board) long No. 8-18×⅜" wafer-head, galvanized, self-countersinking screws. An alternative is 1¼-inch barbed galvanized roofing nails.

FIBERGLASS REINFORCING TAPE is applied over all square-edged and cut joints to make the panel reinforcing continuous. The special tape is 2 inches wide and self-adhesive, and must be alkali-resistant due to the alkaline mortar.

MEMBRANES

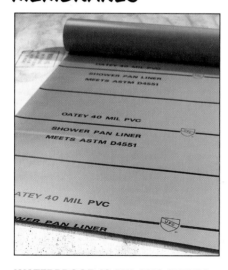

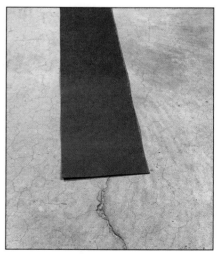

WATERPROOF 40-MIL PVC SHEET is installed under tile in areas which will be soaked, such as shower bases, in order to protect the wood subfloor and joists from water damage.

LAPPING PVC MEMBRANE. The 40-mil PVC sheets come in 4-foot-wide rolls and can be lapped and cemented using the manufacturer-recommended solvent-weld.

15-POUND ROOFING FELT (tar paper) is commonly used to isolate tile from cracks in a concrete slab. Strips 6 to 8 inches wide are centered over the length of the crack and prevent the thin-set from bonding.

ADHESIVES

ADHESIVES are not as glamorous as tile, but are equally important. Without the proper adhesive your tiles will lift. **Organic mastics** are basically glue for wall tiles up to 6"×6". They come premixed in a can and cure by drying. Mastics are fine for wall tile, but should not be used for floors. **Thin-set mortars** are a combination of portland cement, sand, and, sometimes, a **latex additive**. The latex improves the bond and makes the thin-set waterproof and somewhat flexible.

GROUTS

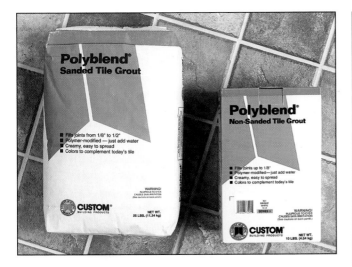

GROUT is what fills the gap between tiles. It looks like thin-set and contains the same materials, but in different proportions. The grout you need depends on the type of tile, width of the grout joint, (use sanded grout for joints wider than ⅛ inch and unsanded for joints ⅛ inch or less) and the location of the installation. Unmodified cement-based grouts must be kept damp for a few days to cure properly. Grouts with latex additive cure without being kept damp. All cement-base grouts should be sealed to prevent staining.

SEALERS

SEALERS protect tile and grout from stains and scuff marks. Only glazed tiles may be left unsealed. There are many types and grades of sealer, so ask for guidance from your tile dealer.

PROJECT PLANNING

As with any building or home repair project, particularly if it is your first time, planning is the key to a happy experience and gratifying result. Here are the questions you will have to answer in tiling a floor.

DESIGN

- Is the tile readily available in sufficient quantity, or does it have to be ordered?
- Can you return any unused tile?
- Do you have enough tile on hand (floor area plus 10 percent is a rule of thumb)?

EVALUATING THE BASE

- Is the existing floor (framing and subfloor) stiff enough, or does it have to be reinforced?

- Is the existing floor surface suitable, or must you replace or cover it?

LAYING CEMENT BACKERBOARD

- Can you transport and handle the heavy panels (3'×5'×½" panel weighs 45 pounds, 4'×8'×½" weighs 96 pounds)?
- Do you have the recommended fasteners and tools to drive them?

MARKING TILE LAYOUT LINES

- Can you make an accurate, to-scale sketch of the existing room?
- Do you have the geometric aptitude required to lay out an orthogonal grid?

MARKING AND CUTTING TILES

- Should you rent a wet saw, and do you have a place to use it that

won't be damaged by water?
- Can you get a helper to make the tile cuts while you set the tile?

SETTING THE TILE

- Will you set the tile by eye, or will you use spacers?
- Can you get a second helper to mix the thin-set while you concentrate on setting the tile?

GROUTING THE JOINTS

- Does the tile require sealing before grouting the joints?
- Will anyone be around to mist the grout twice a day for two days?

SEALING

- Does the tile require sealing, as well as the grout?
- Will you be using a topical (surface) or penetrating sealer?

SPECIAL HEIGHT CONSIDERATIONS

KITCHEN CABINETS

Under-counter dishwashers require 34½ inches from floor to underside of the countertop. If you are tiling a kitchen floor and the cabinets are already in place, you have a decision to make: will you not tile under the dishwasher (making it difficult to remove the dishwasher), or will you shim the cabinets by the thickness of backerboard and tile?

HEIGHT TRANSITIONS

Small changes in floor level are a leading cause of accidents in the home. Since tiling over an existing floor typically increases the thickness of the floor by ½ inch to ¾ inch, you must consider the nature of the transition.

Tile outlets carry an assortment of stock metal extrusions, as well as hardwood "reducers" for trimming exposed edges of tiles.

SHIM KITCHEN CABINETS by the thickness of the tile installation if you wish to slide a dishwasher out.

BASEBOARDS. To avoid having to remove baseboards, tile up to the existing baseboard and install a new shoe.

METAL EXTRUSIONS are available in a variety of shapes and finishes to trim the edges of exposed tile.

HARDWOOD REDUCERS are perfect for making the transition from a hardwood floor to a new tile floor.

EVALUATING WOOD FLOORS AND SUBFLOORS

The recommended setting base for tile is cement backerboard. If the subfloor is at least ⅝-inch plywood, you can install backerboard in thin-set over the subfloor. While tongue and groove hardwood flooring can sometimes be used, is not generally acceptable for tile unless it is covered in a mortar base instead of backerboard; installation should be done by a professional, not a homeowner. In this case the total thickness of the subfloor must be at least 1⅛ inch. If it is less, CC-Plugged with Exterior Glue plywood must be installed over the existing floor.

EXTERIOR-GRADE PLYWOOD is acceptable provided it is clean, solid, and at least ⅝ (¹⁹/₃₂) inch thick.

IF THE SUBFLOOR IS NOT PLYWOOD (lower right photo), tear up and replace with ¾ (²³/₃₂) inch Exterior-Grade plywood.

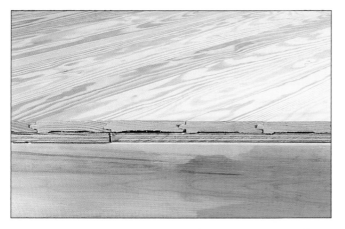

HARDWOOD FLOORING is generally not recommended for do-it-yourself tile installation since it requires a solid mortar base instead of backerboard to ensure stability. The floor must also be level and smooth, which may require sanding.

IF THE SUBFLOOR IS PLYWOOD or solid wood, but too thin, build up thickness with CC Exterior-Grade plywood at least ⅜ inch thick.

WHAT A SUBFLOOR SHOULD NOT BE

Most homes being built today have subfloors of "engineered wood"— variations on oriented-strand board (OSB). Make sure the contractor uses the right plywood for the subfloor if you intend to install tile.

REINFORCING AN EXISTING FRAMED FLOOR

Though the new thin-set mortars with latex additives are more flexible than straight mortar, they are still not rubber. The first requirement for tiling over a wood-framed floor is that the floor not deflect under a load. If the floor squeaks or feels "bouncy," stiffen it up as shown.

SKILL SCALE

EASY	MEDIUM	HARD

SKILLS: Basic carpentry

HOW LONG WILL IT TAKE?

PROJECT: Stiffening a squeaky or bouncy floor

EXPERIENCED . . . . . 2 HRS.

HANDY . . . . 4 HRS.

NOVICE . . . . 6-8 HRS.

STUFF YOU'LL NEED

TOOLS: Hammer, pen or marker, utility knife, circular saw, variable-speed drill, drill bits, Phillips bit, safety glasses

MATERIALS: Glue, drywall screws, scrap plywood, wood wedges, framing lumber

1 SISTERING JOISTS doubles the stiffness of a floor. Drill pairs of pilot holes in new joists every 24 inches and fasten to the old joists with 3-inch drywall screws.

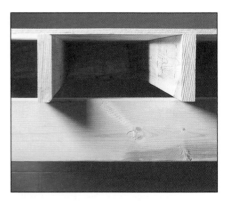

2 ADDING A BEAM cuts the span of the joists in half and more than doubles the floor's stiffness. Ask a contractor to size the new beam.

3 MARK SQUEAK LOCATIONS with a pen while a helper walks on the floor above. A one-person alternative is driving a long nail at the location.

4 DRIVE GLUED WEDGES between joist and subfloor at the marked locations, eliminating the wood-on-wood motion producing the squeaks.

5 TRIM THE WEDGES with a sharp utility knife after the glue has dried. Score the wedge with several passes, then snap it off.

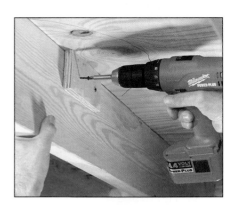

6 SCREW BLOCKING tight up against the subfloor. Predrilled 2"×4"×½" plywood blocks are easily fastened with 1⅝-inch drywall screws.

EVALUATING A CONCRETE SLAB

A concrete slab offers the perfect base for setting tiles, provided it meets three conditions:

- It is flat, because unevenness will be more obvious with a more reflective tile surface.
- It is stable, that is, it has no active cracks which can telegraph through the tile and mortar.
- It is clean so that the thin-set will adhere to the concrete.

IS THE SLAB STABLE?

Rare is the slab which doesn't have at least a few hairline cracks. However, most of these cracks are due to simple shrinkage as the slab cured and pose no problem. The cracks we are worried about are the ones that are still moving due to heaving or settling of the ground beneath, because the motion can crack the tile or grout.

Fortunately, there is a simple test: If the displacement of the two sides of a crack is strictly horizontal, it is a harmless shrinkage crack. If there is vertical displacement, it is an active crack.

IS THE SLAB CLEAN?

Nothing sticks to grease or oil—thin-set included. Mortars, including latex-modified thin-set mortar, will stick to anything water "wets."

To test: After sweeping dust from the slab, dribble water from a glass onto the surface. If the water sinks into the concrete, the surface is free of grease and wax. If the water beads (stands up), the surface is contaminated. If that is the case, ask your tile supplier for an appropriate cleaner.

IS THE SLAB FLAT?

How flat the slab needs to be depends on your personal standard and the nature of the tile. If you are installing cleft stone or crude Saltillo tile, you probably don't even need to check for flatness, but if you are installing glazed tile or polished marble or granite, you will want the slab as flat as a pool table.

Correcting minor dips and hollows is pretty simple, as the photos below and on the following page show. You just have to find and mark the low spots, prime them for adhesion, and pour a self-leveling mortar.

A HARMLESS SHRINKAGE CRACK is indicated if there is no vertical displacement across the crack. This crack probably occurred during the first year as the slab dried out.

A TROUBLESOME ACTIVE CRACK is indicated by vertical displacement—a difference in height—across the crack. The cause is movement of the soil beneath, which will continue.

WATER BEING ABSORBED indicates a grease- and oil-free surface to which thin-set can bond. Mortar will not bond to most paints, either. Be sure to test all areas of the slab even if they look clean.

WATER BEADS indicate oil or wax, which would prevent a good bond between the thin-set and the slab. This slab must be cleaned with a trisodium phosphate (TSP) cleaning product until the water stops beading, followed by a rinse to remove the TSP.

LEVELING A CONCRETE SLAB

ow flat a slab needs to be depends on the sheen of the tile finish, the size of the individual tiles, and your personal standard. If the tile faces are polished (such as polished marble or granite), the slightest waviness will show up in the reflected light. If the tiles are a third or more of the size of the dips and hollows, the tile edges are likely to be misaligned. However, if the tiles themselves are rough and irregular, then slight variations in the level of the floor will be masked by the greater variations in the tiles.

As the photos below show, filling an occasional low spot in a slab is a simple task. If the slab is just plain rough and irregular, however, you should call in a professional slab finisher to apply a skim coat of new concrete to make the floor perfectly smooth so that you can get the results you want when you install the tile.

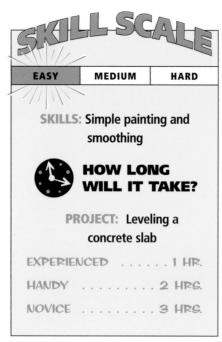

SKILL SCALE

EASY	MEDIUM	HARD

SKILLS: Simple painting and smoothing

HOW LONG WILL IT TAKE?

PROJECT: Leveling a concrete slab

EXPERIENCED . . . . . . 1 HR.

HANDY . . . . 2 HRS.

NOVICE . . . . 3 HRS.

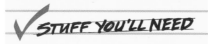

STUFF YOU'LL NEED

TOOLS: Straightedge (4 feet minimum), tape measure, marker, 2-inch brush

MATERIALS: Manufacturer-recommended latex primer, self-leveling mortar

1 DETERMINE FLATNESS. Using a long (minimum 4 feet) straightedge, locate and mark the deepest points of all of the hollows and valleys in the slab.

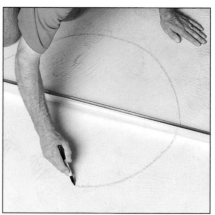

2 MARK PERIMETER. Swinging the straightedge around the deep points, find and mark the perimeters of the hollows. Any sort of marker will work as it will be covered later.

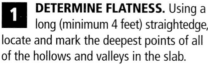

3 APPLY LATEX PRIMER. After making sure the slab is clean (see previous page), brush on the specific latex primer recommended by the manufacturer of the self-leveling mortar. Using any other primer will void the mortar warranty.

4 POUR SELF-LEVELING MORTAR at the center of the primed area. Pour enough so that it spreads on its own nearly to the edges of the area. After it stops spreading, use a straightedge to feather the edges.

PREPARING OTHER FLOORS

O ther possible surfaces include resilient flooring (linoleum, vinyl, or vinyl-asbestos sheet and tile) and a previously tiled floor.

RESILIENT FLOORING

Resilient flooring can serve as a base provided it is of a single layer, is not of the cushion-vinyl variety, is not cracked, and is firmly adhered. Cushioned vinyl and multiple layers are too compressible to provide adequate support, while cracks may indicate an instability, which will cause failure in the tile as well.

To determine the nature of the existing flooring, remove a small sample from under a refrigerator or dishwasher and take it to a flooring store for identification. The existing flooring needs to be firmly adhered and installed over exterior-grade plywood at least ⅝ inch thick. If the subfloor is inadequate, screw a layer of ½-inch, CC-Plugged, Exterior-Grade plywood over the flooring.

You also need to determine whether the flooring contains asbestos. Don't start sanding until you are sure (see the Safety Alert below left). If subfloor and sheet flooring are OK, then remove any wax from its surface and roughen with 40-grit sandpaper. Remove the dust with a damp sponge.

ASBESTOS TILE
Resilient flooring installed before 1986 may contain asbestos. It's not a problem—until you try to remove it. Then, the loose fibers can get into your lungs and cause serious health problems. If you are planning to remove asbestos tile, talk to your state department of environmental affairs or department of health about its removal and disposal. You will have to either have the asbestos tile removed professionally or switch to a different type of flooring.

PREVIOUSLY TILED FLOOR

Removing existing ceramic tiles is also not necessary, provided the tiles are uncracked and solidly adhered, and the surface is flat and smooth.

Remove any cracked or loose tiles and fill the void with thin-set.

Remove any wax or sealant from the tiles, then scarify the surfaces of the tiles with an aggressive Carborundum sandpaper on a belt- or disk sander. Remove the resulting dust with a damp sponge.

ROUGHEN THE SURFACE of soundly adhered, wax-free resilient flooring with 40-grit sandpaper. Be sure to wear a tightly fitting dust respirator.

REMOVE THE DUST of sanding with a damp sponge. To test whether the thin-set will adhere, give the surface the "water-bead" test on page 43.

AN EXISTING TILE FLOOR IS OK, but it must first be cleaned of wax and oil with TSP and a second time with an ammonia-based sealer stripper (don't forget to open the windows!).

SCARIFY THE TILE SURFACE with a course Carborundum sandpaper until the glaze is dull, then remove the sanding dust with a damp sponge.

LAYING BACKERBOARD

The purpose of laying cement backerboard is to provide as stiff, smooth, and continuous a surface as possible as a base for the tile. To that end, three principles must be observed:

■ Orient the backerboard panels perpendicular to the plywood.
■ Don't let backerboard edges fall over plywood edges.
■ Stagger the backerboard panels to avoid four-corner joints.

You will be spreading thin-set adhesive for one backerboard panel at a time, so after you plan the panel layout, mark the positions of the joints on the plywood with a chalk line so you will know where to spread the thin-set.

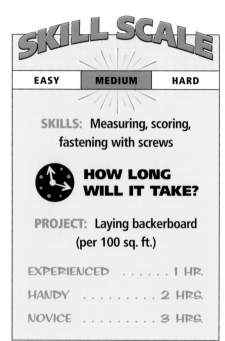

1 CHALK LINE PANEL POSITIONS. After planning where the panel edges should fall (see Steps 2–4), snap chalk lines as guides for the thin-set.

2 ORIENT PANELS PERPENDICULAR TO PLYWOOD. Backerboard is extremely heavy, but use 4'×8' sheets, provided you can handle their weight.

3 WRONG. Avoid four-corner joints because the backerboard corners are the weakest points.

4 RIGHT. Stagger the backerboard panels so that one edge of a joint is always continuous and, therefore, stiff.

SCORING AND CUTTING

Cutting backerboard is similar to cutting drywall, with two differences:

- The sand in the mortar will quickly dull a utility knife, so you should use a carbide scoring knife designed for the purpose.
- The board should be scored on both sides before snapping.

Mark the panel for cutting, align a straightedge with the marks, and score the surface, using the straightedge as a guide. Repeat scoring until the fiberglass is cut through.

Turn the panel over and repeat the process. When the fiberglass on both sides is cut through, snap the panel.

MIXING AND SPREADING ADHESIVE

Pour the recommended amount of water into a 5-gallon bucket, then add the dry mortar. Stir with a paddle attached to a $\frac{1}{2}$-inch drill at a slow speed until the mixture is uniform. Let the mixture rest, or "slake," for 10–15 minutes, then remix. While you are using the mortar, remix every 15 minutes, but do NOT add more liquid.

With the smooth edge of a $\frac{1}{4}$"×$\frac{1}{4}$" square-notch trowel, spread enough mortar to cover the area inside a set of chalk lines. Press the mortar into the plywood at a shallow angle; then comb the mortar in straight furrows, holding the trowel at a 45-degree angle.

5 **MEASURE AND MARK.** Mark the panel for cutting with a felt-tip pen or the scoring tool. Just mark the ends of the cut.

6 **SCORE.** Use a straightedge to guide the carbide scorer or utility knife in a straight line. Score until all of the fiberglass strands are cut.

7 **SNAP PANEL.** After scoring both sides, press down with hand and knee near the score line; lift one edge to snap the panel.

8 **ADD POWDERED MORTAR TO LIQUID.** Follow the manufacturer's instructions for proportions. Use a bathroom scale to measure amounts of the dry mix. Wear a dust respirator when pouring the powder.

9 **MIX WITH PADDLE.** Use a paddle designed for mortar—not paint. Make sure the drill has enough power for the job, and mix at slow speed.

10 **SPREAD ADHESIVE.** Press the mortar into the plywood with the trowel at a shallow angle; then comb it out, holding the trowel at 45 degrees.

FLOORS

47

LAYING BACKERBOARD (CONTINUED)

POSITIONING AND FASTENING

After applying and combing thin-set over the area within a panel's chalk lines, place the panel on edge against the wall or the previous panel and "hinge" it down onto the thin-set. Shift the panel only enough to insert spacers, then apply uniform pressure to bed it in the mortar. The ⅛-inch spaces between panels are to allow the thin-set to bond to the panel edges.

Before the mortar sets, fasten the panel to the subfloor. Some tilesetters use 1¼-inch galvanized roofing nails, but special backerboard screws are better because they minimize the risk of fracturing the board. Apply the fasteners in the pattern printed on the backerboard or as shown below. Remove the spacers when the panel is secure.

11 **GAP AT WALLS.** Leave a ¼-inch gap between the panel edges and the wall. You can remove the shims immediately, so just a couple will do.

12 **GAP AT EDGES.** Space the panel edges about ⅛ inch with 16d common nails. Again, remove the nails as soon as the panels are in position.

13 **USE BACKERBOARD SCREWS:** 1½-inch screws for ½-inch board, 1¼-inch screws for ¼-inch board. Do NOT use ordinary drywall screws.

14 **AROUND THE PERIMETER,** drive screws every 4 inches, spaced ½ inch from panel edges. For speed, start the screws with a hammer, then drive home.

15 **AT THE CORNERS,** keep the screws 2 inches from the intersection. Be careful not to crack the panel by overdriving in this vulnerable area.

16 **IN THE CENTER,** space the screws 6 inches on-center in both directions. Some panels are premarked with recommended screw locations.

FLOORS

FILLING AND TAPING PANEL EDGES

Cement backerboard derives its strength and rigidity from the fiberglass scrim embedded in each face. At the joints where panels meet the reinforcing is discontinuous. This weakness can be largely overcome, however, by splicing the joints with fiberglass tape. The commonly available tape is 2 inches wide, self-adhesive, and alkali-resistant (important because mortar is alkaline).

Some tilesetters take a shortcut by applying the self-adhesive tape to the joint and covering it with thin-set in a single application. Better and stronger, however, is filling the $1/8$-inch joint gap with thin-set, spreading it $1\frac{1}{2}$ inches to either side of the joint, pressing the tape into the wet mortar, then covering the tape with a second coat of thin-set and feathering the edges to a perfectly flat surface.

Whichever method you choose, make sure you feather the joint flat and remove any excess mortar before it sets. If it does set, you are in for a job to remove it so that it doesn't prevent the tile from setting flat on the backerboard.

17 **FILL THE JOINTS** with thin-set using a margin trowel. Spread and smooth the mixture $1\frac{1}{2}$ inches on both sides of the joint.

18 **APPLY FIBERGLASS TAPE** to the joints where one or both edges are square or cut. Embed the tape firmly in the wet thin-set.

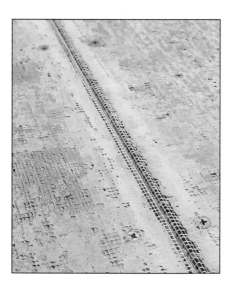

19 **ROUNDED PANEL EDGES** require no tape reinforcing. Simply fill the joints with thin-set where both panel edges are uncut.

20 **COVER THE TAPE** with a second application of thin-set. Use the flat edge of the trowel to spread and feather the mortar for a perfectly flat surface.

Homer's Hindsight

CLEAN YOUR TOOLS
Why do we buy the best, most tenacious adhesives we can find and then think they won't stick to our tools? The first time I mixed and spread latex-modified thin-set, I was so pleased with myself I dropped the tools in a bucket and treated myself to a leisurely lunch. BIG mistake! That lunch cost me $5 plus the cost of a new paddle mixer, margin trowel, square-edged trowel, and pair of pants.
Latex-modified thin-set is good—VERY good!

FLOORS

TILE LAYOUT

The first impulse of a novice tilesetter is to start laying tile at one corner of a room and fill in the squares until reaching the opposite walls. This would be fine if all rooms were perfect rectangles whose dimensions were integer multiples of the tile size, but they are not. Rooms are not perfect rectangles, often contain obstructions such as cabinets, and are of random size.

Laying out the design on paper, and then with chalk on the actual setting surface, allows you to:

- practice layouts at zero cost
- minimize the number of cuts
- avoid unsightly and vulnerable narrow strips
- closely estimate the number of tiles needed

Document the size and shape of the area you wish to tile. On a sheet of graph paper, sketch the plan to scale, as shown below.

TEN TIMES MORE ACCURATE than measuring a single tile and spacer, is measuring 10 tiles and 10 spacers. Simply line up 10 in a row, measure the span, and divide by 10.

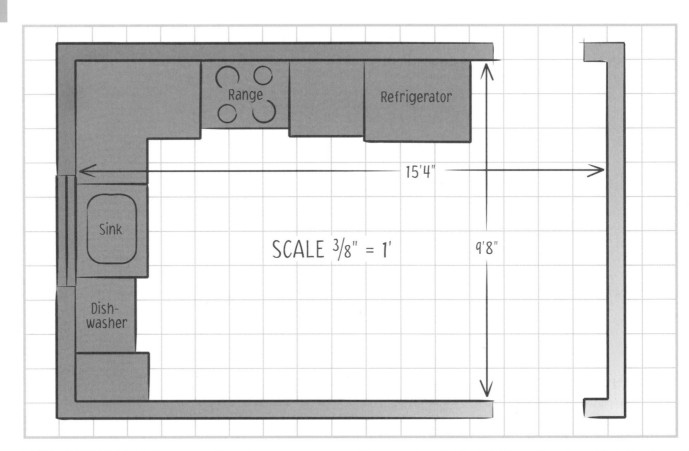

Range

Refrigerator

15'4"

Sink

SCALE ³⁄₈" = 1'

9'8"

Dish-
washer

MAKE A FLOOR PLAN. Draw the walls of the room as accurately as you can on a sheet of grid paper. Include doorways and floor obstructions, such as cabinets and fixtures.

The paper is available with ¹⁄₈-inch, ¹⁄₄-inch, and ¹⁄₂-inch grid spacing. For greatest accuracy, use the largest grid the room will fit. Interpolate dimensions with an architect's scale.

LAYING OUT A KITCHEN FLOOR

Once you have designed a layout, you have to transfer it to the floor. If you use spacers, or if you have a particularly good eye, there is no need to lay every joint line. After establishing reference lines (orthogonals), secondary joint lines enclosing an area of 8 to 12 square feet will be sufficient.

The longest wall in a room is visually important. Measure out from both ends of the wall several tile spaces (allowing for a ¼-inch gap at the wall) and snap a chalk line. Do the same for the next longest wall. If the room is square, these lines will be orthogonal.

From the intersection, measure and mark 3 feet on one line and 4 feet on the other line. If the reference lines are orthogonal, the diagonal distance between the points will be precisely 5 feet. If it is not, adjust the shorter line and snap a different color chalk line until it is.

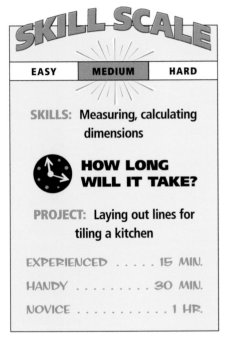

SKILL SCALE

EASY	MEDIUM	HARD

SKILLS: Measuring, calculating dimensions

HOW LONG WILL IT TAKE?

PROJECT: Laying out lines for tiling a kitchen

EXPERIENCED . . . . . 15 MIN.

HANDY . . . . 30 MIN.

NOVICE . . . . 1 HR.

✔ STUFF YOU'LL NEED

TOOLS: Tape measure, chalk line, pencil, permanent marker, knee pads (optional)

A+ WORK SMARTER

DUST OFF THE CHALK LINE

Before you snap the line on the floor, shake off some of the chalk. Too much chalk will make a muddy line that can be hard to read, especially if you're checking for square.

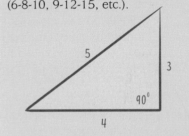

THANK PYTHAGORAS

The Greek mathematician Pythagoras (540–510 B.C.) proved a useful carpentry rule: a triangle with sides in the proportions 3-4-5 always forms a 90–degree angle. For larger triangles, use multiples of 3-4-5, (6-8-10, 9-12-15, etc.).

1 **MEASURE FROM BOTH ENDS** of the longest wall out several tile spaces (allowing a ¼-inch gap at the wall) and mark with pencil.

2 **SNAP A CHALK LINE** between the two points just marked. This line should represent the center of one of the tile joints.

3 **REPEAT STEP 1** for the next longest adjacent wall, and snap a second chalk line. This line also will represent the center of a tile joint.

4 **CHECK THE ANGLE** by marking points 3 feet and 4 feet from the intersection. Measure the diagonal. If it is exactly 5 feet, your marks are accurate. If not, repeat the first three steps.

DESIGN THE LAYOUT. Using either graph paper or a computer drawing program, draw the room to scale. After determining the average dimension of a tile plus the thickness of one joint, fit the tiles to the floor plan. In the plan shown, full tiles run along the bottom wall. If the adjacent floor were either tiled or carpeted, you might bring the joint to the middle of the door opening.

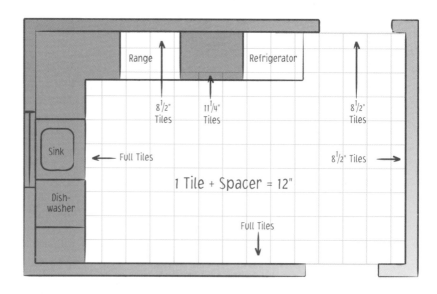

SNAP REFERENCE ORTHOGONALS. Measure several tile spaces (tile plus width of one joint) out from both ends of the longest wall and snap a chalk line (Line A). Allow for a ¼-inch gap between the edge of the tile and the wall. Repeat for the adjacent wall (Line B). Verify that Lines A and B are perpendicular by marking points 3 feet and 4 feet from the intersection and measuring the diagonal. **When measuring the diagonal, make sure the tape is read from the same edge at both ends of the line.** If the diagonal is not exactly 5 feet, adjust Line B until it is.

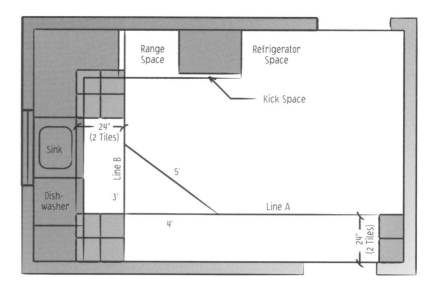

SNAP ADDITIONAL LINES at joint lines to mark off areas of 8 to 12 square feet. These lines ensure that you won't stray too far from your planned design, and they mark areas of tile you can comfortably set at one time. After all lines have been snapped, trace over them with a permanent marker so they won't disappear when you wipe the backerboard with a damp sponge.

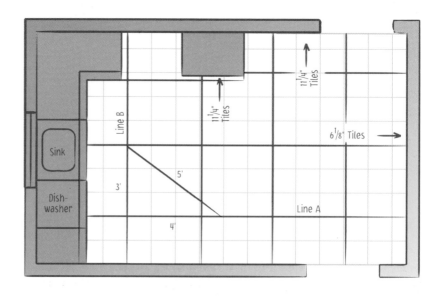

FLOORS

52

LAYING OUT DIAGONAL PATTERNS

Diagonal designs catch the eye, especially when framed with a border. They look as if they use more tile, and they look as if they require a high degree of skill. Actually, neither is true. While they do require more cuts around the perimeter, the straight cuts simply make two triangles from one full tile so, barring mistakes, no tile is wasted. The only extra skill required is that of laying out the diagonal pattern, and that is simple provided you follow the step-by-step directions illustrated here.

Note: You cannot assume the room is a perfect rectangle, so the first step is to establish a pair of reference lines or orthogonals (A1 and A2) through the midpoint the room, as shown in Step One. Once you have established Midline A establish Midline B in the same manner to find the center of the room (Step 2).

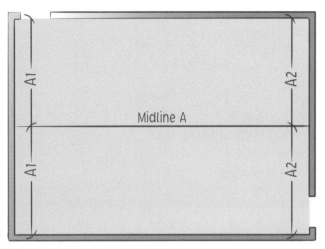

1 **SNAP A CHALK LINE** down the midline of the room. Note that the two A1 distances are equal but may be different than the A2s because the room may not be square.

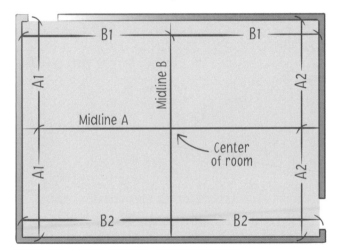

2 **FIND THE CENTER OF THE ROOM** by snapping a second chalk line equidistant from the other pair of walls.

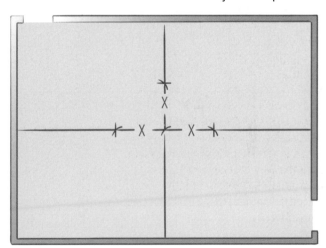

3 **FROM THE MIDPOINT**, measure equal distances in three directions. The larger the distance, the greater the accuracy.

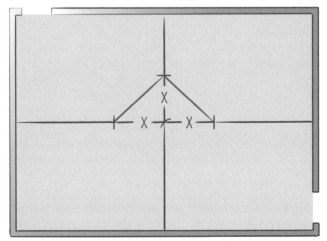

4 **CONNECT THE POINTS** by snapping chalk lines. The new lines are diagonal and orthogonal to each other.

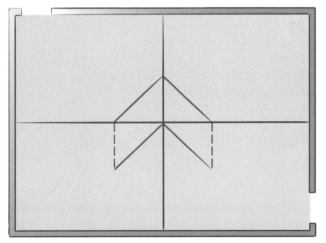

5 **SHIFT THE DIAGONAL LINES** down so their apex is at the center point of the room.

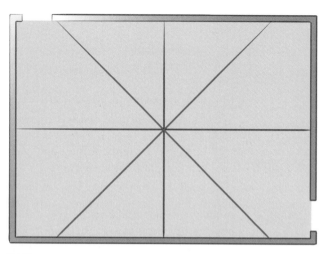

6 **USING THE APEX IN STEP 5,** extend the diagonal lines to the walls by snapping new lines over the old lines.

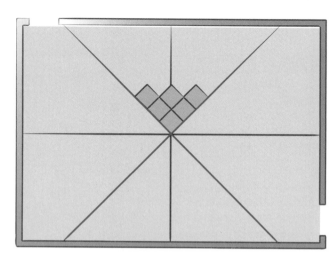

7 **BEGIN SETTING TILE** at the center point, building an inverted pyramid between the diagonals.

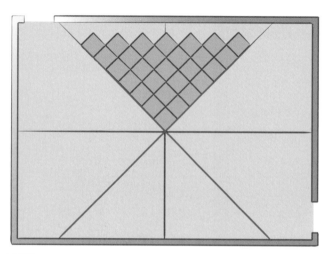

8 **CONTINUE SETTING TILE** until full tiles no longer fit into the remaining space.

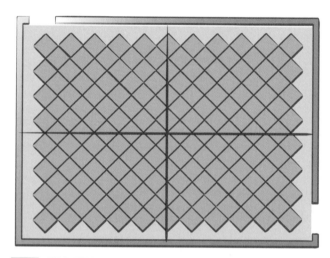

9 **FILL THE REMAINING THREE QUADRANTS** in the same way, building from the center toward the walls.

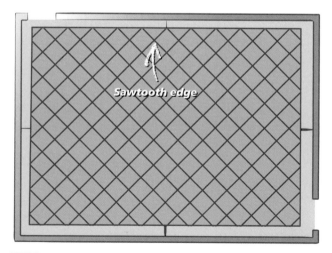

Sawtooth edge

10 **FILL THE SAWTOOTH EDGES** with tiles cut diagonally in half, leaving symmetrical borders around the edge.

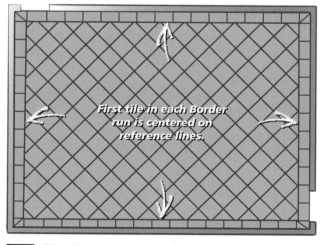

First tile in each Border run is centered on reference lines.

11 **FILL THE BORDER** with the same or different color tile, centering each border row on the red reference lines (shown in Step 10).

MORE LAYOUTS

SMALL ROOM

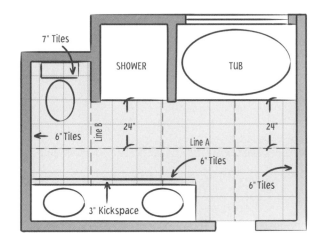

Bathrooms are generally small enough that you can ignore the 3-4-5 triangle for establishing reference lines. Lay out a single reference line along the center of the room in the longest direction to represent the middle of a tile joint. Mark the locations of joint lines every 3 or 4 tiles using a tape measure. Use a framing square to draw the orthogonals.

In this small bathroom, full tiles are used at the entrance and along the tub and shower. The layout was adjusted to avoid having a 2-inch strip of tile at the end of the vanity.

COMBINATION ROOMS

Kitchen and dining room and other room combinations may require that you deal with more visual elements.

If the rooms are joined by a narrow doorway, separate the field tiles at the doorway with a threshold. Full tiles may be installed on both sides of the doorway without visually disturbing the pattern. The joints perpendicular to the doorway must line up.

In the kitchen and dining room, the layout must account for cut tiles along the peninsula counter as well as the perimeter of the room. The width of the bay allows for the use of full tiles if the $\frac{1}{2}$-inch to $\frac{3}{4}$-inch gaps at the walls are covered with baseboards.

Most of the cut tiles are obscured by the cabinet toe kick. The only place a design principle is violated is at the kitchen door, where a less-than-half-width tile is placed.

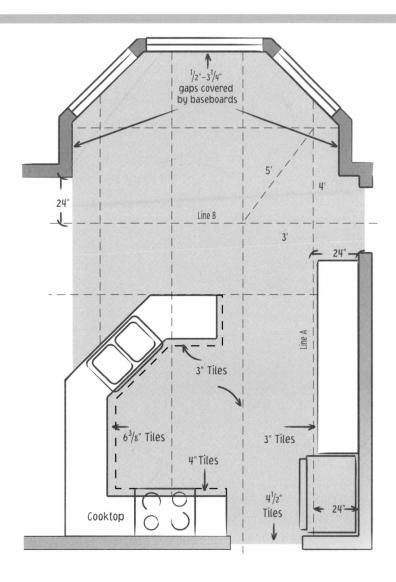

55

CONNECTED ROOMS

Uninterrupted joint lines are key to running a tile design through multiple rooms. The solution is simple: Run the primary reference orthogonals through the doorways into the adjacent rooms.

In the rooms below, Line A runs vertically through the kitchen and the dining room. Using a 3-4-5 triangle, orthogonal reference Line B runs horizontally through both the dining room and the utility room. A second 3-4-5 triangle establishes orthogonal reference Line C vertically in the utility room.

In Option A (below) full tiles are set through the utility room doorway, which requires 6-inch tiles along both walls. Option B installs a wood or marble threshold the width of the wall in the doorway, allowing full tiles to start in the utility room.

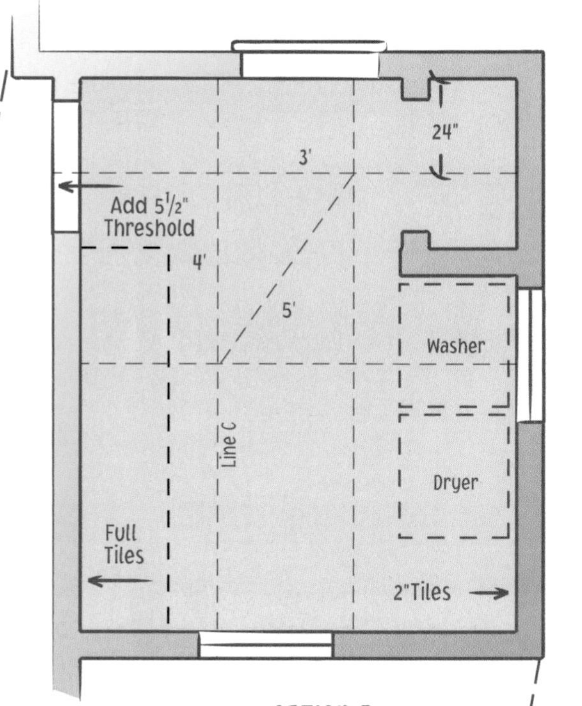

OPTION B

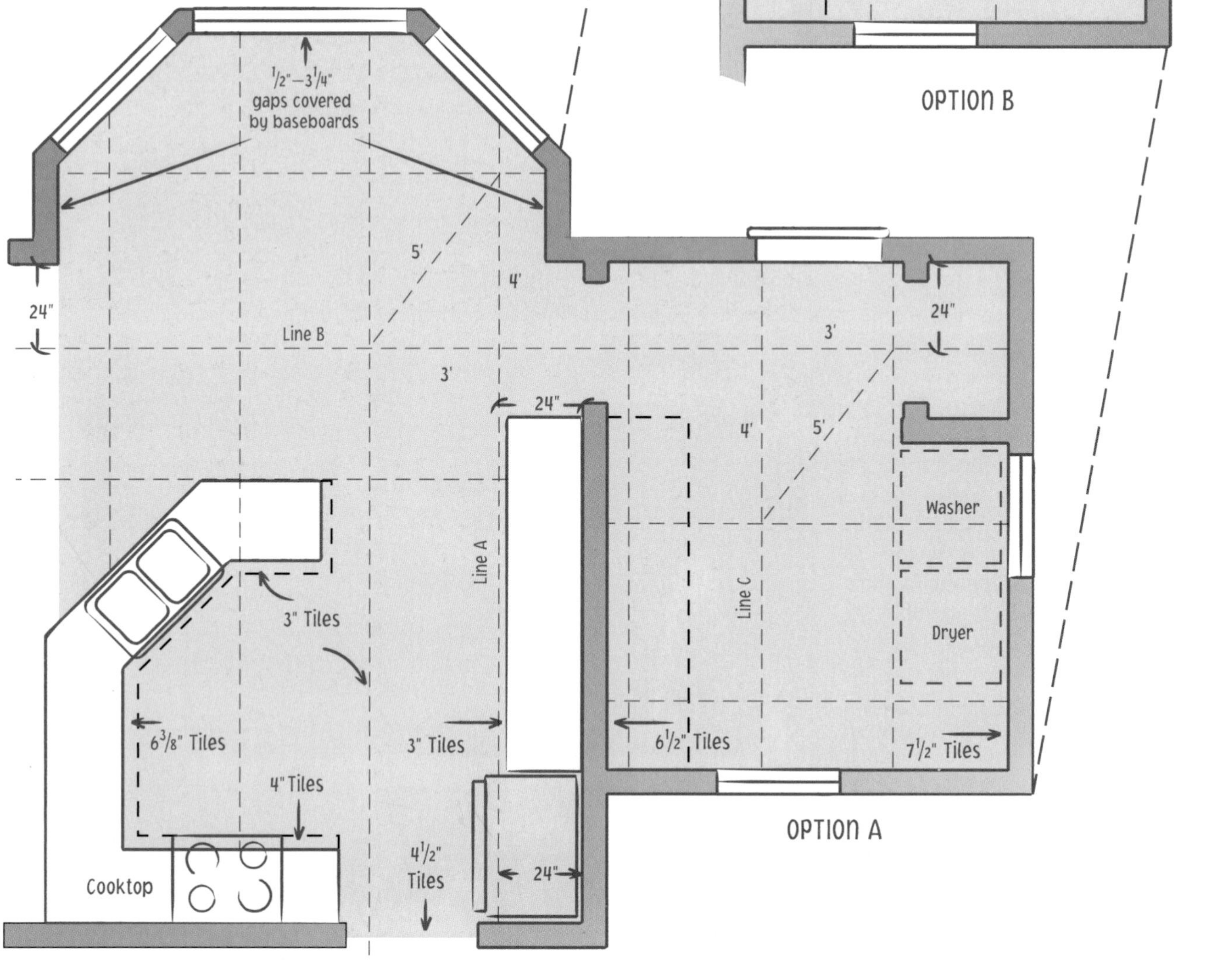

OPTION A

MARKING TILE FOR CUTTING

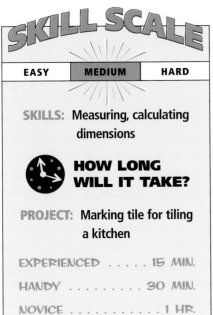
✓ STUFF YOU'LL NEED

TOOLS: Tape measure, combination square, china marker, scissors or a utility knife

MATERIALS: Floor tiles, heavy paper stock or cardboard (a file folder works well)

Most floor layouts require that at least a few tiles be cut. Follow the layout suggestions on pages 50-56 to minimize the cuts.

When an obstruction, such as a pipe, is located away from the wall and you can remove it, cut a hole in the tile and feed the pipe through the set tile.

To notch a tile around a pipe or other obstruction, start by marking a straight cut and then marking for the notches.

To transfer markings to tile for obstructions such as door casings and other complex cuts, slip a sheet of paper under the casing and trace its outline. Cut out the outline, then trace it onto the tile.

When paper doesn't fit under the obstruction, cut and fit the shape of the obstruction in small increments until you approximate the outline. If you have a contour gauge, press it against the obstruction to register the outline. Trace the outline onto the tile.

FLOORS

MARKING HOLES

1 **PLACE THE TILE TO BE CUT** directly over the tile beneath, butting it against the pipe. Mark the center of the pipe onto the front edge of the tile.

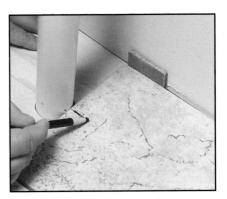

2 **MOVE THE TILE** to the side and butt it against a ¼-inch spacer against the wall to mark the pipe center on the side edge of the tile.

3 **DRAW TWO PERPENDICULAR LINES** through the two edge marks to the edges of the tile using a combination square.

4 **THE INTERSECTION** of the perpendicular lines is the center of the hole to be cut. Draw a circle slightly larger than the pipe to allow for expansion.

MARKING STRAIGHT & L-CUTS

1 **GAPS AT WALLS.** Place tile to be cut on the last tile set. Place marker tile on top, against a spacer tile at the wall. Trace the edge of the marker tile onto the tile to be cut.

2 **OPTION: OUTSIDE CORNERS.** Mark the first cutting line as in Step 1. To mark the second cut, mark the corner on the marker tile, allowing a ¼-inch gap.

3 **OPTION TO STEP 2: SLIDE BACK THE MARKER TILE** and transfer the corner mark to the first cut line. Draw the second cutting line using a combination square.

MARKING NOTCHES

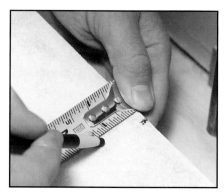

1 **MARK THE WIDTH** of the notch on the edge of the tile, with the tile to be notched lined up with the tile beneath and butted against the pipe.

2 **MEASURE THE DEPTH** of the notch with a tape measure butted against a ¼-inch spacer held against the wall.

3 **MARK THE DEPTH** of the notch on the tile to be notched with the tape measure; then draw the three cut lines from the three marks.

A+ WORK SMARTER

PRACTICE MAKES PERFECT
When marking a complex cut, take the time to get the pattern exactly right before you cut the tile. Transfer the pattern carefully to the tile and be sure to save the cutout in case you make a mistake and have to start over.

MARKING COMPLEX CUTS

1 **MARK THE OUTLINE** of the cut on a heavy paper stock or cardboard. Cut it out with scissors or a utility knife.

2 **TRACE THE OUTLINE** onto the edge of the tile. Apply masking tape to the edge of the tile and trace the outline onto it.

FLOORS

CUTTING THE TILE

SKILL SCALE

EASY	MEDIUM	HARD

SKILLS: Using a snap cutter or wet saw, drilling, and grinding

HOW LONG WILL IT TAKE?

PROJECT: Cutting floor tile for a kitchen

EXPERIENCED	2 HRS.
HANDY	3 HRS.
NOVICE	4 HRS.

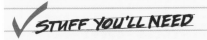

✓ STUFF YOU'LL NEED

TOOLS: Snap cutter or wet saw, tile nippers, hammer, center punch (for holes), carbide hole saw, abrasive stone, safety glasses, dust respirator, ear plugs.

MATERIALS: Floor tile

Snap cutters are great for straight cuts. They create sharp edges you must smooth on exposed edges. A wet saw can be used for straight cuts, L-cuts, and notches. Always wear a dust respirator, safety glasses, and ear plugs when using a wet saw.

CUTTING NOTCHES

Use a wet saw to make notches less than one inch wide by making two parallel cuts and tapping the inside piece with a hammer. Make wider notches by repeating parallel cuts

(Continued on page 60.)

STRAIGHT & L-CUTS (TILE CUTTER OR SAW)

1 **ALIGN THE CUTTING WHEEL,** then pull the wheel toward you with moderate pressure.

2 **LIFT THE CUTTING WHEEL,** lower the pressing tee, and strike the handle to snap the tile.

1 **ADJUST THE FENCE** so the cut mark lines up with the blade. Hold tile with both hands.

2 **ADVANCE THE TILE** into the blade, using the fence as a guide. Avoid chipping tile by cutting slowly.

CUTTING NOTCHES USING A TILE SAW

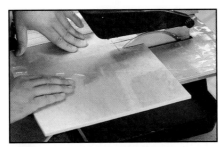

1 **MAKE BOTH SIDE CUTS** straight, but stop exactly at the intersection of the marks.

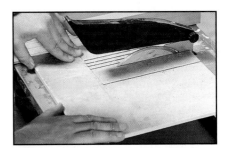

2 **IF THE NOTCH IS WIDER** than 1 inch, make a series of parallel cuts spaced about ¼ inch apart.

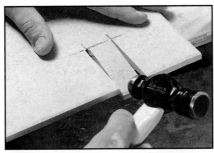

3 **IF THE NOTCH IS NARROW** (less than 1 inch wide), tap the tongue with a hammer to break it off.

4 **BREAK OFF THE SLIVERS,** trim the jagged edge with sideways pressure on the tip of the blade.

about ¼ inch apart and breaking off the interior pieces. Smooth the break with an abrasive stone or rotary grinder. Rod saws can also be used for small jobs.

CURVED CUTS

Curved cuts can be made three ways. Tile nippers nibble away tile in tiny bites. The smaller the bite, the less chance you will break the tile. The nippers produce a ragged edge that must be smoothed with an abrasive stone or rotary grinder.

Use a wet saw to cut tightly spaced parallel cuts up to the curve and snap out the interior pieces.

Rod saws have diamonds on the rod, enabling them to cut in any direction, but they are effective only for softer tiles.

CUTTING HOLES

Make round holes in tile with a carbide hole saw. It works best in a drill press, but a ½-inch hand drill also can be used. In either case, clamp the tile and drill slowly to prevent breaking the tile.

SMOOTHING EDGES

Vitreous tile is as hard as glass. Cutting it with a snap cutter or with tile nippers produces a sharp edge. Unless the cut edge is hidden, it must be smoothed with an abrasive stone or a rotary grinder.

TOOL TIP

ROTARY GRINDING AND CUTTING TOOLS

High-speed rotary grinding and cutting tools are good multi-purpose tools to have on hand. They come with a variety of attachments that make finishing work with stone, metal, or wood fast and easy. Wear goggles and a mask and work in a well-ventilated area.

CURVED CUTS

1 START AT ONE END of the cut line, using about one-quarter of the jaw to make the bite.

2 WORK FROM BOTH ENDS toward the middle. If the nipping is difficult, take even smaller bites.

3 TRIM THE EDGES with a wet saw if the appearance of the cut is important.

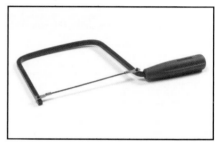

A CARBIDE HOLE SAW, OR ROD SAW, can cut in any direction, but it works well only on soft material such as wall tile.

CUTTING HOLES WITH A HOLE SAW

1 BREAK THROUGH THE GLAZE with a center punch to keep the drill bit from wandering.

2 CLAMP THE TILE firmly to a table or workbench. Go slowly and exert light pressure to avoid breaking the tile.

SMOOTHING EDGES

AN ABRASIVE STONE is used to smooth the edges of a cut tile. Snap cutters tend to leave glass-sharp edges.

A ROTARY GRINDER makes fast work of smoothing tile edges. Use it where you want to bevel an edge deeply.

SETTING TILE

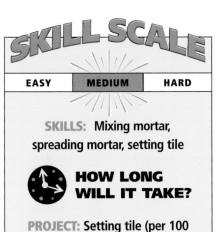
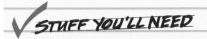

STUFF YOU'LL NEED

TOOLS: ½-inch drill, mixing paddle, 5-gallon bucket, margin trowel, ¼"×¼" square-edge trowel, rubber mallet

MATERIALS: Tile, tile spacers, thin-set mortar with acrylic latex admix, dry-mix grout, short (12–18 inches) length of 2×4

FLAT IS GOOD

You'll never get a good tile job without a flat and level floor. Make sure you fill in all depressions and repair cracks before you lay down the floor. See pages 43-49.

Dry thin-set mortar is mixed with either water or a liquid-latex additive. The mortar is stiffer and heavier than paint, so use a mixing paddle designed for mortar or grout to mix it using the proportions recommended by the manufacturer.

TIPS FOR SETTING TILE

- **Wipe down the backerboard.** Before spreading the mortar, wipe down the backerboard with a damp sponge to remove any dust. Begin near the center of the room spreading enough mortar to cover the area bounded by the set of layout lines (8 to 12 square feet).
- **Pick up the mortar.** Use the flat edge of a square-notch trowel and apply the mortar by pushing it into the face of the backerboard to establish a good bond. Make a layer ⅜ to ½ inch thick.
- **Comb the adhesive into straight lines.** Hold the trowel at 45 degrees to the floor and push the teeth of the trowel to the backerboard. The size of the trowel notches should be the same as the thickness of the tile.
- **Lay the first tile.** After applying and combing thin-set over the area within a set of chalk lines, lay the first tile at the intersection of two lines. Slightly twist the tile back and forth to embed it in the adhesive, and slide the tile into its final position. Some tilesetters then tap the tile lightly with the wood handle of the trowel.
- **Check the adhesive.** Remove the first tile to inspect the mortar on its back. The tile should be completely covered with mortar (see Step 4 on page 62). If it has only parallel ridges, the bed is not thick enough; switch to a trowel with larger notches.
- **Keep the mortar sticky.** As you set the tiles, occasionally touch the mortar to see if it is sticky. If it doesn't stick to your finger, it won't stick to the tiles. Scrape it off the backerboard and reapply a fresh batch of mortar.

  When the mortar bed is thick enough, butt the edge of the second tile against the edge of the first, rotate it down into position, twist it slightly back and forth, and insert the spacers.
- **Level the tiles.** After setting all of the tiles in a section, lay a short piece of 2×4 on the tiles and tap **lightly** with a rubber mallet to level the tiles and to bed them firmly in the adhesive.
- **Remove excess adhesive.** Use a spacer to clean the joints and wipe the faces with a damp sponge to remove the excess.

CLOSER LOOK

PROPER USE OF SPACERS

Spacers may be used flat, requiring only one per four-way intersection. However, removal will require use of a special removal tool and risks disturbing the set tile. It is better to place four spacers on end, as shown. Placed on end, the spacers are easily removed before grouting, allowing for a better grout seal.

1 **MIX THIN-SET MORTAR WITH A PADDLE.** Use a paddle designed for mortar—not paint. Make sure the drill has enough power for the job, and mix at slow speed.

2 **SPREAD ADHESIVE.** Press the mortar into the backerboard with the trowel at a shallow angle in order to make it fully adhere to the backerboard.

3 **COMB THE ADHESIVE** out into straight lines, holding the trowel at 45 degrees to the floor and pushing the trowel teeth to the floor.

4 **LIFT THE FIRST TILE** and check the mortar on its back. Parallel rows show the bed isn't thick enough. Dry areas mean the mortar is too old.

5 **SET REMAINING TILES** by butting edge against edge, hinging down, twisting slightly back and forth, placing spacers, and sliding into the final position.

6 **PLACE SPACERS ON END** so you can remove them easily. Although this requires more spacers, you can reuse them in another part of the project.

GROUTING AND SEALING

| EASY | MEDIUM | HARD |

SKILLS: Mixing and spreading grout

HOW LONG WILL IT TAKE?

PROJECT: Grouting and sealing tile (per 100 sq. ft.)

EXPERIENCED . . . . . 3 HRS.

HANDY . . . . 6 HRS.

NOVICE . . . . 8 HRS.

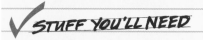

STUFF YOU'LL NEED

TOOLS: Margin trowel, 5-gallon bucket, grout float, grout bag (if tile joints are more than ⅜ inch), sponge, rubber gloves, stiff scrub brush, spray bottle

MATERIALS: Grout with latex additive, clean soft rags and cloths, tile and grout cleaner, penetrating sealer

SANDED OR UNSANDED GROUT—WHICH TO USE

Use sanded grout on joints wider than ⅛ inch. Use unsanded grout on joints ⅛ inch or less.

Grouting is the process of filling the spaces between the tiles. Grout comes in powder form in many premixed colors. Grout that is a different color than the tile emphasizes the design, while grout and tile of the same color makes the design recede. If you need more than a single bag of dyed grout, premix all of the bags to assure a uniform grout color.

SEAL THE TILES

Glazed tiles do not need to be sealed, but if the tile is unglazed and rough or porous such as brick or quarry tile, preseal the faces of the tiles before grouting. Otherwise, you may not be able to remove grout residue. The quickest, easiest way to preseal tile is to lay it all out, butted together with no spaces, and roll sealer onto the tile with a foam roller. Protect the floor beneath from sealer that drips down between the cracks. Before grouting, let the mortar cure for at least 24 hours. Remove the spacers and clean any mortar out of the joints with a bristle brush before applying the grout.

FOLLOW THE DIRECTIONS

Grout comes with or without latex additive. If the package doesn't contain additive, mix the powder with liquid latex instead of water. If the directions call for mixing with water, and your water is hard (contains minerals), use demineralized water.

To mix strong, colorfast grout, use the least amount of liquid possible. Mix thoroughly to minimize color variation. Make only as much as you can use before it begins to set. Store unmixed grout in a dry place for future repairs.

Do not damp cure tinted grout. Damp curing can dissolve the tint and leave an inconsistent color.

USING A GROUT BAG

The grout float doesn't work well on joints wider than ⅜ inch or on tile with irregular edges. Instead, use a grout bag with a tip sized to the joint (the tips are interchangeable). Apply just enough grout to fill the joints, then smooth the joint with the rounded end of a wooden trowel handle or other cylindrical object larger than the joint.

GROUTING AND SEALING (CONTINUED)

1 **MIX THE GROUT** with a margin trowel. Let the mixed grout slake (rest) for 10 minutes to let the dyes develop; then remix. If your water is hard, use demineralized water.

2 **SPREAD GROUT** in sweeping arcs with a rubber grout float held at a shallow angle. Press the grout into the joints, filling them completely. For joints wider than ⅜ inch, use a grout bag.

3 **REMOVE THE EXCESS** grout with the grout float held at a steep angle. Sweep the float diagonally across the tiles to avoid dipping into the joints.

4 **TEST THE GROUT**. When your thumbnail leaves no impression (10 to 15 minutes or per manufacturer's instructions) clean the tiles.

5 **WIPE THE TILES** with a damp sponge (wring dripless) to remove grout residue. If the residue resists, use a scrub pad, but avoid scrubbing the joints.

6 **REMOVE THE HAZE** immediately. Do not take a break. First wipe the haze with a damp cloth, then buff the tiles with a clean, dry cloth.

7 **CURE THE GROUT** by misting it twice a day for three days. Don't mist tinted grout. Misting can dissolve the tint and leave an inconsistent color.

8 **APPLY TILE AND GROUT CLEANER** with a sponge, then scrub the surface with a stiff brush. Rinse thoroughly and let the floor dry before applying the sealer.

9 **APPLY PENETRATING SEALER** after the grout has damp-cured a minimum of 3 days. Apply 6–8 sq. ft. of sealer with a sponge and wipe up the excess before the liquid dries.

64

THE RUSTIC LOOK OF TUMBLED STONE

Tumbled stone tiles, with their characteristic rounded edges and rough-hewn qualities are an elegant option for floors, walls, and countertops. Tiles are usually marble or slate and imported from Italy. The tiles are "tumbled" in abrasives and sometimes bathed in acid to round the edges and accentuate the natural veining. See page 192 for information on contacting manufacturers of the tiles pictured.

EACH TILE IS UNIQUE

Unlike finished marble or granite, flaws—open veins, chips, and depressions—in tumbled tiles are part of the finished look. Colors are natural, ranging from neutral tans to reds, browns, greens, and blacks. Combining field tiles, which are usually 4×4 inch squares, with borders, listellos, or pre-designed and mesh-backed medallions as shown on the upper left offers classic focal points on floors, walls, and countertops.

FOLLOW THE DIRECTIONS

Installed in mortar or thin-set like other tiles, tumbled tiles are usually

COMBINING TUMBLED MARBLE and rock matrix tiles on the floor creates a richness of texture and a timeless feeling in a shower stall.

given a matte finish or left unfinished to accentuate the natural look. But they must be sealed before grouting to prevent stains. Deep veins in the surface can be filled with grout as well. Products called stone enhancers can be applied to accent natural veining and color. Tiles should be cleaned with a damp mop. Avoid detergents. Check with your home center or tile supplier for more detail on options, installation, and maintenance for tumbled tile.

WORK SMARTER

INSTALLATION TIPS

▪ Wash any dust from the backs of the tiles and let them dry before installation.

▪ The stone in darker tiles tends to be softer and tends to be harder in lighter tiles, often making lighter tiles a better choice for flooring.

▪ Do a test. Install a few tiles on a 2'x2' piece of backerboard and let the mortar dry overnight. Look for stains. Pull on the tile to check the bond.

▪ Use white thin-set mortar for light, white, or translucent stones to prevent mortar from showing through the tile.

▪ Mix the tiles from each box together before you begin tiling to keep the pattern and color random.

▪ Use unsanded grout.

▪ Colored grouts can stain stone, so test on a spare tile first. Seal tumbled stone per manufacturer's instructions before grouting to prevent staining.

THE WARMTH OF A TUMBLED MARBLE BACKSPLASH is the perfect complement for a solid surface, easy-to-clean composite countertop.

BUILDING A CUSTOM SHOWER PAN

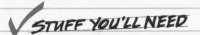

STUFF YOU'LL NEED

TOOLS: Hammer, framing square, tape measure, level, carbide scorer, utility knife, adjustable wrench, scissors, stapler, ½-inch drill, mixing paddle, finishing trowel, notched trowel, grout float, saber saw, marker, wood screed

MATERIALS: ¾-inch exterior plywood, 2×4 studs, pressure-treated 2×4s, pressure-treated 2×6s, backerboard screws, ½-inch cement backerboard, sand mix, mortar, 4-mil poly sheeting (walls), 40-mil CPE shower pan liner, masking tape, CPE adhesive, shower drain, thinset, wall tiles, floor tiles, grout

A shower floor requires a thick, carefully flattened, mortar bed to support the tiles and to prevent them from cracking. A bed consists of three layers. The first is sand mix, a mixture of portland cement and sand that forms a strong substructure. The second layer is a plastic liner. The third layer is regular mortar that goes on top of the liner. Together the three layers provide a dense, watertight surface that won't flex. The bed is covered by a layer of thinset and finally, the tile.

The liner—a flexible 40-mil sheet of CPE plastic—keeps the water from soaking through the tile and mortar into the subfloor. When you buy the drain fitting for the shower stall, make sure you get one called a tile shower drain, that is designed to make the whole system watertight.

Choose the correct tile. Floor tiles can be applied to a wall, but wall tiles are too thin to use on the floor.

Homer's Hindsight

TILE THE WALLS BEFORE YOU FINISH TILING THE FLOOR

One of my customers had laid a perfect mortar bed for the floor tiles, put the tiles in thinset, and then started to tile the walls. Big mistake. Mortar falling off the trowel quickly covered the floor tiles, and when he accidentally dropped the trowel, it chipped a floor tile. Once you get your mortar bed laid, tile the walls before you tile the floor. Things dropping on the mortar bed will do far less damage to it than they would to a tile.

FLOORS

1 **PREPARE THE FLOOR.** If the subfloor is not ¾-inch plywood in good repair, replace it with ¾-inch exterior plywood. (See page 41.)

2 **FRAME THE SHOWER STALL** with 2×4 studs. Install pressure-treated 2×6 blocking on edge between the bases of the studs.

3 **BUILD A THRESHOLD** by facenailing three pressure-treated 2×4s in the shower opening.

4 **CUT A HOLE** in the floor and install and connect the lower piece of the drain, called the drain base. Temporarily tape the opening shut.

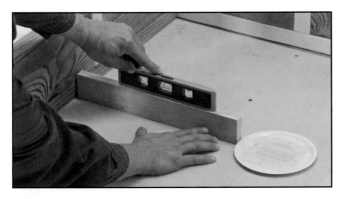

5 **PREPARE FOR THE FIRST MORTAR BASE.** Use a level to transfer the level position of the floor at the drain to the walls and curb to account for any irregularities on the surface of the floor.

6 **MAKE GUIDE MARKS AROUND THE SHOWER BASE.** Measure ¼ inch above the original mark for every foot between the drain and the wall, and make marks around the walls and curb to act as guides for the mortar base.

FLOORS

7 **MIX SAND MIX** with enough water to make a crumbly cement mixture that just holds together.

8 **LAY A SAND MIX BED** between the drain and the marks on the wall to create the slope of the shower.

CLOSER LOOK

TO SEAM CPE SHOWER MEMBRANE:

1. Remove dust, dirt, oil, and water from a 2-inch wide strip along surfaces to be joined.
2. Coat a 2 inch-wide strip on the mating surfaces of both pieces with the recommended adhesive.
3. Immediately join the two surfaces. The adhesive must be wet when you do.
4. Press the surfaces together for 2 to 3 minutes by rolling the seam with a rolling pin.
5. Place a heavy object along the entire seam for 2 to 4 hours.
6. Install the liner. Allow it to cure overnight before conducting the water test described in Step 17.

9 **SCREED THE SAND MIX BASE** with a piece of wood so the bed slopes from the line on the wall to the floor at the drain base but not over it.

10 **FINISH WITH A STEEL TROWEL** to create a smooth surface. Let the bed cure per manufacturer's instructions before applying the plastic liner.

11 CUT THE LINER TO SIZE, seaming it if necessary. On the side walls, the liner should extend 2 inches above finished height of curb. At the curb it should be long enough to go over the curb and about halfway back down to the floor.

12 REMOVE THE TAPE. Apply a bead of 100 percent silicon caulk around the face of the drain base. Screw the drain bolts part way in. (See inset.)

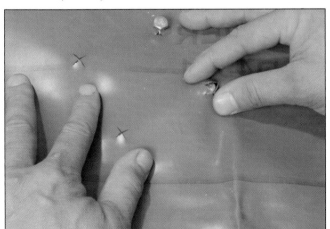

13 PUT THE LINER IN PLACE. Cut a small X over each bolt head so the liner will slip over it. Push the liner into the caulk. Flatten the liner with your hands, working from the drain toward the walls to smooth out the air bubbles.

TO MAKE A HOSPITAL CORNER:

1. Fold and crease one flap.
2. Fold and crease the second flap.
3. Join both flaps at the corner and pinch them together to form a triangle.
4. Press the triangle to one side, then staple in place.

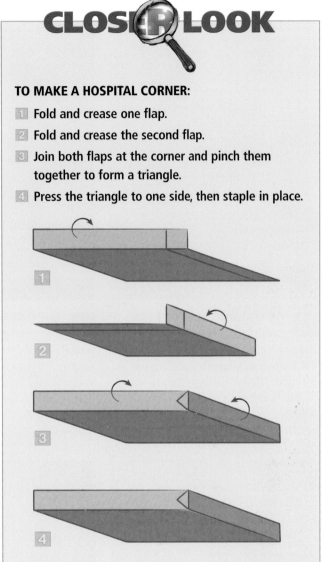

FLOORS

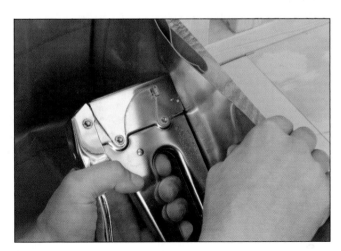

14 MAKE HOSPITAL CORNERS and staple the liner to the wall ½ inch below the edge of the liner.

BUILDING A CUSTOM SHOWER PAN (CONTINUED)

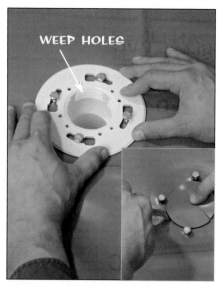

15 **ON OUTSIDE CORNERS OR CURBS,** cut along the corner to allow the material to make the bend. Cut out the excess. Glue on a patch made by the manufacturer that's shaped to fit corners and curbs using the same adhesive you use to make a seam.

16 **CUT OUT THE DRAIN HOLE.** (See inset.) Put the clamping ring (the second part of the drain) over the bolts and tighten. The clamping ring has weep holes to drain away any water that might gather underneath the finished surface. Allow the liner to cure overnight before applying the mortar bed.

17 **TEST FOR LEAKS.** Plug the drain with a test plug, available in the plumbing department, and fill the pan to the top of the curb. The plug goes far enough into the drain to keep the water from draining out through the weep holes. Check for leaks after 4 hours. Patch as needed. (See "Closer Look," page 68.)

18 **STAPLE 4-MIL POLY TO THE WALLS,** letting it overlap the liner by 2 inches. Staple it to the studs just above the top of the liner, but don't staple through the liner.

19 **INSTALL ½-INCH BACKERBOARD ON THE WALLS AND CURB.** Leave 1 inch between the bottom edge of the wall and the liner. Don't drive any screws through the shower pan liner. Install backerboard on both sides of the curb before you install the top of the curb. The curb panels need to be screwed in, but use no more than three screws on each.

20 **PUT THE DRAIN BARREL IN** and set the top at finished height—1½ inches above the liner, plus the combined thickness of the tile and thinset.

70

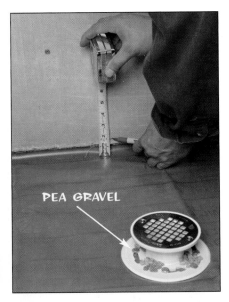

21 MARK THE WALLS, CURB, AND DRAIN BARREL 1½ inches above the liner. Cover the area around the drain with pea gravel to keep the mortar from sealing the weep holes. You will cover the gravel with the final mortar bed.

PEA GRAVEL

22 FILL THE PAN WITH MORTAR to the level of the marks you made. Use a cement product designed for mortar beds. Cover the pea gravel, being careful not to plug the weep holes.

23 SCREED AS BEFORE, creating a flat surface that slopes toward the drain and is even with the marks on the wall and drain.

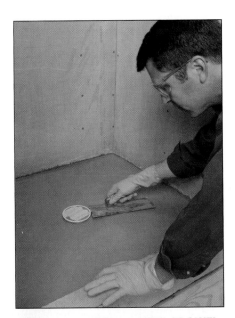

24 FINISH WITH A STEEL TROWEL, creating a smooth plane between the marks on the wall and those on the drain. Let the mortar cure for 24 hours.

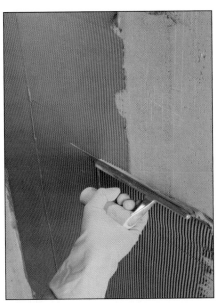

25 TILE THE WALLS. Although you can tile the floor before you tile the walls, most professionals tile the walls first to avoid damaging the floor tile in case a tool is dropped. It will also be easier to clean up mortar spills. Protect the shower floor with cardboard. Use a notched trowel to apply latex modified thinset and set the wall tiles. (See Chapter 3, "Walls," page 73.)

26 SET THE FLOOR TILE in thinset, cutting the tile to fit around the drain. Let the mortar cure, as directed on the bag, and then apply grout first to the wall and then to the floor.

WALLS

The grade of the tile used for a wall is not as important as it is for floors because no one, except possibly Spiderman, actually walks on a wall. Also, the substrate for wall tile does not need to be as stiff as that required for floors because weight is less of an issue. A single layer of cement backerboard applied directly over framing is often adequate. Check your local codes before proceeding.

A LITTLE PRACTICE CAN'T HURT

Wall tiles tend to slide downward during installation because of gravity. Mixing the mortar correctly so that it has "hang" (ability to support a tile's weight) helps, but depends to some degree on temperature and humidity. Practice your mortar-mixing and tilesetting skills on a floor or small wall area before tackling an entire wall or shower stall. Once you have gained confidence, you will find directions in this chapter that will allow you to tackle the complex projects.

GET THE RIGHT TILE FOR THE JOB

Pay particular attention to the water absorption rate of the tile you are buying. For areas that could get wet, you should buy tile that is labeled either vitreous or impervious.

CHAPTER THREE CONTENTS

74	**Choosing Wall Tile**
75	**Tile Ratings**
75	Reading a Rating Label
76	**Tools for Tiling Walls**
76	Tools for Measuring and Laying Out
77	Tools for Setting and Grouting
78	Tools for Cutting and Shaping
78	Using a Rotary Cutter
80	**Wall Tiling Materials**
80	Backerboard and Fasteners
80	Adhesives, Grouts, and Sealers
81	**Project Planning**
82	**Preparing the Base**
82	Drywall
83	Plaster
83	Masonry
84	**Installing Backerboard**
86	**Tile Layout Lines**
88	**Marking and Cutting the Tiles**
90	**Setting and Grouting**
94	**Tiling a Tub or Shower Surround**

CHOOSING WALL TILE

Wall tiles are available in a variety of sizes, colors, shapes, patterns, and textures. With the exception of areas that will be wet, almost anything goes. The biggest challenge may be narrowing your selection from thousands of available designs.

The photograph, right, shows only a few choices; see **Decorative Tile Gallery,** page 20, for more.

Hand-crafted decorative tiles can be expensive, and an entire wall of decorative tiles is likely to be visually overwhelming. Many attractive installations use decorative tiles as accents, borders, or murals set into a background of inexpensive field tiles.

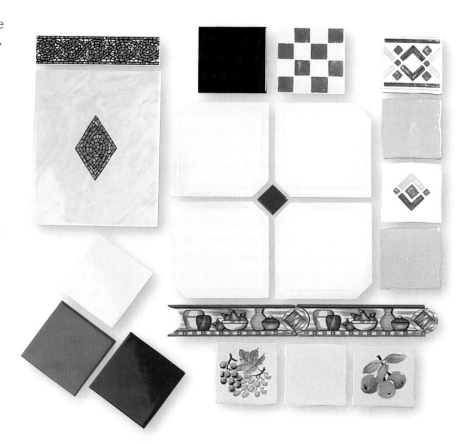

BUYER'S GUIDE

TILE CHARACTERISTICS

TYPE OF TILE	COST	RELATIVE DURABILITY	WATER ABSORPTION	MAINTENANCE
Glazed wall	Low to medium	Low to high	Medium	Low
Glazed decorative	High	Low to medium	Medium	Low
Porcelain	Medium	High	Low	Low
Quarry	Low to medium	High	Medium	Low
Terra-cotta	Low to medium	Low	Medium to high	High
Natural stone	Low to high	High	Low to high	Medium to high
Cement-bodied	Low	High	Low	Low to medium

TILE RATINGS

Although any tile that appeals to you can be used on walls in dry locations, most tile—particularly floor tile—is labeled with one of six ratings. Here is a guide:

■ PEI Wear Rating—resistant to abrasion so it's suitable for foot traffic.
■ Water Absorption—percentage of water absorbed, a measure of suitability for wet areas.

■ Coefficient of Friction—slip resistance on a scale of 0 to 1.0, a measure of safety for floors.
■ Tone—whether the color of the tile is variable or uniform.
■ Frost Resistance—whether a tile is warranted against damage by freezing and thawing.

Use the guide below to help you select the appropriate tile for your application.

READING A RATING LABEL

GRADE: #1 Standard—suitable for most applications; #2 Second—structurally similar to #1, but with minor glaze or size imperfections; #3 Decorative—thin wall tile, suitable only for wall applications.

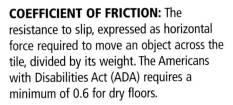

PEI: Wear Rating: 1, 2—not suitable for floors (walls only); 3—all residential; 4—residential and light commercial (restaurants, etc.); 4+—commercial and heavy traffic (airports, etc.).

WATER ABSORPTION: Percentage by weight: nonvitreous, more than 7%; semi-vitreous, 3–7%; vitreous, 0.5–3%; impervious, less than 0.5%. Only vitreous and impervious tiles should be used in wet and freeze/thaw applications.

COEFFICIENT OF FRICTION: The resistance to slip, expressed as horizontal force required to move an object across the tile, divided by its weight. The Americans with Disabilities Act (ADA) requires a minimum of 0.6 for dry floors.

TONE: The multi-shade icon indicates the tile has variations in tone. This is true of most tile, except for those of pure color, such as white or black. Squares all the same shade indicates no tone variation.

FROST RESISTANCE: A snowflake shows the tile is frost-resistant and is suitable for use in exterior freeze/thaw applications. It does not guarantee the tile won't lift, however, as that is also a function of the adhesive and the conditions when set.

RECOMMENDED RATINGS FOR WALL TILES

CONDITIONS/ TYPICAL AREAS	GRADE	PEI	WATER ABSORPTION	COEFFICIENT OF FRICTION	TONE	FROST PROOF YES/NO
Interior, clean and dry areas (living room, dining room, hall)	1 or 2	1+	any	NA	Any	No
Interior, smoky or greasy areas (kitchen)	1 or 2	2+	less than 7%	NA	Any	No
Interior, wet areas (tub/shower enclosures, pools)	1 or 2	2+	less than 3%	NA	Any	No

TOOLS FOR TILING WALLS

Quality tools will pay for themselves over time. The amount you spend should depend upon how often you plan to use them. Professional tools can last a lifetime if properly cared for. Ease of use may be as important as durability.

Consider how many times you will need the tool. If the purchase cost divided by the rental cost is greater than the number of times to be used, rent it.

USING SAFETY GLASSES AND DUST RESPIRATORS

Always wear safety glasses and a dust respirator when you are creating dust and debris. Flying chunks of mortar or tile can damage your eyes and airborne particles can damage your respiratory system. Dust respirators are less effective when worn over a beard.

BUYER'S GUIDE

TOOL	USE FOR	PRICE	IMPORTANCE
MEASURING AND LAYING OUT			
Chalk line	layout, cut lines	$	must have
China marker	marking tile cuts	$	or felt-tip or pencil
Combination square	marking tile cuts	$$	nice to have
Framing square	establishing square	$$	must have
Tape measure	measuring	$$	must have
4-foot level	establishing level, vertical	$$	can use small level
CUTTING AND SHAPING			
Abrasive stone	smoothing cut edges	$$	nice to have
Carbide (glass) bit	small holes in tile	$$	only for small holes
Carbide hole saw	large holes in tile	$$	must if hole is inside tile
Carbide-grit rod saw	curved tile cuts	$$	nice to have
Dust respirator	respiratory protection	$	must have
Ear plugs	hearing protection	$	must have
Mason's hammer	shaping rough stone	$$	must for cleft stone
Safety glasses	eye protection	$	must have
Snap cutter	straight tile cuts	$$$	must, or wet saw
Tile nippers	intricate tile cuts	$$	must have
Wet saw	straight tile cuts	$$$	nice to have
SETTING AND GROUTING			
Caulking gun	caulking joints	$	must have
Grout float	spreading grout	$$	must have
Margin trowel	mixing and spreading grout	$	nice to have
Mortar mixing paddle	mixing grout	$$	must have
Nonabrasive pad	removing excess grout	$	must have
Notched trowel	applying mortar	$$	must have
Round-corner sponge	removing excess grout	$	must have
Rubber gloves	hand protection	$	must have
½-inch drill	mixing adhesives	$$$	must have

TOOLS FOR MEASURING AND LAYING OUT

Ⓐ 4-FOOT LEVEL
To establish level and vertical.

Ⓑ CHALK LINE
To snap tile layout lines.

Ⓒ CHINA MARKER (WAX PEN
To make temporary cut marks on t of a tile.

Ⓓ COMBINATION SQUARE
A guide for marking straight, notc and L-cuts.

Ⓔ FRAMING SQUARE
For establishing perpendicular anc a guide for cutting.

Ⓕ TAPE MEASURE
For accurate measuring.

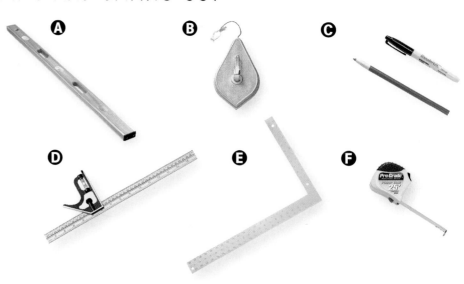

TOOLS FOR SETTING AND GROUTING

(A) ½-INCH ELECTRIC DRILL
For mixing and applying large amounts of adhesive and grout.

(B) CAULKING GUN
Used for caulking tub and tile joints.

(C) CLEAN, SOFT CLOTH
For removing grout haze.

(D) DUST RESPIRATOR
Wear respirators when working with mortar and chemical powders.

(E) FOAM PAINTBRUSHES
For applying sealer.

(F) GROUT FLOAT
For filling grout joints.

(G) MARGIN TROWEL
For mixing and applying small amounts of adhesive and grout.

(H) MORTAR MIXING PADDLE
For mixing and applying large amounts of adhesive and grout.

(I) NONABRASIVE SCOURING PAD
For removing stubborn grout residue.

(J) NOTCHED TROWEL(S)
For spreading adhesive to setting bed.

(K) ROUND-CORNER SPONGE
For removing grout residue and applying sealer.

(L) RUBBER GLOVES
For protecting hands from grout and other caustic materials.

(M) SAFETY GLASSES
Wear safety glasses when working with hand and power tools.

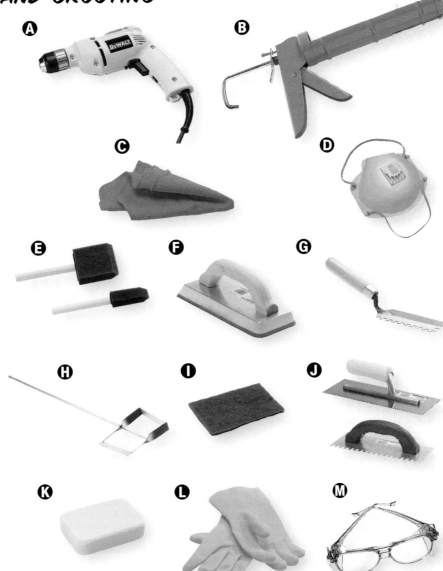

WALLS

TOOL TIP

TROWEL SIZE GUIDE FOR THESE TILES	NOTCH	TROWEL	MORTAR PATTERN
Mosaic and smaller tile (less than 2"×2")	³⁄₁₆"×⁵⁄₃₂" V-notch		
4¼"×4¼" wall tile	¼"×³⁄₁₆" V-notch		
Wall tile larger than 6"×6" Flat-backed floor tile to 8"×8" Marble and granite	¼"×¼" square-notch		

TOOLS FOR CUTTING AND SHAPING

Ⓐ ABRASIVE STONE
Smooths sharp edges of cut tiles.

Ⓑ CARBIDE HOLE SAW
Drills large holes through tiles, such as for water pipes. Available in a variety of sizes.

Ⓒ CARBIDE (GLASS) BIT
Drills small holes through tiles.

Ⓓ CARBIDE-GRIT ROD SAW
Makes intricate cuts. The rod can be removed and fed through a hole.

Ⓔ DUST RESPIRATOR
Wear respirators when working with mortar and chemical powders.

Ⓕ EAR PLUGS
Protect hearing from damaging sounds such as power tools.

Ⓖ ROTARY GRINDING AND CUTTING TOOL
Smooths and bevels sharp tile edges. Cuts tile with special attachments.

Ⓗ SAFETY GLASSES
Wear safety glasses when working with hand and power tools.

Ⓘ SNAP CUTTER
Scores and snaps tiles in straight lines.

Ⓙ SPIRAL SAW
Quickly and easily cuts soft wall tile.

Ⓚ TILE NIPPERS
Makes curved or intricate cuts by nibbling away tile.

Ⓛ WET SAW
Quickly and easily makes straight, notched, and L-shape cuts.

USING ROTARY CUTTERS AND SPIRAL SAWS

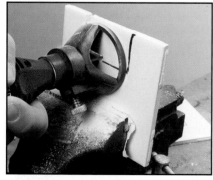

A ROTARY CUTTER cuts through soft wall tile as if it were wood. Clamp the tile between wood strips in a vise.

USE TWO HANDS. Cutting tools tend to wander, so use both hands in intricate cuts and when you want a straight cut.

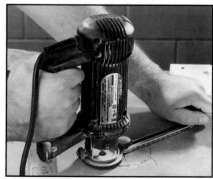

CUT CIRCLES WITH A SPIRAL SAW with the circle accessory. Locate the accessory's pivot at the center of the circle and swing the arc.

FOUR WAYS TO CUT TILE

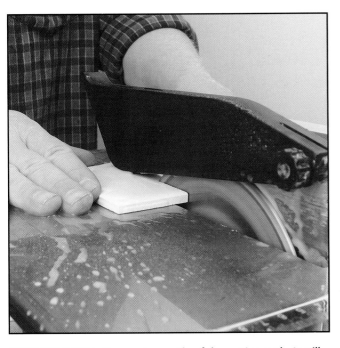

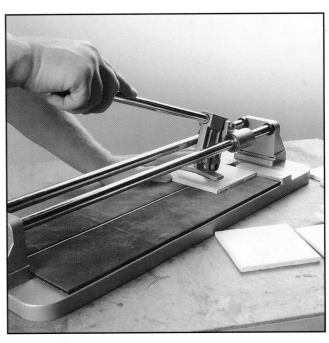

THE WET SAW is the most versatile of the cutting tools. It will cut through the hardest tile with ease. With practice, you can use it to make straight, L-shape, notched, square, and even intricate cuts. See pages 33-34 for making the various cuts. Unless you're doing a lot of tiling, this is a rental.

THE SNAP CUTTER is the quickest, easiest tool for making straight cuts. While it leaves little mess, it does leave sharp cut edges that, if exposed, must be smoothed. For details on its use, see page 35.

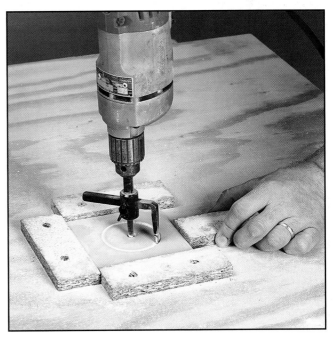

TILE NIPPERS may seem about as sophisticated as a hammer, but make curved and intricate cuts by biting away chunks of the tile. The tool is a must unless you have a wet saw. See page 35 for instructions on its use.

AN ADJUSTABLE CARBIDE HOLE DRILL cuts circular holes up to 3 inches in diameter in soft wall tile, but requires great care. Nail cleats around the tile rather than holding by hand. For harder tile, use a carbide hole saw, as shown on page 35.

WALLS

79

WALL TILING MATERIALS

BACKERBOARD AND FASTENERS

CEMENT BACKERBOARD, a rigid and water-resistant, glass-fiber reinforced cement panel, is a perfect base for setting tile. It has two thicknesses (¼ inch and ½ inch) and three panel sizes (3'×5', 4'×4', and 4'×8').

SPECIAL FASTENERS for cement backerboard are 1¼-inch (1½-inch for ½-inch board) long No. 8-18×⅜-inch wafer-head galvanized self-countersinking screws. You also can use 1¼-inch barbed galvanized roofing nails.

15-POUND ROOFING FELT 4-mil polyethylene sheeting or a 40-mil CPE shower pan membrane can be used for waterproofing wall framing, depending on the severity of the application—with a steam bath requiring the most waterproofing.

ADHESIVES, GROUTS, AND SEALERS

Ⓐ FLEXIBLE THIN-SET MORTAR
For setting backerboard and tile in difficult situations. Contains latex additive.

Ⓑ LATEX ADDITIVE
Increases adhesion, strength, and flexibility of thin-set mortars and grouts.

Ⓒ THIN-SET MORTAR
For setting backerboard and tile in most situations. Requires latex additive.

Ⓓ BONDING MORTAR
For setting backerboard and tile in most situations. Contains latex additive.

Ⓔ CERAMIC TILE MASTIC
For setting ceramic tile.

Ⓕ SANDED GROUT
For filling grout joints wider than ⅛ inch.

Ⓖ NON-SANDED GROUT
For filling grout joints narrower than ⅛ inch.

Ⓗ SEALERS
For protecting tile and grout from stains and scuff marks.

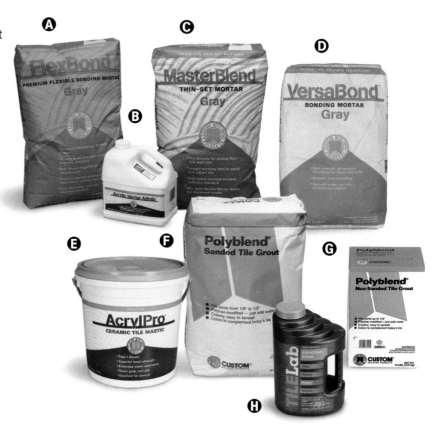

PROJECT PLANNING

lanning is the key to success for every project. Two factors make this especially true for tiling walls. First, when you start to spread mortar, you have a limited time before the mortar sets up. Second, undoing a mistake is not a matter of pulling nails and refastening; it is a matter of destroying and throwing away tiles, and beginning all over again. Here are some considerations.

DESIGN
- Is the tile readily available in sufficient quantity, or does it have to be ordered?
- Can you return any unused tile?
- Do you have enough tile on hand (wall area plus 10 percent)?

EVALUATING THE BASE
- Is the existing wall surface suitable or must you replace or cover it?
- Is the existing floor surface suitable or must you replace or cover it?

LAYING CEMENT BACKERBOARD
- Can you transport and handle the heavy panels (3'×5'×½" panel weighs 45 pounds, 4'×8'×½" weighs 96 pounds)?
- Do you have the recommended fasteners and tools to drive them?

MARKING TILE LAYOUT LINES
- Can you make an accurate, to-scale sketch of the existing wall?
- Do you have the geometric aptitude required to lay out an orthogonal grid?

MARKING AND CUTTING TILES
- Should you rent a wet saw, and do you have a place to use it that won't be damaged by water?
- Can you get a helper to make the tile cuts while you set the tile?

SETTING THE TILE
- Will you set the tile by eye, or will you use spacers?
- Can you get a second helper to mix the thin-set while you concentrate on setting the tile?

GROUTING THE JOINTS
- Does the tile require sealing before grouting the joints?
- Will someone be around to mist the grout twice a day for 2 days?

SEALING
- Does the tile require sealing, as well as the grout?
- Will you be using a topical (surface) or penetrating sealer?

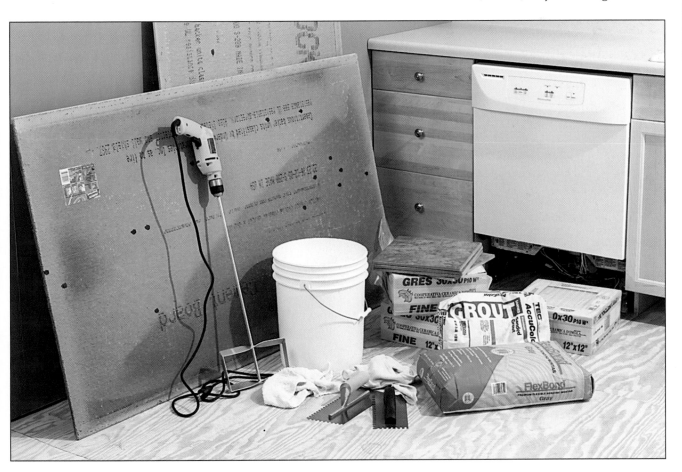

PREPARING THE BASE

DRYWALL

If the wall is in a moist location, staple 4-mil polyethylene to the wall as a moisture barrier; then cover it with ¼-inch backerboard as an ideal base for the tile. Fasten the backerboard to the studs through the drywall. In areas where there will be no moisture, sound drywall is an adequate base for wall tile. Small dings and scratches don't matter; they will be filled and covered with thin-set mortar. Wallpaper is another matter. The moisture in the thin-set will likely dissolve the wallpaper adhesive, and the wallpaper—tile and all—may come tumbling down.

WALLS

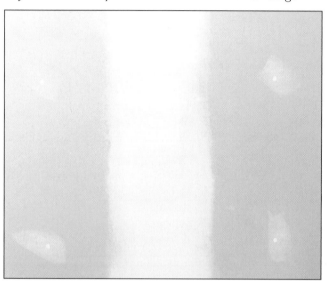

DRYWALL needs to be clean and solid without loose paint, wall, or wallpaper adhesive residue. New, properly taped drywall is ideal.

REMOVE wallpaper with a 4- to 6-inch scraper. If the scraper is metal, round off the corners to avoid damaging the drywall. Sand off any wallpaper adhesive residue with 80-grit sandpaper; then remove the dust with a clean, damp cloth.

PAINT must be sanded with 80-grit sandpaper in order to remove loose paint and to give the paint gripping ability. Don't sand through the paint. Wear a dust respirator when sanding.

REMOVE SANDING DUST with a clean, damp sponge. Kitchen walls are often greasy from cooking; wash them with TSP and let dry before sanding.

PLASTER

Plaster that is solid, hard, and not cracked is an ideal setting surface for wall tile. If the plaster powders when you dig into it with a screwdriver, or if it contains cracks that span more than a single stud space (about 16 inches), either remove it or cover it with drywall or ¼-inch cement backerboard. If the room is subject to moisture, staple 4-mil polyethylene sheeting to the wall before fastening the drywall or backerboard.

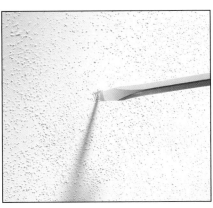

PLASTER must be clean, hard, and not cracked. If not, fasten ¼-inch backerboard to the studs through the plaster.

HARD PLASTER is nearly as hard as concrete and doesn't powder when you dig at its surface with a screwdriver.

SOFT PLASTER, which contains too high a ratio of lime, powders easily and is not a good setting bed for tile.

MASONRY

Masonry (concrete, concrete block, and brick) walls provide the best setting surfaces for tile, provided they are clean, flat, and not cracked. Unfortunately, most masonry walls—even poured concrete—are not flat. Minor bumps and hollows can be ground or filled, but larger ones require a professionally applied skim-coat of mortar, or furring and backerboard.

If the masonry is oily or greasy, wash it with a TSP solution, followed by a clean water rinse.

If the masonry is painted, you will, unfortunately, have to remove the paint in order for the mortar to stick.

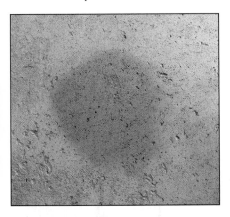

CLEAN CONCRETE is indicated by water readily being absorbed. If water wets the wall, so will thin-set mortar.

OILY OR GREASY CONCRETE causes water to bead on its surface. Thin-set mortar will not bond to a greasy surface.

A SKIM-COAT OF MORTAR applied by a professional is the best way to flatten an irregular masonry wall.

INSTALLING BACKERBOARD

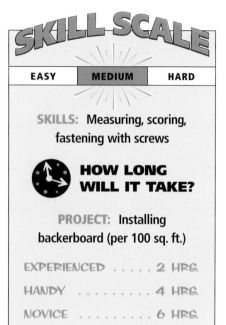

SKILL SCALE

EASY	MEDIUM	HARD

SKILLS: Measuring, scoring, fastening with screws

HOW LONG WILL IT TAKE?

PROJECT: Installing backerboard (per 100 sq. ft.)

EXPERIENCED . . . . . 2 HRS.

HANDY . . . . 4 HRS.

NOVICE . . . . 6 HRS.

✓ STUFF YOU'LL NEED

TOOLS: Marker, chalk line, tape measure, straightedge, carbide scorer (or utility knife with extra blades), ½-inch drill, mixing paddle, ¼"×¼" square-notched trowel, margin trowel, safety glasses

MATERIALS: ½-inch cement backerboard, thin-set mortar with acrylic latex admix, 16d nails, fiberglass tape, backerboard screws or galvanized roofing nails

I f the wall you plan to tile is not suitable (see Preparing the Base, pages 82-83), install ½-inch backerboard. Backerboard provides a quality surface for setting tile. The board is mortar, reinforced on both faces with fiberglass scrim (screen); the mortar provides the hardness; and the fiberglass the stiffness needed for a strong, sturdy tile application.

Installing backerboard is similar to installing drywall. In spite of the hardness, the panels are easily screwed and nailed. Cutting the panels consists of scoring and snapping.

Backerboard is notable for its weight. A 4×8-foot sheet of ½-inch backerboard weighs 98 pounds. The ¼-inch board weighs approximately half that much. Most home centers carry the smaller and popular 3'×5' and 4'×4' panels.

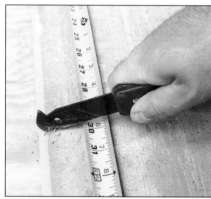

1 **MEASURE AND MARK** both edges of the panel; then snap a chalk line or draw the cut line using a long straightedge.

2 **SCORE THE PANEL** along the line with a carbide scorer or a utility knife if you have a lot of extra blades. Cut through the fiberglass strands.

3 **SNAP THE PANEL** after scoring both sides. Place your knee next to the cut line and lift the panel edge to snap the panel.

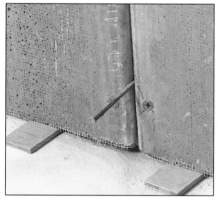

4 **SPACE PANELS** ¼ inch off the floor and ⅛ inch apart at the seams. A 16d common nail provides a convenient ⅛-inch spacer.

5 **FASTEN THE PANELS** with either 1¼-inch-long No. 8-18×⅜" wafer-head galvanized backerboard screws or 1¼-inch galvanized roofing nails.

6 **SPACE FASTENERS** every 8 inches over studs and around the perimeter. Keep back ½ inch from the panel edges and 2 inches from corners.

7 **FILL THE JOINTS** with thin-set mortar using the margin trowel. Press the mortar into the joint, then spread it to 3 inches.

8 **BED 2-INCH FIBERGLASS TAPE** in the wet thin-set and smooth it out with the margin trowel.

9 **PANEL EDGES WITH EXPOSED FIBERGLASS SCRIM** on the rounded edges don't require fiberglass tape application.

10 **COVER THE TAPE** after the thin-set dries. Smooth with the flat edge of a square-tooth trowel, leaving no bumps to interfere with the tile.

WORK SMARTER

SPEED THINGS UP BY PRESETTING THE SCREWS

Most of the time required to drive backerboard screws is taken up by fumbling in your nail apron for the screws. Although the screws pull themselves into the panel once the threads engage, they have a hard time penetrating the rocklike surface.

For these reasons, you will find it much faster to preset the screws by tapping them in about one quarter of the way with a hammer. You can cut the time in half again by giving the presetting operation to an assistant.

WALLS

Homer's Hindsight

MISSED OPPORTUNITY?

The outside walls of kitchens and baths in cold parts of the country can never have too tight a vapor barrier on the warm sides. If you surface the wall with cement backerboard, a nearly perfect vapor barrier can be easily added by simply tacking up a continuous sheet of 4-mil poly sheeting before installing the backerboard. **Don't forget!**

TILE LAYOUT LINES

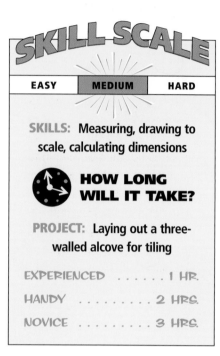

SKILL SCALE

EASY	MEDIUM	HARD

SKILLS: Measuring, drawing to scale, calculating dimensions

HOW LONG WILL IT TAKE?

PROJECT: Laying out a three-walled alcove for tiling

EXPERIENCED . . . . . . 1 HR.

HANDY . . . . 2 HRS.

NOVICE . . . . 3 HRS.

Proper layout before installing wall tiles is crucial. It allows you to:

- balance the design for a pleasing appearance
- minimize the number of cuts
- estimate the number of tiles

First document the size and shape of the area you plan to tile (here a 4×6-foot alcove). Measure and sketch the plan to scale, either on gridded graph paper or on a computer.

Divide the midheight dimension by the tile size. If the resulting fraction is less than half a tile, shift the midheight line by one-half tile and snap a new horizontal line.

Measure the width of the back wall, divide by two, then mark a midwidth line with a felt-tip pen. Divide the midwidth dimension by the tile unit dimension. If the resulting fraction is less than half a tile, shift the vertical centerline by one half tile and snap a new vertical reference line.

STUFF YOU'LL NEED

TOOLS: Tape measure, chalk line, felt-tip pen, 4-foot level

MATERIALS: Powdered chalk in several colors, tile

Snap additional horizontal and vertical lines to break the wall into rectangles of 8 to 12 square feet.

Fasten a straight piece of 1×2 strapping with its top edge at the level of the first joint line above the floor. Double-check to make sure the strapping is level, and let it support your first row of tile.

After the upper rows have been set, remove the strapping (don't disturb the tile) and set the bottom row, hanging each tile from the one above with masking tape.

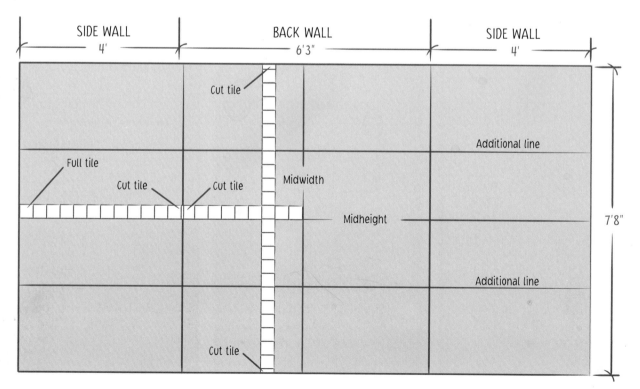

SCALE: ½" = 1'

1 **MEASURE THE TILE.** Butt 10 tiles together and measure the total length of the row. The total length divided by 10 is the unit dimension to use for layout.

2 **DRAW A MIDHEIGHT LINE.** Measure the height of wall to be tiled and draw a horizontal line through the midpoint. Extend the line to all three walls using a 4-foot level.

CROOKED CORNERS

Crooked walls are everywhere whether your house is new or old. If the corner is not plumb, you'll have to cut tiles to fit for the last row. This only will be a problem with smaller tiles, where a corner is out of plumb by ½ inch or more. If the wall is extremely out of square, stick with tiles that don't have patterns or borders which could draw the eye straight to what seems like a mistake.

There are two solutions:

- Remove the drywall or base material down to the studs and reinstall it, shimmed out to vertical. (Lots of work, but may be the only solution!)
- Use larger tiles so the variation from top to bottom on the last row is a less noticeable percentage of the width of the total tile.

3 **DRAW A MIDWIDTH LINE.** Measure the width of the back wall and draw a vertical line through the midpoint using a 4-foot level.

4 **MEASURE THE HALFWIDTH** to find the width of the cut tiles at the ends. If less than one-half tile, shift the vertical by one-half tile and snap a new line. Repeat for the halfheight reference.

WALLS

5 **SNAP MORE LINES** vertically and horizontally to mark off 8- to 12-square-foot rectangles.

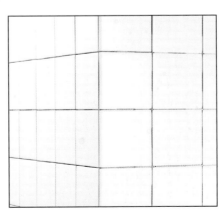

6 **START OUTSIDE CORNERS** with full tiles, both for appearance and so that the edges will be rounded.

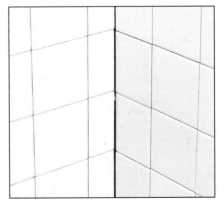

7 **INSIDE CORNERS** can accept cut tiles because the cut edges will be concealed.

MARKING AND CUTTING THE TILES

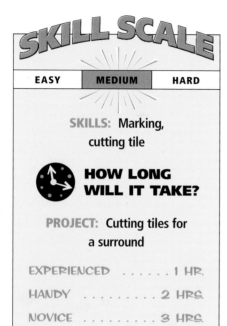

SKILL SCALE

EASY	MEDIUM	HARD

SKILLS: Marking,
cutting tile

HOW LONG WILL IT TAKE?

PROJECT: Cutting tiles for
a surround

EXPERIENCED . . . . . . 1 HR.

HANDY . . . . 2 HRS.

NOVICE . . . . 3 HRS.

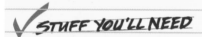

✓ STUFF YOU'LL NEED

TOOLS: China marker, scissors or
utility knife, combination square,
snap cutter or wet saw, tile
nippers, carbide hole saw or
rotary cutter, safety glasses,
dust respirator

MATERIALS: Cardboard, tile

TIME SAVER

UNUSUAL SHAPES

If you have a lot of irregular
cuts, consider purchasing a
carpenter's contour gauge—a
set of small pins which slide in
and out to record any shape.
The gauge is then placed on the
tile and the shape transferred
with a marker.

Snap cutter or wet saw? The question is one of utility and ease of use rather than price.

The snap cutter makes only straight cuts, but those comprise most of the cuts you will make. Once you set the snap cutter's fence, you can cut about 10 tiles per minute. The snap cutter also is silent and clean.

One of the disadvantages is that snap cutters can't make L-shaped, notch, or irregular cuts. Snap cuts have sharp edges that require smoothing if exposed.

The wet saw cuts about as quickly as the snap cutter, and it can make the more intricate L-shaped, notch, irregular, and square cuts. It also produces a clean cut with slightly rounded edges—you rarely have to smooth edges. The wet saw is messy, however, spewing a mist of water and tile dust.

Ask to demo a snap cutter and a wet saw before purchasing either one.

1 **MARK A STRAIGHT CUT** by placing tile to be cut over tile last set, butting the marker tile against a ¼-inch spacer, and tracing the edge of the marker tile.

2 **DRAW A TEMPLATE** for complex cuts. Cardboard is thick enough to provide an edge for tracing later.

3 **CUT THE TEMPLATE.** Cut the cardboard along the line with scissors or a sharp utility knife. Fit the cut template and make adjustments.

4 **TRACE THE TEMPLATE.** Trace the template onto the face of the tile with a china marker, using the edge of the cardboard as a guide.

88

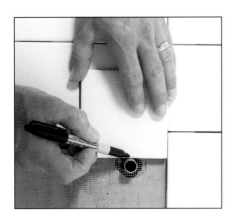

5 **MARK A HOLE** by holding the tile over the last tile set and sliding forward to butt against the pipe. Mark the pipe center on the tile edge.

6 **MAKE THE SECOND MARK** by sliding the tile sideways against the pipe and marking the pipe's center on the tile's vertical edge.

GOOD IDEA

CUTTING TILE
You are ready to set tile and your helper hasn't arrived with the snap cutter yet? Or the rental store is about to close and you have to return the snap cutter? No problem—just score the tile with an ordinary glass cutter and straightedge. Snap the scored tile over a dowel.

7 **MARK THE HOLE CENTER** by transferring the two edge marks to the face of the tile with a combination square. The intersection marks the center.

8 **TRACE THE HOLE** on the tile face using a washer the size of the hole. A washer works well because you can see the marked intersection.

9 **USE A WET SAW** if you have one for all of the straight cuts. See page 33 for instructions on its use.

10 **A SNAP CUTTER** makes simple straight cuts but leaves an irregular edge which must be smoothed. See page 35 for instructions.

11 **USE TILE NIPPERS** to make irregular cuts at the edges of the tiles. See page 35.

12 **USE A ROTARY CUTTER** or a carbide hole saw to make holes in the interior of a tile. See page 78.

WALLS

SETTING AND GROUTING

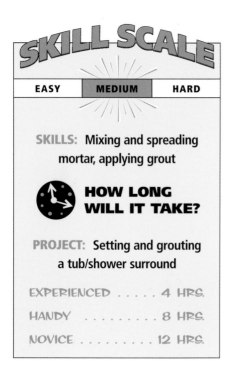

SKILL SCALE

EASY	MEDIUM	HARD

SKILLS: Mixing and spreading mortar, applying grout

HOW LONG WILL IT TAKE?

PROJECT: Setting and grouting a tub/shower surround

EXPERIENCED . . . . . 4 HRS.

HANDY . . . . 8 HRS.

NOVICE . . . . 12 HRS.

✓ STUFF YOU'LL NEED

TOOLS: ½-inch drill, mortar-mixing paddle, ¼"×¼" square-notched trowel, margin trowel, 5-gallon bucket, grout float, rubber gloves, sponge, spray bottle, safety glasses, dust respirator

MATERIALS: Tile, thin-set mortar with acrylic latex admix, dry-mix grout with acrylic latex admix, 1×3 strapping, masking tape, penetrating sealer, drop cloth

Gravity makes wall tiling messier than floor tiling. Properly mixed thin-set will adhere in a thin layer to the surface of the wall. But thick blobs from applying and combing the mortar weigh too much to stay on the wall. So a fair proportion of thin-set ends up on the floor.

Before setting tile on a wall, protect every surface below the operation. Cover surfaces with drop cloths and tape the cloth in place.

When tiling a tub surround, do NOT use polyethylene sheeting as your drop cloth. Polyethylene is slippery and will make the sloped bottom of the tub dangerous. Use a canvas drop cloth or an old sheet or blanket instead.

SAFETY ALERT!

CAUSTIC MORTAR

Mortar is very caustic and can burn holes in your skin, so wear rubber gloves if you are tempted to pick up blobs of thin-set. If you don't wear gloves and do get your hands into the mortar, rinse them with white vinegar, which will neutralize the alkalinity.

1 **FASTEN 1×3 STRAPPING** at the midheight reference line to start the middle of the tile field off level. You can also position the straightedge just below the bottommost tile joint and eliminate the hanging of tiles shown in Step 6.

2 **MIX LATEX-MODIFIED THIN-SET MORTAR** at slow speed with a mortar paddle and variable-speed drill. Weigh out and mix one quarter of the bag at a time. After mixing, let mixture slake (rest) for 10 minutes, then mix again.

3 **APPLY THIN-SET** to an area bounded by reference lines not more than 15 square feet at a time. Press the thin-set into the backerboard with the straight edge of a square-notched trowel held at a shallow angle to the surface.

4 **RAKE THE THIN-SET INTO STRAIGHT LINES** with the notched edge of the trowel. Hold the trowel at a steep angle to the surface, and press down so that the teeth contact the backerboard, ensuring a uniform thickness of mortar.

5 **LIFT THE FIRST TILE** and check the back to make sure the thin-set wets the entire surface. If the thin-set on the tile is in rows, the mortar bed is not thick enough. Scrape off the first application and use a trowel with a larger notch size.

6 **AFTER SETTING THE TILE** above the straightedge, let it set for 12 hours; then remove the straightedge. The bottom tiles are set from the middle down, supporting each with a strip of masking tape attached to the tile above.

SETTING AND GROUTING (CONTINUED)

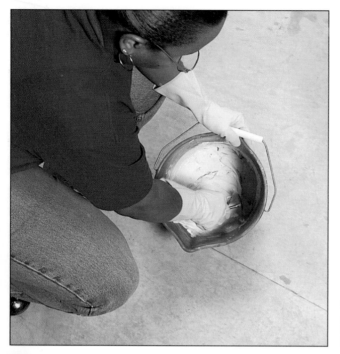

7 **MIX THE POWDERED GROUT** with the recommended liquid using a margin trowel. Follow the manufacturer's directions. After mixing, let the grout rest for 10 minutes, then remix. Add liquid only if the grout is too stiff to spread.

8 **SPREAD THE GROUT** with a rubber grout float. Pick up about a cup of grout with the float and smear it on the tile. Hold the float at a shallow angle to the tile and press the grout into the joints with several sweeps.

9 **REMOVE EXCESS GROUT** with diagonal sweeps of the rubber float, held at a steep angle to the tile. Hold the float diagonal to the tiles so the edge of the float doesn't cut into the joints and remove grout.

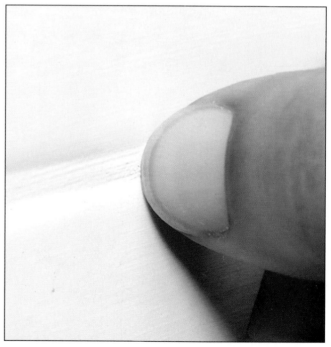

10 **GIVE THE GROUT THE THUMB TEST.** The grout will require five to 15 minutes to set up. It is hard enough to start the final cleanup when your thumbnail leaves no impression.

11 **WIPE THE TILES** with a damp—not dripping wet—sponge, rinsing it often in the clean water. If the grout is too resistant to sponge, use a plastic scrub pad, but avoid scrubbing the grout in the joints.

12 **REMOVE THE HAZE** left after sponging, first with a damp rag, then with a clean dry rag. Continue damp and dry wiping until the tile is reflective as glass. Check by holding a lamp to the surface.

13 **CURE THE GROUT** by misting it with water several times a day for three days. Damp curing maximizes the strength and minimizes the water absorbability of the grout. Do not mist tinted grout. Misting can dissolve the tint and leave an inconsistent color.

14 **APPLY PENETRATING SEALER** to grout with a sponge. Wipe off excess before it dries. If the tile is not glazed, seal the tile as well.

TILING A TUB OR SHOWER SURROUND

SKILL SCALE

EASY	MEDIUM	HARD

SKILLS: Design, installing backerboard, basic tilesetting

HOW LONG WILL IT TAKE?

PROJECT: Tiling a tub or shower surround

EXPERIENCED . . . . 10 HRS.

HANDY . . . . 14 HRS.

NOVICE . . . . 18 HRS.

✓ STUFF YOU'LL NEED

TOOLS: Chalk line, carbide scorer (or utility knife with plenty of blades), ½-inch drill, mixing paddle, ¼"×¼" square-edged trowel, 4-foot level, 5-gallon bucket, stapler, caulking gun, grout float, spray bottle, snap cutter or wet saw, sponge or plastic scrub pad, safety glasses, dust respirator

MATERIALS: ½-inch cement backerboard, thin-set mortar with acrylic latex admix, backerboard screws, fiberglass tape, 4-mil poly or 15-lb. felt, asphalt roofing cement, tile, dry-mix grout with acrylic latex admix, masking tape, penetrating sealer, marker, soap tray

Most bathroom tiling jobs average about 80 square feet and involve all of the basic tilesetting skills: designing, measuring, laying out, installing backerboard, setting tile on a vertical surface, and cutting holes as well as making straight cuts. Once you have everything on hand, a weekend should be enough time for the job.

Installation procedures and requirements for putting backerboard on vertical surfaces varies from manufacturer to manufacturer. Follow the instructions provided by the manufacturers when installing their products.

1 APPLY ASPHALT roofing cement to the flange of the tub edge. The cement will seal the tub to the 15-lb. felt (or 4-mil poly if an outside wall) shown in the next step.

2 STAPLE 15-POUND FELT to the studs. Bed the first layer in the cement, and overlap succeeding sheets by at least 2 inches. Use only enough staples to hold in place.

PLAN AHEAD FOR SAFETY BARS

Tub and shower safety bars must be securely fastened to framing. Avoid the expense of ripping out and retiling down the road by installing solid 2×6 or 2×8 blocking between the studs of the back wall and the wall opposite the shower controls. The bars and blocking should be centered 33 inches to 36 inches above the floor.

3 **INSTALL ½-INCH CEMENT BACKERBOARD.** Fasten to studs with galvanized backerboard screws.

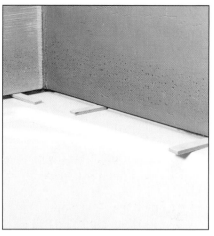

4 **SHIM BACKERBOARD** ¼ inch above the tub so that water on the rim won't wick up behind the panels.

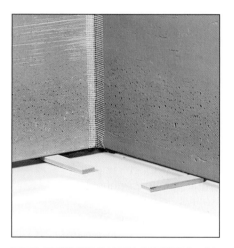

5 **REINFORCE THE CORNERS** with fiberglass tape bedded in and skim-coated with thin-set.

6 **CAULK THE GAP** with clear or white silicone, which is flexible enough to allow minor tub movement.

7 **DETERMINE THE ACTUAL TILE SIZE** by butting 10 tiles, measuring the total length, and dividing by 10.

8 **MEASURE AND MARK** the horizontal midheight on all three walls. For more detail, see page 86.

9 **MEASURE AND MARK** the midwidth of the back wall. Use a 4-foot level to draw a vertical line.

10 **SHIFT THE VERTICAL LINE** by one-half tile if the midwidth divided by the size of the tile results in less than one-half tile at the corners.

11 **DRAW A VERTICAL JOINT LINE** at the midpoint of the side wall, starting with a full tile at the outside corner. Repeat on the other side wall.

12 **SET THE BOTTOM ROW** on a ¼-inch shim strip. First check to see if the rim of the tub is level. If it is not, shim the strip itself until it is level.

TIME SAVER

MARKING CUTS FOR AN INSET
To mark the cuts for an inset, lay out a close-fitted array of field tile. Place the inset on top. Align the inset with the field below. Trace the inset edges onto the field tiles with a china marker. Sketch the layout on paper, and number the back of each tile and its location in the sketch.

13 **SET A SOAP TRAY** after the tile has set, supporting its weight with masking tape. Do NOT install a tray with a towel bar that may be mistaken for a hand hold.

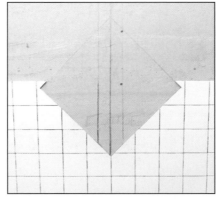

14 **SET PRECUT TILE** around an inset design. The surrounding field tiles have been marked and precut as described in Time Saver, above right.

15 **SET DESIGN TILES.** Although the design has been carefully traced, the notched field tiles at the corners may have to be recut and reset at this point.

16 **START THE SIDE WALLS** with a horizontal straightedge. Line up the top of the straightedge with one of the joints in the back wall.

17 **MARK, CUT, AND SET** tile around the shower arm. See the instructions for marking and cutting a hole on page 89.

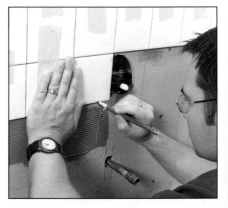

18 **REMOVE THE STRAIGHTEDGE** and hang the rows below, using masking tape. Mark the holes for the shower controls as shown on page 89.

WALLS

96

19 **MIX THE GROUT** with a margin trowel. Let the grout rest for 10 minutes, then remix. Add liquid only if the grout is too stiff to spread. Wear rubber gloves for this and the next four steps.

20 **SPREAD THE GROUT** with a grout float. Hold the float at a shallow angle to the tile and press the grout into the joints.

21 **REMOVE THE EXCESS** with the rubber float held at a steep angle to the tile. Make sure the direction is diagonal to the tiles. Allow the grout to set 10 to 15 minutes, then clean.

22 **WIPE UP THE EXCESS GROUT** with a damp sponge. If the grout is too resistant to the sponge, use a plastic scrub pad, but avoid scrubbing the grout in the joints.

23 **RINSE, RINSE, RINSE.** Use very clean water. The more you rinse the sponge, the less haze you will have to remove later. Wring every drop of water from the sponge so it is barely damp.

24 **REMOVE THE HAZE** left after sponging, first with a damp cloth, then with a dry cloth. Alternate damp and dry wiping until the tile is as reflective as glass.

25 **CURE THE GROUT** by misting with water several times a day for three days. Damp curing increases the strength of the grout.

26 **APPLY PENETRATING SEALER** to the grout joints with a sponge. Wipe off the excess within 10 minutes so the sealer doesn't dry on the tile.

27 **CAULK** the tub and tile joint with bath and tube caulk that matches either the tile or the tub. Smooth the bead, if necessary, with a wet finger.

4 COUNTERTOPS

Tile is often used to surface countertops in kitchens, baths, and wet bars. Before settling on tile, however, consider how you will be using your countertop. If you do a lot of food preparation and entertaining, the surface will be subjected to food stains, cooking oils, animal fats, citric acid, glass and metal cookware, and knives. Conversely, its brittle, unyielding surface will be hard on dropped dishes and glassware, as well as knives used for chopping and slicing. And unless the grout joints are flush, wiping the countertop will be a difficult chore.

CHOOSE THE RIGHT MATERIALS

All of these problems can be solved by the proper choice of materials. Due to exposure to water, the recommended setting base is cement backerboard set in thin-set mortar over $3/4$-inch exterior-glue plywood. To resist water, oils, and acids, the tile must be rated either impervious or vitreous, and grout must contain latex additive. (Epoxy grout is suitable as well, but can be difficult to work with until you've had some tiling experience.)

SCRATCH RESISTANCE IS IMPORTANT

Floor tiles generally have a high enough wear rating to resist scratching, but wall tiles generally do not. If you choose wall tile for your countertop, provide wood or plastic chopping surfaces that are either portable or set into the tiled surface. One option to a solid countertop is tiling the surface in 12"×12" squares of polished granite squares.

CHAPTER FOUR CONTENTS

100	**Tile for Countertops**
	100 Countertop Trim
102	**Tools for Tiling Countertops**
	102 Tools for Measuring and Laying Out
	103 Tools for Cutting and Shaping
	103 Tools for Setting and Grouting
104	**Countertop Tiling Materials**
	104 Backerboard and Fasteners
	104 Adhesives, Grouts, and Sealers
105	**Project Planning**
106	**Preparing the Base**
107	**Tile Layout Lines**
108	**Laying Backerboard**
112	**Marking and Cutting Tile**
113	**Setting the Tile**
114	**Grouting the Joints**
115	**Sealing the Joints**

TILE FOR COUNTERTOPS

W hen selecting tile for a countertop, consider the intended uses— kitchen countertop, vanity top? Will it be subject to standing water? Do you foresee cutting and slicing on it? Will you drag cast-iron cookware across it, or will the toughest thing it encounters be a wet sponge?

Surfaces that are frequently exposed to water require vitreous tile or a nonporous natural stone. The grout and adhesive must also be nonporous (latex- or acrylic-modified).

Mechanical abuse, such as cutting, slicing, and exposure to china and cast-iron cookware, means the surface has to be hard, and that the color should extend through the body of the tile.

Glazed wall and decorative tiles do not meet these requirements. Choices for hard-working surfaces are limited to porcelain tile, quarry tile, and granite.

TILE CHARACTERISTICS

TYPE OF TILE	COST	RELATIVE DURABILITY	WATER ABSORPTION	UPKEEP
Glazed wall	Low to medium	Low to high	Medium	Low
Glazed decorative	High	Low to medium	Medium	Low
Porcelain	Medium	High	Low	Low
Quarry	Low to medium	High	Medium	Low
Natural stone	Low to high	High	Low to high	Medium to high

CLOSER LOOK

INSTALL A CUTTING BOARD
Rather than chop or cut directly on tile countertops, install a wood or plastic cutting board. Cut a maple cutting board to fill an integral number of tile spaces and set it into the gap with silicone adhesive. Because the board shrinks and swells, caulk the board and tile joints as shown.

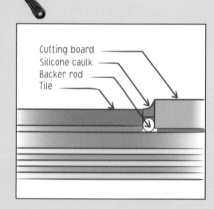

Cutting board
Silicone caulk
Backer rod
Tile

COUNTERTOP TRIM

Make sure there are trim pieces that coordinate with the tile you choose. V-cap and L-sink trims are designed especially for edging countertops. If these are not available, or if your tile is natural stone, your dealer can supply oak L-trim in 5-foot and 8-foot lengths.

If you have a dishwasher, be sure the bottom of the trim is at least 34¼ inches above the finished floor. Otherwise you may not be able to open the dishwasher or remove it in case of a plumbing problem.

The best way to increase the clearance is to install a thicker plywood base.

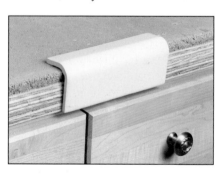

V-CAP is designed specifically for edging countertops. It has a raised lip to prevent spills from running over the edge.

L-SINK TRIM. Ask your dealer for trim ideas. Sometimes a different style or color of trim enhances the installation.

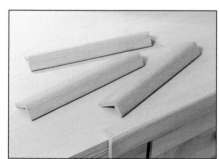

OAK TRIM goes with any color tile, but you must caulk the joint between trim and tile because the wood swells when wet.

COUNTERTOPS

▶ **PORCELAIN TILES** are made of highly refined clay and are fired at very high temperatures. As a result, they are dense and hard, and highly resistant to wear and scratching. They are also among the most water-resistant tiles; they don't absorb water or oil and harbor mold and bacteria. Unfortunately, most are not very colorful and do little to brighten a kitchen or bath.

◀ **QUARRY TILE** originally was quarried stone. Quarry tile today is clay extruded through a die, cut to size, and fired in a kiln. The tile is extremely hard and stands up well to abuse. It is fairly nonporous, (absorbs little water). Color selection is limited.

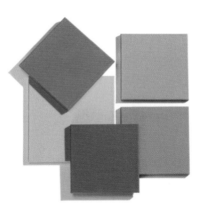

▶ **NATURAL STONE** includes granite, marble, and slate. Granite and marble are available in polished (shiny and slippery) and honed (dull and less slippery) finishes. Both slate and marble are fairly soft and porous compared to granite. In addition, marble is vulnerable to common kitchen acids such as vinegar and citrus juice. Polished granite is a good choice for kitchen countertops.

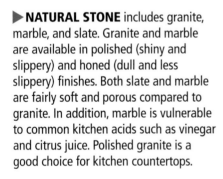

◀ **GLAZED TILES** are generally machine-made of clay, pressed in a die, and fired in a kiln. The glaze adds color and a hard, but fragile, surface. Most glazed tiles are intended for walls and are too soft and too water absorbent to be used on kitchen countertops. If you decide to use them because of their bright colors, provide wood or plastic cutting surfaces in or on the countertop (see Closer Look, opposite).

COUNTERTOPS

101

TOOLS FOR TILING COUNTERTOPS

Tiling tools are available in a range of quality and durability. For a small job, you may be able to use throwaway tools. For jobs requiring repetitive operations, such as cutting dozens of tiles or troweling thin-set, spend just a bit more for tools with better grips. And if you plan to do more tiling projects, professional-level tools will last longer and will yield more polished results.

Another option is to purchase a set of good basic hand tools, especially if they have multiple uses, and to rent professional tiling tools when you need them. Ask the tiling experts at your home center for advice.

Regardless of the quality and how much you pay for them, however, the best tools will be quickly ruined by failure to clean off mortar and grout. You will find mortar especially difficult to remove. Have a 5-gallon bucket of water on hand to dip and scrub your trowels and mixing tools in.

BUYER'S GUIDE

TOOL	USE FOR	PRICE	IMPORTANCE
MEASURING AND LAYING OUT			
Chalk line	layout, cut lines	$	must have
China marker	marking tile cuts	$	or felt-tip or pencil
Combination square	marking tile cuts	$$	nice to have
Framing square	establishing square	$$	must have
Tape measure	measuring	$$	must have
4-foot level	establishing level, vertical	$$	can use small level
CUTTING AND SHAPING			
Abrasive stone	smoothing cut edges	$$	nice to have
Carbide (glass) bit	small holes in tile	$$	only for small holes
Carbide hole saw	large holes in tile	$$	must if hole is inside tile
Carbide-grit rod saw	curved tile cuts	$$	nice to have
Dust respirator	repiratory protection	$	must have
Ear plugs	hearing protection	$	must have
Rotary grinding tool	smoothing cut edges	$$$	nice to have
Safety glasses	eye protection	$	must have
Snap cutter	straight tile cuts	$$$	must, or wet saw
Spiral saw	cutting soft tile	$$$	nice to have
Tile nippers	intricate tile cuts	$$	must, or wet saw
Wet saw	straight tile cuts	$$$	nice to have
SETTING AND GROUTING			
Caulking gun	caulking joints	$	must have
Grout float	spreading grout	$$	must have
Margin trowel	mixing and spreading grout	$	nice to have
Mortar mixing paddle	mixing grout	$$	must have
Nonabrasive pad	removing excess grout	$	must have
Notched trowel	applying mortar	$$	must have
Round-corner sponge	removing excess grout	$	must have
½-inch drill	mixing adhesives	$$$	must have

TOOLS FOR MEASURING AND LAYING OUT

Ⓐ 4-FOOT LEVEL
To establish level and vertical.

Ⓑ CHALK LINE
To snap tile layout lines.

Ⓒ CHINA MARKER (WAX PENCIL)
To make temporary cut marks on the face of a tile.

Ⓓ COMBINATION SQUARE
A guide for marking straight, notch, and L-cuts.

Ⓔ FRAMING SQUARE
For establishing perpendicular and as a guide for cutting.

Ⓕ TAPE MEASURE
For accurate measuring.

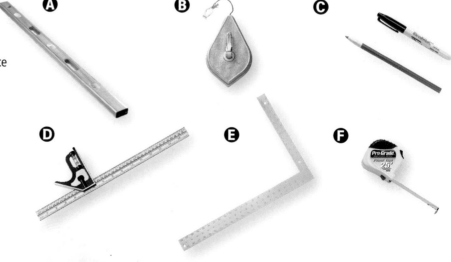

TOOLS FOR CUTTING AND SHAPING

Ⓐ ABRASIVE STONE
Smooths sharp edges of cut tiles.

Ⓑ CARBIDE HOLE SAW
Drills large holes through tiles, such as for water pipes. Available in a variety of sizes.

Ⓒ CARBIDE (GLASS) BIT
Drills small holes through tiles.

Ⓓ CARBIDE-GRIT ROD SAW
Makes intricate cuts. The rod can be removed and fed through a hole.

Ⓔ DUST RESPIRATOR
Wear respirators when working with mortar and chemical powders.

Ⓕ EAR PLUGS
Protect hearing from damaging sounds such as power tools.

Ⓖ ROTARY GRINDING AND CUTTING TOOL
Smooths and bevels sharp tile edges. Cuts tile with special attachments.

Ⓗ SAFETY GLASSES
Wear safety glasses when working with hand and power tools.

Ⓘ SNAP CUTTER
Scores and snaps tiles in straight lines.

Ⓙ SPIRAL SAW
Quickly and easily cuts soft wall tile.

Ⓚ TILE NIPPERS
Makes curved or intricate cuts by nibbling away tile.

Ⓛ WET SAW
Quickly and easily makes straight, notched, and L-shape cuts.

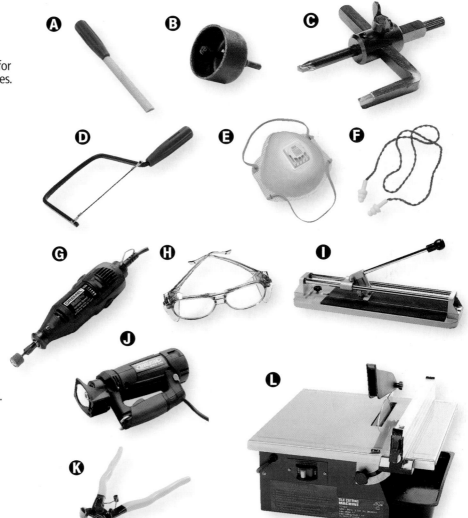

TOOLS FOR SETTING AND GROUTING

Ⓐ ½-INCH ELECTRIC DRILL
For mixing adhesive and grout.

Ⓑ CAULKING GUN
For caulking joints.

Ⓒ GROUT FLOAT
For filling grout joints.

Ⓓ MARGIN TROWEL
For mixing and applying adhesive and grout.

Ⓔ MORTAR MIXING PADDLE
For mixing and applying adhesive and grout.

Ⓕ NONABRASIVE SCOURING PAD
For removing stubborn grout residue.

Ⓖ NOTCHED TROWEL(S)
For spreading adhesive to setting bed.

Ⓗ ROUND-CORNER SPONGE
For removing residue and applying sealer.

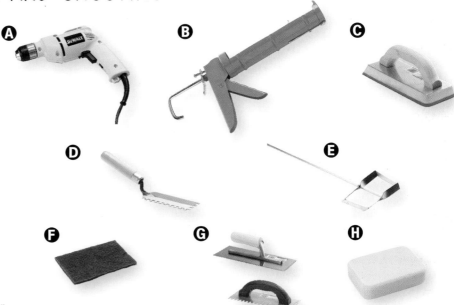

COUNTERTOP TILING MATERIALS

BACKERBOARD AND FASTENERS

CEMENT BACKERBOARD provides a base for setting tile. The rigid, water-resistant, glass-fiber-reinforced panels are available in two thicknesses (¼ inches and ½ inches) and three sizes (3'×5', 4'×4', and 4'×8').

BACKERBOARD FASTENERS are 1¼ inches (1½ inches for ½-inch board) long No. 8-18×⅜" wafer-head galvanized self-countersinking screws. Some tilesetters use 1¼-inch barbed galvanized roofing nails instead.

SELF-ADHESIVE FIBERGLASS TAPE is applied over all square-edge and cut joints to make the reinforcing continuous between panels. The tape is 2 inches wide and must be alkali-resistant due to the alkaline mortar.

ADHESIVES, GROUTS, AND SEALERS

Ⓐ FLEXIBLE THIN-SET MORTAR
A thin-set mortar with powdered acrylic latex additive and is used on ceramic tile, laminates, and plywood.

Ⓑ LATEX ADDITIVE
Increases thin-set mortar's bond strength, flexibility, and resistance to water.

Ⓒ THIN-SET MORTAR
A basic thin-set mortar without latex admix; it is commonly used over backerboard.

Ⓓ SANDED GROUT
For filling grout joints that are from ⅛ inch to ½ inch.

Ⓔ NON-SANDED GROUT
For filling grout joints narrower than ⅛ inch. Also used on soft glazed tile and polished marble to avoid scratching.

Ⓕ PENETRATING SEALERS
Penetrates grout and porous tile and stone to protect against water and stains. It also increases slip resistance.

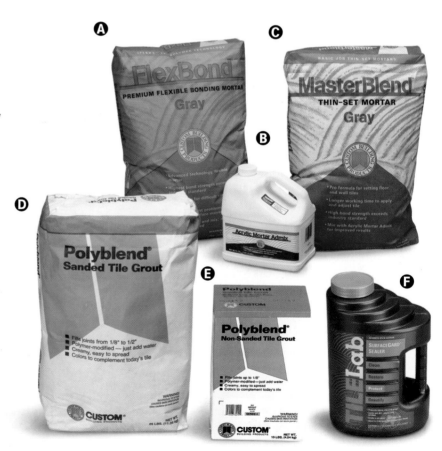

PROJECT PLANNING

Tiling a countertop can be accomplished in a weekend if you plan thoroughly. Even a small countertop can be the focal point of your kitchen or bath. If it is an L- or U-shape counter, it will have both inside and outside corners, as well as a sink cutout. Establishing a detailed layout is critical.

Answer these questions before starting your project:

DESIGN
- Is your chosen tile water- and scratch-resistant enough to serve as a countertop?
- Is the tile readily available, or does it have to be ordered?
- What will you use for edge trim? Trim tile is generally available only for wall tile.
- Can you return unused tiles?
- Do you have enough tile on hand to finish the job?

EVALUATING THE BASE
- Is the existing countertop surface suitable, or must you replace or cover it?
- How will you install the sink? How you will trim around it?
- Do you have the sink?
- Are there any existing wall outlets that will interfere with the backsplash?

LAYING CEMENT BACKERBOARD
- Do you have the recommended fasteners and tools to drive them?

MARKING AND CUTTING TILES
- Should you rent a wet saw? Do you have a place to use it that won't be damaged by water?
- Can you get a helper to make the tile cuts while you set the tile?

SETTING THE TILE
- Will you set the tile by eye, or will you use spacers?
- Can you get a helper to mix the thin-set while you set the tile?

GROUTING THE JOINTS
- Does the tile require sealing before grouting the joints?
- Will someone be around to mist the grout twice a day for 3 days?

SEALING
- Is your sealer food-safe?

COUNTERTOPS

PREPARING THE BASE

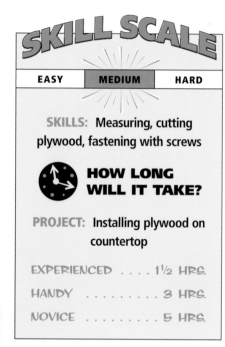

SKILL SCALE

EASY	MEDIUM	HARD

SKILLS: Measuring, cutting plywood, fastening with screws

HOW LONG WILL IT TAKE?

PROJECT: Installing plywood on countertop

EXPERIENCED . . . . 1½ HRS.

HANDY . . . . 3 HRS.

NOVICE . . . . 5 HRS.

✓ STUFF YOU'LL NEED

TOOLS: Tape measure, table saw, variable-speed drill and Phillips© bit, drills, pad sander, safety glasses

MATERIALS: ¾-inch exterior plywood, 1¾-inch drywall, Phillips screws, carpenter's glue, 40-grit sandpaper and a damp cloth (for existing laminate countertop)

The minimum requirement for a tiled countertop is a ¾-inch exterior plywood base. If no countertop exists, rip a 4×8-foot sheet in half and fasten a strip of the same plywood to the back edge as a backsplash. A countertop over 8 feet long or an L-shape countertop may be formed by gluing and screwing a ¾-inch plywood splice plate from below.

With an existing countertop that is less than ¾ inch thick, glue and screw a minimum ¾-inch exterior plywood over the original surface for a rigid surface.

To prepare for cement backerboard over an existing laminate countertop at least ¼ inch thick and in good condition:

- Check that the laminate is soundly adhered (if not, scrap the whole countertop).
- Clean and degrease the laminate surface.
- Sand the laminate with 40-grit sandpaper.
- Remove all sanding dust with a damp cloth.

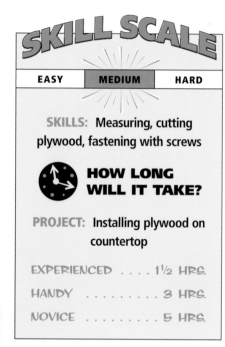

1 **FASTEN** the base to the cabinet with the front edge projecting 1 inch beyond the face of the cabinet.

2 **EXTEND A COUNTERTOP** that is longer than 8 feet or around a corner by attaching a ¾-inch plywood splice plate at the butt.

3 **FORM A BACKSPLASH** by gluing and screwing a strip of ¾-inch plywood to the rear of the countertop.

4 **UPGRADE** a worn base by gluing and screwing to it an exterior plywood layer at least ½ inch thick.

TILE LAYOUT LINES

SKILL SCALE

EASY	MEDIUM	HARD

SKILLS: Snapping chalklines

HOW LONG WILL IT TAKE?

PROJECT: Laying out

EXPERIENCED . . . . 20 MIN.

HANDY . . . . 30 MIN.

NOVICE . . . . 1 HR.

STUFF YOU'LL NEED

TOOLS: Chalk line

MATERIALS: Piece of tile

V-cap trim, sink cutout template

The more accurate your layout the more you'll be happy with the end result. Solid preparation is the key to success

The first principle in laying out a countertop is simple: No cut tiles on the front edge. The second principle is applied when there is a sink: Adjust the sink location, if possible, so that cut tiles are of equal size on the left and right.

To tile an existing countertop that has a sink size and location that will remain the same, determine whether to have full tiles at the corner or equal size tiles at the sink. Sinks and their mountings are so variable this book cannot address all of the ways to edge them. Your best option is to take an accurate sketch of the sink's rim or, better yet, the actual sink, to your tile supplier to work out the details.

Another layout requirement may be that of an inset chopping block. Rather than cutting tiles, design the opening so that it is an integral number of tiles in both width and depth. Then cut the chopping block to leave a ¼-inch gap all around. The gap will be caulked with silicone to allow for the block's expansion.

1 **HOLD THE V-CAP** against the front edge of the counter and mark the location of the joint. Repeat for other end.

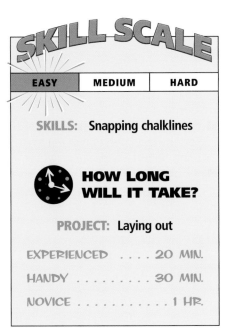

2 **SNAP A CHALK LINE** between marks to indicate the first joint line. Repeat for the other leg if the counter is L-shape.

3 **THE INTERSECTION** of chalk lines indicates the starting point for laying the tile, assuring full tiles on both front edges.

4 **SHIFT THE SINK TEMPLATE** to make the side tile cuts equal. To avoid less than half-width tiles, shift the template one-half tile.

COUNTERTOPS

LAYING BACKERBOARD

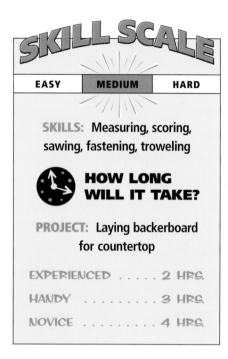
The purpose of backerboard is to provide adhesion for tiles. The ¾-inch plywood subsurface establishes the stability for the surface; therefore, the backerboard can be applied in manageable pieces. If you can handle the weight, a 4'×8' backerboard panel cut into 2'×4' strips is the ideal size.

After making the sink cutout in the plywood, dry fit 2'×4' sections of backerboard to the plywood and trace the plywood cutout on the underside of the backerboard. Make the backerboard cutout, place the cut pieces back on the plywood, and drop the sink into the hole.

Spread the thin-set, then set and align the backerboard panels with 16d spacer nails. If the counter is longer than 8 feet, spread the thin-set and set the backerboard in two sessions.

With all of the backerboard pieces carefully aligned to the front edge of the counter, and the sink sitting in the cutout, fasten each piece with two backerboard screws or nails to hold it in place (some tilesetters use 1¼-inch galvanized roofing nails instead of backerboard screws).

Install the remaining fasteners 4 inches on-center, ½ inch in from the panel edges, and every 6 inches in both directions in the interior. Don't fasten within 2 inches of a panel corner to avoid breaking off a corner.

If the thin-set has begun to stiffen, mix another small batch to bed the fiberglass reinforcing tape. With the margin trowel, spread a 3-inch-wide layer of thin-set over a joint between two panels. Apply a strip of 2-inch-wide self-adhesive fiberglass reinforcing tape to the thin-set, and lightly wet it into the mortar. Apply more thin-set over the tape, and smooth and feather the thin-set to just cover the tape.

Repeat this process over all joints that contain at least one cut backerboard edge. Rounded edges with exposed mesh don't require reinforcing.

Consider covering the base cabinets and appliances with plastic to protect them from splatters of thin-set.

1 **MEASURE AND MARK** the counter dimensions on the backerboard. If you can handle the weight, 4'×8' sheets cut in half are the correct width.

2 **THE EDGES** of the backerboard and plywood or existing laminate countertop must line up at the front and at both ends.

3 **TRACE THE PLYWOOD HOLE**
onto the backerboard and cut with a dry-cutting diamond blade. Round the corners if necessary. Wear a dust respirator and safety glasses.

4 **BACKERBOARD FOR BACKSPLASH** should clear the counter backerboard by ⅛ inch and allow for the radius bullnose trim at top.

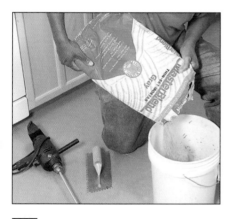

5 **ADD THE DRY THIN-SET MIX**
to the acrylic latex admix in a 5-gallon bucket. Pour in half of the liquid, then weigh and add half of the bag contents. Wear a dust respirator.

6 **MIX** the thin-set with a mortar mixing paddle and a ½-inch variable-speed drill. Use slow speed (150-200 rpm) to avoid incorporating air.

7 **SPREAD AND COMB THIN-SET**
onto the plywood base with a ⅛"×⅛" square-notched trowel.

8 **SPREAD** thin-set onto the back of the backsplash backerboard strip. This will allow you to position the strip ⅛ inch above the countertop backerboard.

TIME SAVER

ELIMINATE MEASUREMENTS

Don't transfer measurements from a sink cutout in a plywood countertop to the backerboard that will form the base for the tile. Instead, place the uncut backerboard (you may need a helper to steady it) over the plywood. Line up the back edge and one of the ends. Then trace the cutout from underneath into the bottom face of the backerboard with a black felt-tip pen.

FRAGILE CUTOUT

When the sink cutout is made, the backerboard will be fragile. To avoid breaking the narrow strips at the front and back of the cutout, slide the cut backerboard onto a 2-foot-wide strip of ¾-inch plywood. Then, using the plywood as a stretcher, slide the backerboard into place on the countertop. Another way is to remove the narrow strips from the front and back of the sink cutout before the break and install them separately. The installed strips will be strong, provided they are well fastened and bedded in thin-set to the plywood.

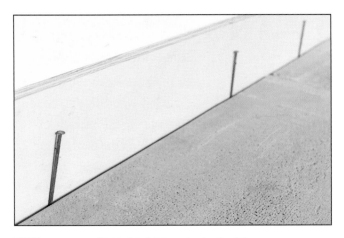

9 **LEAVE A ⅛-INCH GAP** at the back of the countertop backerboard for expansion. The horizontal and vertical strips of backerboard must not touch.

10 **LEAVE ⅛-INCH JOINTS** between sections of backerboard. A 16d common nail provides perfect spacing. Don't drive the nails into the plywood, however.

11 **USE SPECIAL BACKERBOARD SCREWS** to fasten the backerboard to the plywood. The self-tapping screws have wafer heads that firmly hold without projecting above the surface.

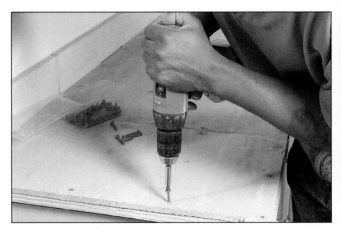

12 **FASTEN THE SCREWS** 4 inches on-center, ½ inch from edges, all around the panel. Tap the screws lightly with a hammer to start, then drive home with a power driver, just to the surface.

13 **STAY 2 INCHES FROM THE CORNERS** to avoid breaking the panel. If you break a corner, start again with a whole panel.

14 **DRIVE MORE FASTENERS** every 6 inches in both directions in the field. Some tilesetters substitute 1¼-inch galvanized roofing nails for the interior fasteners.

15 **FILL THE JOINTS** between sections of backerboard with thin-set. Using a margin trowel held at a shallow angle, force the thin-set into the joint, then spread a layer 3 inches wide.

16 **REINFORCE BACKERBOARD** with 2-inch-wide, alkali-resistant, fiberglass tape at any joint with a square-edge panel. Apply a skim coat over the tape with a trowel.

TIME SAVER

NO TAPING NECESSARY

Backerboard with rounded panel edges that have exposed fiberglass reinforcing don't require the application of fiberglass tape and will make for speedier installation.

17 **WRAP THE EDGES OF THE COUNTERTOP** with fiberglass tape. Apply a coat of thin-set, tape, then a top skim coat to bury the tape in mortar.

WORK SMARTER

FOR A STAINLESS SINK

Many kitchen sinks are made of stainless steel. To reinforce the thin steel, the sinks have vertical stiffening bars welded under the rim on all four sides.

For a more rigid installation, make the sink cutout in both the plywood and the backerboard just large enough (except for the back of the rim where the faucets are mounted) to fit the sink bowl.

To accommodate the stiffeners, place (don't attach yet) the backerboard on the plywood and line up the edges and openings. Then center the sink in the cutout. With a felt-tip pen, trace the locations of the sink stiffeners on the backerboard. Remove the sink, place the backerboard where you can work on all sides, and cut a groove along the stiffener lines. Use a dry-cutting masonry blade on a 4-inch grinder to make the cut, and make sure the groove is just deep enough to take the stiffener.

Now the sink will sit flush on the backerboard, and the tile will lip over the sink rim perfectly.

MARKING AND CUTTING TILE

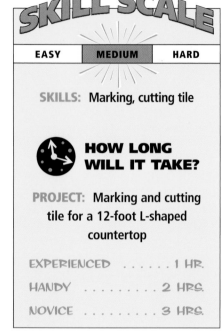

It would be great if countertops were built based on tile size and grout spacing. No awkward corners. No cutting tiles. Well, they aren't and that is why there are snap cutters and wet saws.

When laying tile, it is best to use a wet saw rather than a snap cutter. There are likely to be several difficult cuts. A snap cutter will make the job difficult and time-consuming.

Get used to making cuts by first cutting a series of tile strips at the back of the counter or along the sides. Next, lay out and cut the more difficult and awkard cuts around the sink.

When marking and cutting the back row of countertop tiles, allow a ¼-inch horizontal gap between the countertop and the backsplash. A ⅛-inch vertical gap will be needed between the countertop tile and the bottom of the backsplash tile. This is necessary to allow for slight movement of the joint, once it is filled with silicone sealant.

1 **ALIGN TILE TO BE CUT** with the last tile set, then hold a spacer tile against the backerboard of the backsplash.

2 **SLIDE A MARKER TILE** over the tile to be cut and against the spacer tile at the back.

3 **TRACE THE EDGE** of the marker tile onto the tile to be cut with a china marker or felt-tip pen.

4 **CUT THE TILE** with a wet saw (see Using a Wet Saw, page 33) or a snap cutter (see Using a Snap Cutter, page 35).

SETTING THE TILE

You frame a house before you start working on the inside. The same is true with tiling a countertop. Start with the V-cap, framing the border of the countertop. After the V-cap is in place, work on the interior.

Set the field tiles in small sections. Mix only the amount of thin-set needed for each section.

Install the field tiles starting from the intersection of the layout lines at the inside corner of the sink. Continue setting the field tiles, expanding outward to the end of the counter and around the sink.

Treatment of the sink edges depends on the way the sink is hung from or set on the countertop. Show your tile dealer the sink, and get his advice on the details.

1 **TO SET THE V-CAP,** butter both the countertop inside the layout line and the vertical back of the V-cap.

2 **TO SET THE FIELD TILES,** spread and comb thin-set onto the countertop, then place the tile and twist into place.

3 **TO SET THE BACKSPLASH,** spread and comb thin-set onto the backerboard, set the vertical tiles onto ⅛-inch shims.

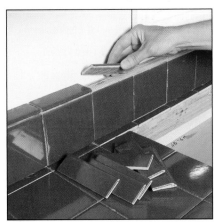

4 **TO SET THE BULLNOSE TRIM,** back-butter the trim pieces; press in place. Clean up excess mortar immediately.

COUNTERTOPS

GROUTING THE JOINTS

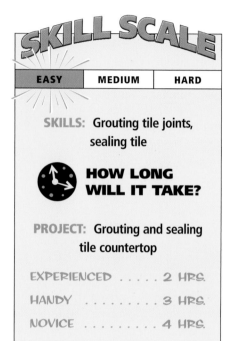

SKILL SCALE

EASY	MEDIUM	HARD

SKILLS: Grouting tile joints, sealing tile

HOW LONG WILL IT TAKE?

PROJECT: Grouting and sealing tile countertop

EXPERIENCED . . . . . 2 HRS.

HANDY . . . . 3 HRS.

NOVICE . . . . 4 HRS.

✓ STUFF YOU'LL NEED

TOOLS: Margin trowel, rubber grout float, round-cornered sponge, nonabrasive pad, clean cloth, rubber gloves, bucket for mixing, bucket for rinse water, dust respirator, safety glasses

MATERIALS: Powdered grout with acrylic latex admix, tile and grout sealer, tile and grout cleaner, tile and grout penetrating sealer

Do not damp cure tinted grout. Damp curing can dissolve the tint and leave an inconsistent color.

114

Choosing a grout color involves more than just interior design. White grout will emphasize a darker tile, but requires frequent cleaning and sealing to prevent staining. White grout also may emphasize joint-line swelling and shrinkage. Grout that closely matches the tile color masks stains and de-emphasizes joint-line changes.

High-glaze tile scratches easily, so it's not a good choice for countertops. If you do use it, however, use a polymer-modified, non-sanded grout to avoid scratches while grouting.

The face of unglazed tile should be sealed before grouting because the grout will be impossible to remove otherwise. If you have a lot of tile to seal, butt it all together on the floor and apply the sealer with a foam roller.

When the front lip of V-cap extends below the bottom of the plywood, there is nothing behind the V-cap to grout against. Hold a short length of wood corner molding against the back and bottom of the V-cap as you force the grout into the joint from the front with the grout float.

1 **SEAL UNGLAZED TILE** before grouting the joints. Apply penetrating sealer with a sponge; don't let it run into the joint.

2 **MIX THE GROUT** with an acrylic latex additive. Let the grout slake 10–15 minutes, then remix. Wear a dust respirator and safety glasses.

3 **APPLY GROUT** with a rubber grout float. Hold the float at a shallow angle and force the grout into the joints.

4 **REMOVE EXCESS GROUT** with the float held nearly vertical. Sweep diagonally to avoid dipping into the joints.

SEALING THE JOINTS

Accidents happen. Especially in the kitchen. Food gets on the countertop during meal preparation. Liquids are spilled, creating potential stains. We take shortcuts and use the countertop as a cutting board. All of this can discolor or shorten the life of grout.

Proper curing, sealers, and additives extend the life of grout. Curing hardens the grout. Sealers minimize staining. Acrylic latex additives waterproof it.

GOOD IDEA

Before grouting, test the hardness of the tile surface by scrubbing the face of a spare tile with wet grout and a plastic scrub pad. If the grout dulls the finish, you will have to be very quick and very gentle in removing the excess grout and grout haze. Rinse the sponge often and use plenty of soft clean rags.

1 **TEST THE GROUT.** When your thumbnail leaves no impression (10–15 minutes or per manufacturer's instructions) clean the tiles.

2 **USE SHORT STROKES** with a clean, damp—not wet—sponge. Try to keep the sponge away from the grout.

3 **RINSE, RINSE, RINSE** after wiping each tile. Wring the sponge dripless to avoid damaging the grout.

4 **REMOVE THE RESIDUAL HAZE** with a clean, dry cotton cloth. If the haze resists, remove with an acid tile cleaner.

5 **DAMP CURE** after 24 hours. Mist the grout twice a day for three days. Don't mist tinted grout. This can leave an inconsistent color in the grout.

6 **APPLY A FOOD-SAFE SEALER** with a sponge. Follow the instructions, and reapply several times a year.

CHAPTER

5 *PATIOS*

*P*atio is the Spanish word for an interior courtyard in a home that is open to the outdoors. Today it usually refers to a paved area adjacent to the home intended for outdoor living. Whether it's actually a courtyard or adjacent to your home, a patio is an outdoor living space for the family to enjoy.

EASY ISN'T ALWAYS THE WAY TO GO

It's possible to put in a patio simply by laying bricks, flagstones, or other pavers on the ground. While simple to install, this method will lose its charm quickly as grass and weeds begin to appear between the pavers. The surface will shift due to movement of the soil beneath, and it will soon become impossible to find a level spot to set your furniture, which creates a potentially hazardous situation.

It's a good idea to build a patio as you would any other room in your home—with a proper foundation and using tile with the proper qualities for resisting weather-related damage.

GETTING GOOD RESULTS

The right tile, set in water-resistant, latex-modified thin-set mortar, and sealed with a penetrating sealer, will create an attractive and comfortable outdoor room, increasing your living space and enhancing the value of your home.

Tiling a concrete patio is no more difficult than tiling any other floor. This chapter will lead you every step of the way, from selecting the type of tile that will last installation procedures, to cleaning up for that first cookout.

CHAPTER FIVE CONTENTS

118 **Tile for Patios**

119 **Choosing Patio Tile**

120 **Tools for Tiling Patios**

    120 **Tools for Measuring and Laying Out**

    121 **Tools for Cutting and Shaping**

    121 **Tools for Setting and Grouting**

122 **Patio Tiling Materials**

    122 **Adhesives, Grouts, and Sealers**

122 **Project Planning**

123 **Evaluating the Slab**

    123 **Jointing a Slab**

124 **Establishing Layout Lines**

    124 **Slabs without Expansion Joints**

    125 **Slabs with Expansion Joints**

126 **Marking and Cutting Tile**

127 **Mixing the Mortar**

128 **Setting the Tile**

130 **Grouting the Joints**

132 **Using Cleft Stone Instead of Tile**

TILE FOR PATIOS

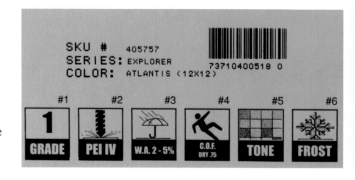

atios are outdoor floors that may be exposed to standing water as well as freeze/thaw conditions. Four qualities to consider when selecting patio tile are:

- **PEI WEAR RATING:** The tile's resistance to abrasion (suitability for foot traffic).
- **WATER ABSORPTION:** The percentage of water the tile can absorb (suitability for wet locations).
- **COEFFICIENT OF FRICTION:** Slip resistance on a scale of 0 to 1.0. Look for a rating of at least 0.6.
- **FROST RESISTANCE:** Warranty against damage by freezing and thawing (a requirement in freeze/thaw regions). Beware that in rating systems other than the one at right, the term **frost resistant** may not imply a warranty against frost damage.

Most floor tiles at your home center will display rating labels like those at right. If you have any question about the suitability of a certain tile for a patio, ask the salesperson for advice.

WORK SMARTER
A+

BACK-BUTTERING

Applying mortar to the back of tile increases the thickness of mortar to guarantee that the tile is covered with the mortar. Back-buttering is recommended when the back of the tile is uneven and when maximum adhesion to the substrate is required—both common conditions in tiling patios.

GRADE: #1 Standard—suitable for most applications; #2 Second—structurally similar to #1 with minor glaze or size imperfections; #3 Decorative—thin wall tile, suitable for wall applications only.

PEI WEAR RATING: 1, 2—not suitable for floors (walls only); 3—all residential; 4—residential and light commercial; 4+—commercial and heavy traffic.

WATER ABSORPTION: Percentage by weight: nonvitreous, more than 7%; semivitreous, 3–7%; vitreous, 0.5–3%; impervious, less than 0.5%. Use only vitreous and impervious tiles in wet and freeze/thaw applications.

COEFFICIENT OF FRICTION: The resistance to slip, expressed as horizontal force required to move an object across the tile, divided by its weight. The Americans with Disabilities Act (ADA) requires a minimum of 0.6 for dry floors.

TONE: The multi-shaded icon indicates variations in tone. This is true of most tile, except for those of pure color, such as white or black. No tone variation is indicated if all squares are the same shade.

FROST RESISTANCE: A snowflake indicates frost-resistance and suitability for use in exterior freeze/thaw applications. It does not guarantee that the tile won't lift, however, because that is also a function of the adhesive and the conditions when set.

118

CHOOSING PATIO TILE

▶ **NATURAL STONE** is available as square-cut "tile" and as random-shape cleft stone. Tiles include granite, marble, and slate. Granite and marble are available in polished (too slippery for patios) and honed (less slippery) finishes. Tumbled marble tiles, slate, and cleft stone are the least slippery. Most stone, except for granite, is porous and will spall (split) when subjected to water and freeze/thaw cycling.

◀ **TERRA-COTTA TILES** are popular tiles for patios in the South. Made of natural clay fired at very low temperatures, most terra-cotta tiles are produced in Mexico. Their appeal is the low cost, earth-tone colors, and rustic hand-made charm. Low density and high water absorption require frequent sealing to prevent staining and prohibit use in freeze/thaw areas.

▶ **CEMENT-BODIED TILES** made of mortar are commonly used in patios. Durable versions are available that resemble brick, glazed tile, or stone. Cement-bodied brick, a variety of cement-bodied tile made to look like brick, comes in common brick face and side. These tiles can be used on concrete patios and concrete block fireplaces.

◀ **QUARRY TILE** is quite popular for patios because of its earth tones and low cost. The extremely hard, unglazed tile is ideal for flooring. Most quarry tile can be used outdoors, even in freeze/thaw areas; check the Frost Resistance rating of the particular stock you consider for your project.

TOOLS FOR TILING PATIOS

Tools required for tiling a patio depend on the surface and the location. Of the list at right, only half will probably be needed for any specific patio job. Buy tools only after you have fully planned the job and know what is needed. Then ask the tiling experts at your local home center for advice. Most speciality tools can be rented—do so if you're only doing a job once.

USING SAFETY GLASSES AND DUST RESPIRATORS

Always wear safety glasses and a dust respirator when you are creating dust and debris. Flying chunks of mortar or tile can damage your eyes and airborne particles can damage your respiratory system. Dust respirators are less effective when worn over a beard.

BUYER'S GUIDE

TOOL	USE FOR	PRICE	IMPORTANCE
MEASURING AND LAYING OUT			
Chalk line	layout, cut lines	$	must have
China marker	marking tile cuts	$	or felt-tip or pencil
Combination square	marking tile cuts	$$	nice to have
Framing square	establishing square	$$	must have
Tape measure	measuring	$$	must have
4-foot level	establishing level, vertical	$$	can use small level
CUTTING AND SHAPING			
Abrasive stone	smoothing cut edges	$$	nice to have
Carbide (glass) bit	small holes in tile	$$	only for small holes
Carbide hole saw	large holes in tile	$$	must if hole is inside tile
Carbide-grit rod saw	curved tile cuts	$$	nice to have
Dust respirator	respiratory protection	$	must have
Ear plugs	hearing protection	$	must have
Mason's hammer	shaping rough stone	$$	must for cleft stone
Safety glasses	eye protection	$	must have
Snap cutter	straight tile cuts	$$$	must, or wet saw
Tile nippers	intricate tile cuts	$$	must have
Wet saw	straight tile cuts	$$$	nice to have
SETTING AND GROUTING			
Caulking gun	caulking joints	$	must have
Grout float	spreading grout	$$	must have
Margin trowel	mixing and spreading grout	$	nice to have
Mortar mixing paddle	mixing grout	$$	must have
Nonabrasive pad	removing excess grout	$	must have
Notched trowel	applying mortar	$$	must have
Round-corner sponge	removing excess grout	$	must have
½-inch drill	mixing adhesives	$$$	must have

PATIOS

TOOLS FOR MEASURING AND LAYING OUT

Ⓐ 4-FOOT LEVEL
To establish level and vertical.

Ⓑ CHALK LINE
To snap tile layout lines.

Ⓒ CHINA MARKER (WAX PEN
To make temporary cut marks on t of a tile.

Ⓓ COMBINATION SQUARE
A guide for marking straight, notc and L-cuts.

Ⓔ FRAMING SQUARE
For establishing perpendicular anc a guide for cutting.

Ⓕ TAPE MEASURE
For accurate measuring.

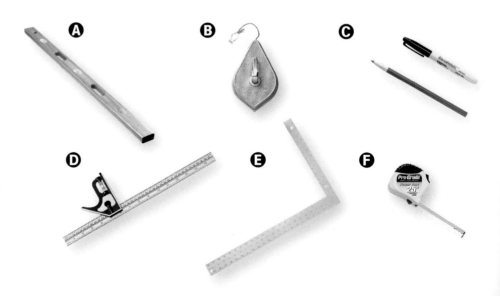

TOOLS FOR CUTTING AND SHAPING

Ⓐ ABRASIVE STONE
Smooths sharp edges of cut tiles.

Ⓑ CARBIDE HOLE SAW
Drills large holes through tiles, such as for water pipes. Available in a variety of sizes.

Ⓒ CARBIDE (GLASS) BIT
Drills small holes through tiles.

Ⓓ CARBIDE-GRIT ROD SAW
Makes intricate cuts. The rod can be removed and fed through a hole.

Ⓔ DUST RESPIRATOR
Wear respirators when working with mortar and chemical powders.

Ⓕ EAR PLUGS
Protect hearing from damaging sounds such as power tools.

Ⓖ ROTARY GRINDING AND CUTTING TOOL
Smooths and bevels sharp tile edges. Cuts tile with special attachments.

Ⓗ SAFETY GLASSES
Wear safety glasses when working with hand and power tools.

Ⓘ SNAP CUTTER
Scores and snaps tiles in straight lines.

Ⓙ SPIRAL SAW
Quickly and easily cuts soft wall tile.

Ⓚ TILE NIPPERS
Makes curved or intricate cuts by nibbling away tile.

Ⓛ WET SAW
Quickly and easily makes straight, notched, and L-shape cuts.

TOOLS FOR SETTING AND GROUTING

Ⓐ ½-INCH ELECTRIC DRILL
For mixing adhesive and grout.

Ⓑ CAULKING GUN
For caulking joints.

Ⓒ GROUT FLOAT
For filling grout joints.

Ⓓ MARGIN TROWEL
For mixing and applying adhesive and grout.

Ⓔ MORTAR MIXING PADDLE
For mixing and applying adhesive and grout.

Ⓕ NONABRASIVE SCOURING PAD
For removing stubborn grout residue.

Ⓖ NOTCHED TROWEL(S)
For spreading adhesive to setting bed.

Ⓗ ROUND-CORNER SPONGE
For removing residue and applying sealer.

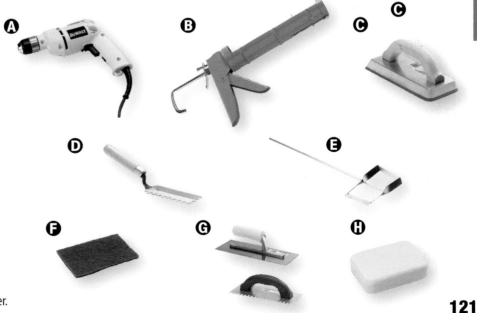

121

PATIO TILING MATERIALS

ADHESIVES, GROUTS, AND SEALERS

Ⓐ FLEXIBLE THIN-SET MORTAR
A thin-set mortar with powdered acrylic latex additive; used on ceramic tile, laminates, and plywood.

Ⓑ LATEX ADDITIVE
Increases thin-set mortar's bond strength, flexibility, and resistance to water.

Ⓒ THIN-SET MORTAR
A basic thin-set mortar without latex admix; it is commonly used over backerboard.

Ⓓ SANDED GROUT
For filling grout joints that are from ⅛ inch to ½ inch.

Ⓔ NON-SANDED GROUT
For filling grout joints narrower than ⅛ inch. They also are used on soft glazed tile and polished marble to avoid scratching.

Ⓕ PENETRATING SEALER
Penetrates grout and porous tile and stone to protect against water and stains. It also increases slip resistance.

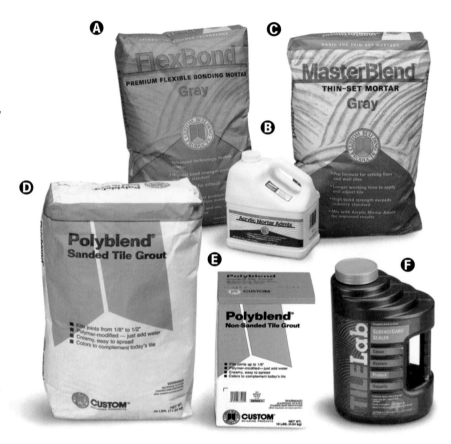

PROJECT PLANNING

Mortar is unforgiving. Once you spread it, you have a limited time before it sets up or gets too stiff to work. When it adheres to the tile and backboard, it can be removed only with a sledgehammer or muriatic acid. Make sure you think through the entire project before beginning so you get it right the first time.

Address these issues before starting a patio project:

DESIGN
■ Is the tile you have chosen appropriate for the environmental conditions in your area?
■ Is it available in sufficient quantity, or does it have to be ordered?
■ Can you return tile you don't use? (Keep a couple of tiles for repairs.)
■ Do you have enough tile on hand to complete the job?

EVALUATING THE BASE
■ Is the existing base suitable, or must you repair or prepare it?

■ Do you need to add control joints to the base?

MARKING TILE LAYOUT LINES
■ Can you make an accurate, to-scale sketch of the existing base?
■ Can you establish layout lines?
■ Do you have someone who can help with the layout?

SETTING THE TILE
■ Will you set the tile by eye, or will you use spacers?
■ Is there water available for cleanup and misting the surface?

EVALUATING THE SLAB

Concrete slab is the only suitable base for a tiled patio. The outdoor slab will be subject to rain, drought, perhaps snow and ice, and cycles of freezing and thawing. To survive these conditions, the slab should sit on well-drained soil (not clay or silt, and well above the water table) and slope away from the house at a minimum of ¼ inch per foot. If the soil is not well-drained, make it so by pouring the slab on top of a 4-inch-thick bed of gravel.

The slab should be reinforced against cracking by adding chopped fiberglass to the concrete mix or by placing 6"× 6" welded mesh an inch above the slab bottom.

Even with reinforcing, however, large slabs will crack. For this reason concrete and masonry structures include control joints—either cast or cut into large surfaces—to control where the cracks occur. A rule for exterior slabs is that there be a control joint every 8 feet in both directions.

If you pour the slab, place full-depth asphalt-impregnated control strips every 8 feet. If the slab already exists and it doesn't have control joints, snap chalk lines and cut joints with a concrete saw (available as a rental tool). Cut the joint about an inch deep, then force foam backer rod into the joint, followed by butyl caulk, as shown in the photos, right.

asphalt-impregnated strip
(repeated at 8" both ways)

slope away from building
at ¼" per foot

← 4"concrete slab
← welded mesh or fiberglass
← 4"crushed stone or well-drained earth

CAUSTIC MORTAR

As you might expect, cutting concrete is not exactly like cutting butter. It is more of a long, slow, grinding-away process than it is cutting. Clouds of fine concrete dust will fill the air. Wear a tight-fitting mask to ensure the dust doesn't get into your lungs. The saw will also emit a sound like a banshee. OSHA requires the operator to wear ear protection. Do it.

JOINTING A SLAB

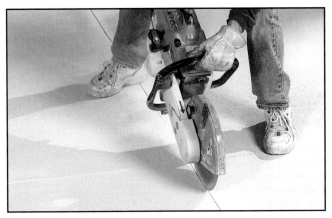

1 **CUT THE CONTROL JOINTS** along the chalk lines, using a rented gas-powered concrete saw. The depth of the cut should be at least ½ inch.

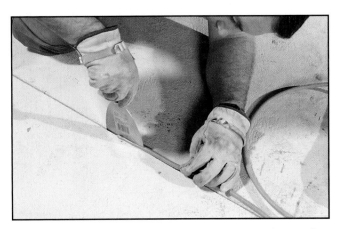

2 **STUFF FOAM BACKER ROD** into the control joint after cleaning it of dust and debris. Leave a depth of ¼ inch for the caulk.

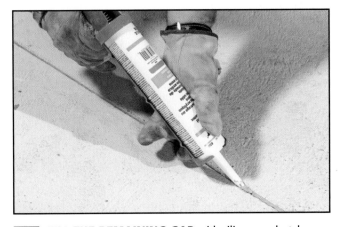

3 **FILL THE REMAINING GAP** with silicone or butyl caulk, either of which will remain flexible for at least 20 years. Smooth the caulk with a wetted finger.

ESTABLISHING LAYOUT LINES

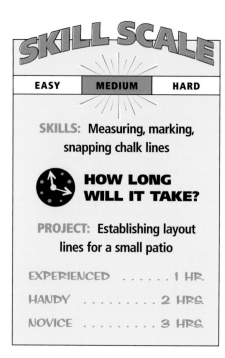

SKILL SCALE

EASY	MEDIUM	HARD

SKILLS: Measuring, marking, snapping chalk lines

HOW LONG WILL IT TAKE?

PROJECT: Establishing layout lines for a small patio

EXPERIENCED ......1 HR.

HANDY ....2 HRS.

NOVICE ....3 HRS.

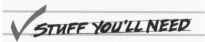

✔ STUFF YOU'LL NEED

TOOLS: Tape measure, chalk line, mason's twine

MATERIALS: None

SLABS WITHOUT EXPANSION JOINTS

Careful planning at the design stage will ensure a patio that lasts. Consider the following for the best layout:

- Locate full tiles where they will be most visible.
- Locate full tiles at doorways.
- Don't use less than half tiles.

You can't always satisfy all three criteria. In the following example, full tiles are placed along the most visible planter border and front patio edge.

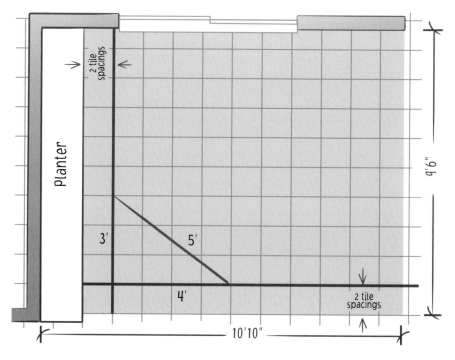

1 **SNAP THE FIRST** reference orthogonal several grid spaces from a row with full tiles. In this project, full tiles are located at the outside.

2 **SNAP A SECOND** reference line several grid spaces from the edge of the adjacent slab edge. The design has full tiles at the slab edges.

3 **MEASURE** 3 feet and 4 feet from the intersection to check for orthogonal. Readjust if needed.

SLABS WITH EXPANSION JOINTS

When laying out tile on a slab with expansion joints, the joints take precedence over tile layout because the slab will crack at the joints. If you tile over the joints, the tile will also crack. Match the tile joints to the slab joints and caulk, rather than grout, the joints.

If you saw the joints, locate the cuts where you want tile joints. The joints will serve as the reference orthogonals for your layout.

Check the orthogonals using the 3-4-5 triangle method. If an adjustment is required, make it to the shorter line.

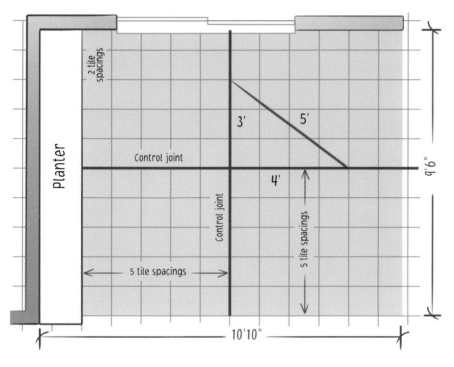

WHERE DID THAT LINE GO?
You know the feeling, "I shoulda done it myself!" I decided to cut joint lines into a slab I planned to tile. After figuring the tile spacing, I snapped chalk lines along a planned tile joint. Then I called a friend who I knew had a concrete saw. He said he'd be over in a few days to do the job.

Then it rained. I forgot about the chalk lines. When my friend came over there were just faint traces of the chalk, but he cut the lines anyway. I now had concrete joints about an inch from where I planned the tile joints.

What to do? I laid a 4-inch strip of 15-pound felt over the joint so the mortar wouldn't stick, and I've never had a problem.

1 **STRETCH MASON'S TWINE** (strong, stretchy 3-strand nylon line) over the center of the longest control joint in the slab.

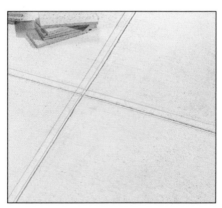

2 **STRETCH A SECOND LINE** over the orthogonal control joint. Establish orthogonal, then snap chalk lines.

3 **MARK** points 3 feet and 4 feet from the intersection of strings. Measure between points. If not 5 feet, adjust one of the strings, then snap the chalk lines.

MARKING AND CUTTING TILE

✓ STUFF YOU'LL NEED

TOOLS: Tape measure, chalk line, felt-tip pen, scissors, wet saw, combination square, china marker, safety glasses, dust respirator

MATERIALS: Chalk, cardboard, tile, masking tape

OOPS!

THAT'S WHY IT'S A "WET" SAW

I showed up at the tile job in nice new clothes. I soon discovered that a wet saw throws a spray of dust and water. But I saved my clothes with an old camper's trick: I cut holes for my head and arms and wore a trash-bag poncho.

Patios usually involve only straight and L-cuts. The type of cutter to use depends on the kind and thickness of tile. A snap cutter is all you need for straight cuts in normal ⅜-inch-thick floor tile. If the tile is cement-bodied and/or more than ⅜-inch thick, however, you will need a wet saw. L-cuts also require a wet saw. Wet saws can be purchased or rented depending on how much you expect to use the tool.

1 **PLACE TILE TO BE CUT** on last set tile. Place marker tile on top, against a spacer tile at wall. Trace edge of marker tile onto tile to be cut.

2 **A WET SAW** cuts through the hardest tile as if it were butter. If you don't own one, rent one. See page 33 for detailed instructions on its use.

3 **MAKE A TEMPLATE** from cardboard for complex cuts.

4 **CUT AND FIT** the template. If you trim too much, use the first template as a guide, adjusting as necessary.

5 **APPLY MASKING TAPE** to the tile; then trace the cut lines onto the masking tape with a felt-tip pen.

MIXING THE MORTAR

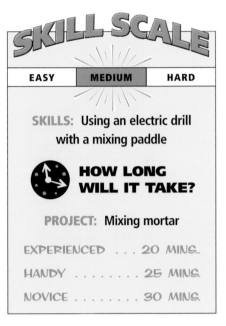

SKILL SCALE

| EASY | MEDIUM | HARD |

SKILLS: Using an electric drill with a mixing paddle

HOW LONG WILL IT TAKE?

PROJECT: Mixing mortar

EXPERIENCED . . . 20 MINS.

HANDY . . . . 25 MINS.

NOVICE . . . . 30 MINS.

Dry form thin-set mortar is mixed with either water or a liquid-latex additive. Latex makes the mortar resistant to water and, therefore, freezing and thawing. Have enough for your project, and don't dilute it with water.

Mortar is much stiffer and heavier than paint. If you attempt to mix it with a paint-mixing paddle, you will probably end up breaking the paddle. Use a mixing paddle specifically designed for mortar or grout.

Also, though you may have a versatile ⅜-inch variable speed drill, don't take a chance. You may get away with mixing a bag or two, but by the end of the day, chances are you will have burned out the motor before you finish the job.

STUFF YOU'LL NEED

TOOLS: 5-gallon bucket, ½-inch drill, mixing paddle

MATERIALS: Latex-modified thin-set mortar

HOLD ON TO THAT DRILL
Drills can get away from you if you don't hold on tightly. Always use to hands on the extension handles whenever you are mixing grout.

PATIOS

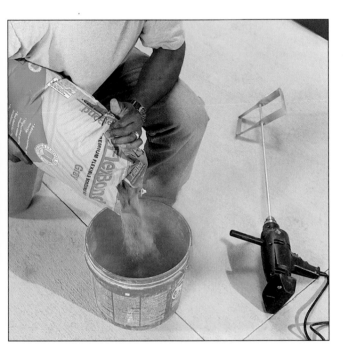

1 **ADD THE DRY MORTAR** to water in a 5-gallon plastic bucket. Use the proportions recommended by the manufacturer.

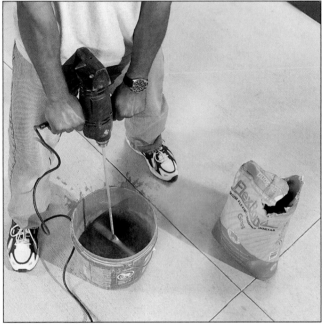

2 **MIX THE MORTAR.** Use a paddle designed for mortar, not paint, and mix at slow speed. After mixing, let the mortar rest for 10 minutes, then mix again before use.

127

SETTING THE TILE

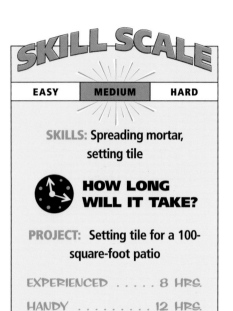

SKILL SCALE

EASY	MEDIUM	HARD

SKILLS: Spreading mortar, setting tile

HOW LONG WILL IT TAKE?

PROJECT: Setting tile for a 100-square-foot patio

EXPERIENCED . . . . . 8 HRS.

HANDY . . . . 12 HRS.

NOVICE . . . . 16 HRS.

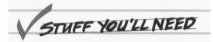

✓ STUFF YOU'LL NEED

TOOLS: Chalk line, 5-gallon bucket, ½-inch drill, mixing paddle, ¼"×¼" square-notch trowel

MATERIALS: Latex-modified thin-set mortar, grout with latex additive, tile

WORK SMARTER

SAVE YOUR KNEES

You may need your knees later in life. Short of playing in the NFL, there is nothing harder on knees than working on rough concrete. Get a set of knee pads from a home center or gardening center.

Before settling for our rather ordinary basketweave pattern, check out the gallery of patterns on pages 15 to 17. They don't require any additional tile. However, some do require additional concentration!

Lay the first tile at the intersection of the lines. Twist the tile back and forth slightly to make sure it is embedded in the mortar. Remove the first tile and inspect its back. If you find only parallel ridges, the bed is not thick enough. Once you are satisfied that the mortar bed is thick enough, place the second tile with a couple of spacers placed on end so that you can remove them easily.

After setting all of the tiles in an area, lay a short 2×4 on top of the tiles and **lightly** tap with a rubber mallet to level the tiles.

1 **START AT THE INTERSECTION** of reference lines and spread mortar over an 8- to 10-square-foot area. Press the mortar into the slab with the trowel held at a shallow angle.

2 **COMB THE MORTAR** in straight lines, holding the trowel at a 45-degree angle to the slab, forcing the teeth of the trowel against the concrete.

3 **LAY THE FIRST TILE** at the intersection of the lines. Twist the tile to make sure it's imbedded in the mortar. Remove and inspect the back. If you find only parallel ridges, the bed is not thick enough. Once the mortar bed is thick enough, place the second tile with a couple of spacers placed on end so you can remove them easily.

4 **PLACE SPACERS ON END** so they will be easy to remove. Use two in the long joints, one in the short joints. Spacers can be removed and reused after 30 minutes.

128

5 **PULL UP A TILE** occasionally to make sure the mortar is wetting the tile as well as the slab. If it isn't, pull up the last batch of set tiles and start over with fresh mortar. After setting all of the tiles in an area, lay a short 2×4 on top of the tiles and **lightly** tap with a rubber mallet to level the tiles.

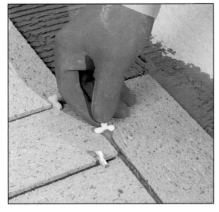

6 **USE A SPACER** to remove excess mortar before it hardens. Mortar remaining in the joint will show through the grout—particularly if the grout is light color.

Homer's Hindsight

DON'T BOX YOURSELF IN!

If your patio is in an enclosed corner of the house, make sure you don't end up there. You shouldn't walk on the tile for 24 hours because disturbing a tile the slightest amount will break the mortar bond. If you must, snap a pair of reference lines in the enclosed corner and start your tiling there, rather than at the center of the slab.

A+ WORK SMARTER

PREPARING TO GROUT

Before grouting, let the thin-set mortar cure for at least 24 hours. Remove the spacers and clean any mortar out of the joints with a spacer or a bristle brush before applying the grout.

If the tile is rough or porous, such as brick, the grout is likely to get into pores and crevices and be difficult to remove after it has set. Seal the face of porous tile before grouting. Don't let the sealer run into the joints, however, because the sealer will prevent the grout from adhering to the joint.

Also seal the control joints and the joints between the patio and the building foundation. Stuff foam backer rod into the joint (it comes in a wide range of sizes); then caulk over it with colored silicone caulk.

1

2

3

4

PATIOS

GROUTING THE JOINTS

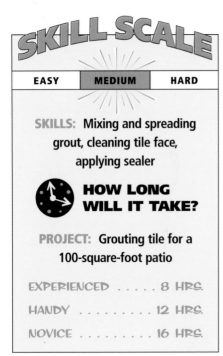

SKILL SCALE

EASY	MEDIUM	HARD

SKILLS: Mixing and spreading grout, cleaning tile face, applying sealer

HOW LONG WILL IT TAKE?

PROJECT: Grouting tile for a 100-square-foot patio

EXPERIENCED . . . . . 8 HRS.

HANDY . . . . 12 HRS.

NOVICE . . . . 16 HRS.

✓ STUFF YOU'LL NEED

TOOLS: 5-gallon bucket, ½-inch drill, mixing paddle, rubber gloves, water supply, sponge, rags, small bucket, sponge mop

MATERIALS: Unmixed dry grout, sealer

Grout is as important for an outdoor patio as for a kitchen or bathroom floor. Water penetrating the joints between tiles may creep under the tile and, if it freezes, break the bond between tile and slab. Grout also keeps dirt from collecting where it would allow grass and weeds to grow.

Tile for a patio should be nonporous. It can, however, be very rough textured. If it is, you will find cleaning up the grout residue nearly impossible. Presealing the tile before setting will make cleanup a lot easier.

The simplest way to preseal tile is to lay it out, tightly fitted with no gaps, and then apply sealer with a roller. Don't do this on the slab, however, as sealer which runs between the cracks will seal the slab, preventing a bond between the setting bed and the slab.

1 **MIX THE GROUT** at slow speed in a 5-gallon bucket with a mortar paddle and ½-inch drill. Let the grout rest for 10 to 15 minutes to let the dyes develop; then remix.

2 **SPREAD THE GROUT** with a rubber grout float held at a shallow angle. Press the grout into the joints to fill them. For joints wider than ⅜ inch, use a grout bag (see page 131).

3 **REMOVE EXCESS GROUT** with the grout float held at a steep angle. Sweep the float across the tiles diagonally so that the float doesn't dip into the joints.

GROUT ESTIMATOR
(COURTESY OF CUSTOM BUILDING PRODUCTS, INC.)

(Sq. ft. per pound of sanded grout)

Tile size, inches	Joint width, inches			
	⅛	¼	⅜	½
1×1×¼	2.5	1		
2×2×¼	3.5	2		
4¼×4¼×5⁄16		3		
6×6×½		2.5	1.75	1.25
4×8×½		2.25	1.5	1
8×8×⅜		4.5	3	2
12×12×⅜	14	7		
16×16×⅜		9	5.75	3.75
24×24×⅜		13	9	6

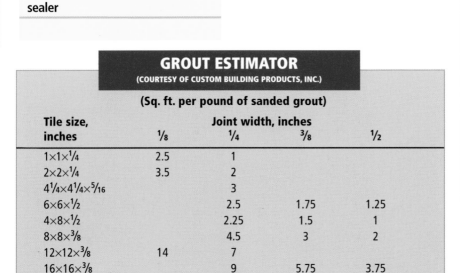

130

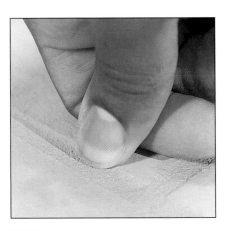

4 **TEST THE GROUT**. When your thumbnail leaves no impression (10 to 15 minutes or per manufacturer's instructions) clean the tiles.

5 **REMOVE GROUT RESIDUE** with a damp—not wet— sponge. If the mortar has set up too much, use a plastic or stainless steel scrub pad, staying out of the the joints.

6 **RINSE, RINSE, RINSE.** Keep the water almost clean enough to drink and you will have a much easier job of removing the inevitable slight haze.

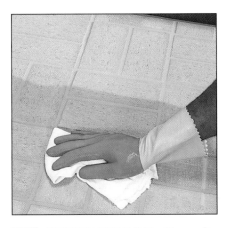

7 **REMOVE THE HAZE** with a soft, clean cotton rag, such as old cotton T-shirts. If you run out of clean rags, launder them and use them again.

8 **DAMP CURE THE GROUT** by misting (not drenching) several times a day for three days. If the patio receives direct sunlight, cover it with plastic sheeting between mistings.

9 **APPLY PENETRATING SEALER** with a sponge mop. Wipe up the excess before it dries. Follow the manufacturer's directions for number of applications.

CLOSER LOOK

FOR WIDER GROUT JOINTS

Use a grout bag to fill joints wider than ⅜ inch or with rounded or irregular edges. Apply just enough grout to fill the joints so you won't have to remove excess.

Smooth the joint with the end of a PVC pipe or the rounded end of a wooden trowel handle. Any cylindrical object with a diameter 2–3 times the joint width will work.

USING CLEFT STONE INSTEAD OF TILE

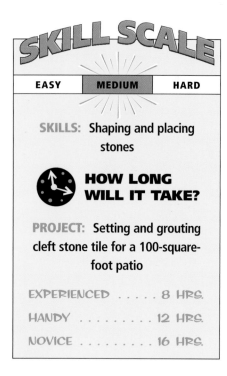

SKILL SCALE

EASY	MEDIUM	HARD

SKILLS: Shaping and placing stones

HOW LONG WILL IT TAKE?

PROJECT: Setting and grouting cleft stone tile for a 100-square-foot patio

EXPERIENCED . . . . . 8 HRS.

HANDY . . . . 12 HRS.

NOVICE . . . . 16 HRS.

For a truly rustic, indigenous look, surface your patio with natural stone from the local area. Many regions of the United States are known for certain types of stone. New Hampshire is the "granite state," for example, and Vermont is known for its slate and marble.

One reason to choose local material is shipping cost. One cubic foot of most rock weighs about 170 pounds. Even if the stone were free at the source, it would cost thousands of dollars to have an average patio's worth shipped interstate. Instead, if you are lucky, you may find an excavation contractor who will let you pick through the rubble from a blasting operation.

Cleft stone has random shape and thickness, which is its charm and its weakness. Unless the stone is slate, the surface will be uneven. Patio furniture will have to be shimmed in order not to rock and wobble.

The solution to fitting the randomly shaped stones together is to treat them as pieces of a jigsaw puzzle. Arrange the largest pieces first, fill in the spaces with smaller stones, then cut even smaller pieces to fit the remaining gaps.

The problem of variable thickness is easily solved by the use of a variable thickness of mortar bed.

Whether you need to apply penetrating sealer depends on the nature of the stone and the climate. In areas subject to freezing and thawing, use mortar with latex additive and a nonporous variety of stone, such as granite, and apply sealer several times a year. If there is never more than an occasional frost where you live, water penetrating the stone and mortar is unlikely to cause a problem.

✓ STUFF YOU'LL NEED

TOOLS: Chalk line, 5-gallon bucket, ½-inch drill, mixing paddle, felt-tip marker, mason's hammer, trowel, safety glasses

MATERIALS: Natural stone, 2 x 4 (for height gauge)

1 **START BY SPREADING THE LARGEST STONES** randomly over the surface of the slab. This is the quickest way to fit the stones together.

2 **FIT THE REMAINING LARGE STONES** like pieces of a puzzle between the first set of larger stones. Don't worry about the inevitable empty spots.

3 **TO FILL THE VOIDS,** place large stones over the empty spaces and sketch the required cut lines on the stone surfaces with a felt-tip marker.

4 **SHAPE THE STONES** to the marked cut lines with a mason's hammer. Use the pointed end of the hammer to chip away outside the line.

5 **MAKE A HEIGHT GAUGE** that just clears the thickest stone. Use it to set the height of each stone as it is laid. Make it just long enough to span the widest stone.

6 **DROP A THICK BED OF MORTAR** on the slab where a stone will be placed. Turn the stone over and apply mortar to its underside to wet the stone and make a thick bed.

7 **PLACE THE BACK-BUTTERED STONE** back in place. If the stone surface is below that of the other stones, pick it up and add mortar to the bed.

8 **USING THE HEIGHT GAUGE,** tamp the stone down to the proper height. After all of the stones have been set, grout the voids between the stones with the same mortar.

MORE TILING PROJECTS

134

CHAPTER 6 MORE TILING PROJECTS

Tile isn't just for walls, floors, and countertops. It's a versatile tool rich with potential for creating special decorative accessories that will enhance both the inside and outside of your home. Whether you are looking for a simple project to involve the entire family, an elegant touch to add beauty to your home, or a craft you might turn into extra money, you will find it here.

The projects on the following pages range in complexity from cutting tile into squares for coasters, (See "Coasters with Felt Backs", page 141.) to facing a fireplace (see "Fireplace Surround," page 152.) to constructing a unique indoor/outdoor checkerboard (see "Outdoor Checkerboard," page 172).

A RANGE OF TILING SKILLS

Many of these projects require minimal skills and an inexpensive materials budget. Some can be completed in an hour—none require more than a weekend.

Start with something simple and as your skill and confidence levels grow, you can tackle a kitchen floor, countertop, or patio.

CHAPTER SIX CONTENTS

136 **Selecting Tile for Projects**

137 **Tools**

138 **Planning and Materials**

    138 Adhesive, Grouts, and Sealers

    138 Mosaic Tile

139 **Techniques**

    137 Laying Cement Backerboard

    137 Tile Layout Lines

    138 Marking and Cutting Tile

    138 Setting and Grouting

141 **Coasters with Felt Backs**

142 **Tiling a Tabletop**

144 **Mural Backsplash**

    145 Mural Samples

146 **Window Treatment**

148 **Door Casing Rosettes**

149 **Chair Rail**

150 **Framed Mirror**

151 **Staircase Risers**

152 **Fireplace Surround**

    153 Fireplace Inspiration

154 **Fireplace Hearth**

156 **Stove Base**

158 **Gas Stove Alcove**

160 **Stove Heat Shield**

162 **Plant Pot**

164 **Birdbath**

166 **Garden Bench**

168 **Tile Name Sign**

170 **Wind Chimes**

172 **Outdoor Checkerboard**

MORE TILING PROJECTS

SELECTING TILE FOR PROJECTS

Tile was originally clay fired at high temperature, resulting in hard, durable, waterproof building materials. Tile was plain or finished with a decorative glaze of melted silicates and dyes. Today, tile includes cut and polished stone and concrete shapes.

Tile varies widely in physical properties and in its suitability to projects. The table, right, lists characteristics; the best guidance comes from knowledgeable tile suppliers and artisans.

TYPE OF TILE	COST	RELATIVE DURABILITY	WATER ABSORPTION	MAIN-TENANCE
Glazed wall	Low to medium	Low to high	Medium	Low
Porcelain	Medium	High	Low	Low
Quarry	Low to medium	High	Medium	Low
Terra-cotta	Low to medium	Low	Medium to high	High
Natural stone	Low to high	High	Low to high	Medium to high
Ceramic mosaic	Medium	High	Low	Low
Cement-bodied	Low	High	Low	Low to medium
Decorative	High	Low to medium	Medium	Low

TILE CHARACTERISTICS

GLAZED TILES have a decorative surface coating of fused glass and metal oxides. They are not waterproof nor tough enough for traffic.

PORCELAIN TILES are dense and hard, and they wear well. Because they are water resistant, they can be used in wet and freezing conditions.

QUARRY TILE is a hard, unglazed, low-cost tile that is ideal for flooring. Most quarry tile can be used outdoors, even in freeze and thaw areas.

TERRA-COTTA TILES are water-absorbent and not durable. They are used mostly in decorative indoor applications.

NATURAL STONE includes granite, marble, and slate, and is available in polished (glasslike), honed (matte), and tumbled (rough) finishes.

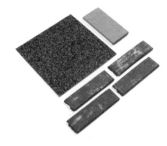

CEMENT-BODIED TILES are made of mortar, not clay, and are cured, not fired. They are durable and waterproof, and can be used outdoors.

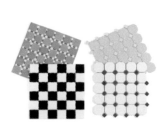

CERAMIC MOSAIC TILE is clay-based tile 2 inches square or smaller. Small tiles are held together in sheets to facilitate setting.

DECORATIVE TILES are generally glazed and decorated by hand; characteristics are similar to those of wall tile.

136

TOOLS

ost tools used for tiling are also used in carpentry and masonry. Assembling tools for a tile project need not be expensive.

The exception is the wet saw—a miniature table saw with a diamond blade that cuts through tile, masonry, and stone. Hobbyists' wet saws cost under $100. Borrow or rent a wet saw first to determine if you need it.

Ⓐ ABRASIVE STONE
Smooths sharp edges of cut tiles.

Ⓑ CAULKING GUN
To apply caulk.

Ⓒ CHALK LINE
To snap tile layout lines.

Ⓓ CHINA MARKER
To make temporary cut marks on the face of a tile.

Ⓔ COMBINATION SQUARE
A guide for marking straight, notch, and L-shape cuts.

Ⓕ DUST RESPIRATOR
Wear respirators when working with mortar and chemical powders.

Ⓖ EAR PLUGS
Protect hearing from damaging sounds such as power tools.

Ⓗ FRAMING SQUARE
For use in establishing perpendicular and as a straightedge.

Ⓘ GROUT FLOAT
For filling grout joints.

Ⓙ MARGIN TROWEL
For mixing and applying small amounts of mortar and grout.

Ⓚ NOTCHED TROWEL
For spreading adhesive to setting bed.

Ⓛ ROTARY GRINDING AND CUTTING TOOL
Smooths and bevels sharp tile edges. Cuts tile with special attachments.

Ⓜ SAFETY GLASSES
Wear safety glasses when working with hand and power tools.

Ⓝ SPIRAL SAW
Quickly and easily cuts soft tile.

Ⓞ TAPE MEASURE
For all measurements.

Ⓟ TILE NIPPERS
Makes curved or intricate cuts by nibbling away tile.

Ⓠ WET SAW
Makes straight, notched, and L-shape cuts.

BUYER'S GUIDE

TOOL	USE FOR	PRICE	IMPORTANCE
Abrasive stone	smoothing cut edges	$$	nice to have
Caulking gun	caulking joints	$	must have
Chalk line	layout, cut lines	$	must have
China marker	marking tile cuts	$	can use felt-tip
Combination square	marking tile cuts	$$	nice to have
Dust respirator	respiratory protection	$	must have
Ear plugs	hearing protection	$	must have
Framing square	establishing square	$$	must have
Grout float	spreading grout	$$	must have to grout
Margin trowel	mixing/spreading	$	must have
Notched trowel	applying mortar	$$	must have
Rotary grinding tool	smoothing cut edges	$$$	nice to have
Safety glasses	eye protection	$	must have
Spiral saw	cutting soft tile	$$$	nice to have
Tape measure	measuring	$$	must have
Tile nippers	intricate tile cuts	$$	must have
Wet saw	straight tile cuts	$$$	can use snap cutter

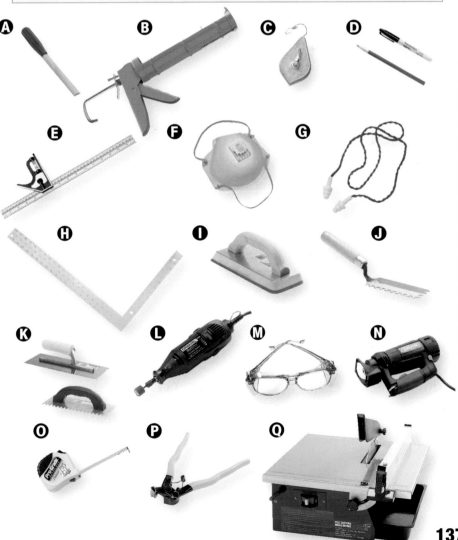

137

PLANNING AND MATERIALS

Most of the projects in this chapter can be completed in a day or a weekend, provided you plan the process and have all the tools and materials. Answer these questions as you plan your project:

- Is the tile readily available locally, or does it have to be ordered?
- Can you return unused tiles?
- Do you have enough tile on hand (plus at least 10 percent overage)?

- Is the surface suitable for tile or must you prepare or cover it?
- Do you have all of the required tools on hand?
- Do you have buckets, sponges, brushes, and clean cloths to mix and clean the mortar?
- Do you have a helper you can call upon when needed?
- Do you understand every step of the project? Should you discuss it with your tile supplier?

ADHESIVES, GROUTS, AND SEALERS

Tile projects require three materials: adhesive (generally thin-set mortar, sometimes silicone) to adhere the tile to substrate, grout to fill the joints between the tiles, and sealant to prevent the tile and grout from absorbing water or stains. Ask your tile supplier to recommend the specific adhesive, grout, and sealer best for your application.

A LATEX ADDITIVE
Mix with thin-set mortar to increase adhesion, flexibility, and water resistance.

B NON-SANDED GROUT
Use unsanded grout for joints less than ⅛ inch wide.

C SANDED GROUT
Use to fill joints that are from ⅛ inch to ½ inch wide.

D SEALER
Penetrates grout and porous tile to protect against water and stains.

E THIN-SET MORTARS
Use as adhesive to set tile on cement backerboard or concrete. Mix with water or latex additive.

MOSAIC TILE

MOSAIC TILE is tile 2 inches square and smaller. Most are attached to web-backed sheets to facilitate setting large areas. You can remove the backing by soaking in water, or you can make random mosaic tiles, as shown below.

PLACE DECORATIVE WALL TILES in a burlap bag on the floor, and strike the tile, through the bag, with a rubber or wooden mallet. Continue until the broken pieces are of the desired size.

TRIM BROKEN TILES with tile nippers to remove sharp projections or to shape pieces to fit into a mosaic pattern.

TECHNIQUES

LAYING CEMENT BACKERBOARD

Many projects require a base cement backerboard—a fiberglass-reinforced cementitious panel that serves as rigid substrate for tile. The panels are sold in ¼-inch and ½-inch thickness, and 3'×5' and 4'×8' sizes. A 4'×8' panel weighs about 98 pounds.

Cut backerboard by scoring both sides and snapping it. Use a carbide scoring tool to cut backerboard; the material will dull a utility knife. Backerboard can also be cut with a masonry blade and a circular saw or grinder.

If the tiled surface will bear traffic, the backerboard is imbedded in thin-set mortar and screwed or nailed to the material beneath. If the tile will not bear weight, the backerboard is screwed or nailed to the supporting structure.

TILE LAYOUT LINES

Design the tile arrangement on paper before laying it out, unless you use a random placement. When you are satisfied with the arrangement, transfer the design to the tile substrate with chalk lines or a felt-tip pen.

Laying out the design on paper and with chalk on the setting surface allows you to:
- practice layouts at zero cost
- minimize the number of cuts
- avoid narrow strips
- estimate the number of tiles needed

For small projects, a single pair of orthogonal (at a right angle) reference lines will suffice. Lines represent tile joint centers. Begin at the intersection of the lines and build outward in both directions to fill the quadrant with tile.

For projects larger than 8 to 12 square feet, secondary lines are snapped to enclose rectangles that can be set from one position and within the working time of the mortar.

If a reference line is slightly in error, snap a corrected line in a different color.

MARKING AND CUTTING TILE

Use a snap cutter (basically a miniature glass cutter) or a wet saw (a small table saw with a diamond blade that is cooled by water) to make straight cuts.

Snap cutters can only be used to make straight cuts, although they are very good at that tile task. A versatile wet saw allows straight, L-shape, notch, square, and complex curved cuts. For a description of how each of these tools works, turn to page 59.

Specialized tile-cutting tools include: tile nippers for nibbling complex curves, carbide rod saws (which cut like a coping saw), and carbide drills and hole saws for making circular holes. The use of these tools is described on page 60.

When marking a tile cut line, use a marking medium that doesn't permanently stain the tile.

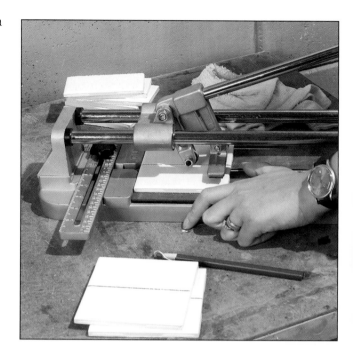

SETTING AND GROUTING

Thin-set mortar comes in dry form and is mixed with water or liquid-latex additive. Small amounts can be mixed by hand with a margin trowel. To mix large amounts, use a $^3/_8$-inch drill and a mortar-mixing paddle in a 5-gallon plastic bucket.

Apply thin-set with the appropriate size trowel (see Trowel Size Guide, page 36). Press the mortar into the substrate with the trowel to wet the surface; then comb out the mortar in uniform, straight lines with the toothed edge of the trowel.

To set tile, twist it back and forth slightly to embed it in the mortar. Remove the first set tile and inspect the back; if you find only parallel ridges, the mortar bed is not thick enough.

Let mortar cure for 24 hours before grouting. Preseal porous tile so you can remove grout traces. Pour grout on the tiles. With a rubber grout float held at a shallow angle, spread the grout and press it into the joints. Remove the excess by diagonally sweeping the float across the tiles. When the grout hardens, wipe the tiles with a damp sponge. Remove the remaining haze immediately with a clean, damp cloth.

COASTERS WITH FELT BACKS

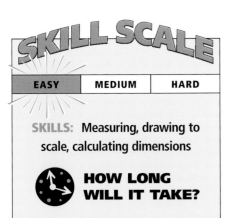
A great first project for adults or children, a set of coasters makes a wonderful handcrafted Christmas or housewarming gift.

The fun part is selecting the tile from which to make the coaster set. Use floor tiles without a pattern to make coasters that are similar. To personalize a set of coasters, choose decorative floor tile with a scene. The tile coasters can be used to form a puzzle—two gifts in one. Floor tile also comes in 8"×8" and 6"×6" sizes; both can be cut into four equal pieces.

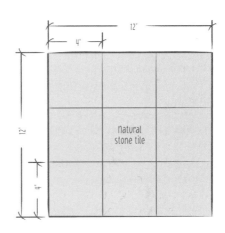

natural stone tile

1 **DIVIDE** the tile into nine equal squares on the back side. The tile doesn't have to measure exactly 12 inches square, but the squares should be equal.

2 **CUT THE TILE** with a wet saw. Align the blade with the middle of the mark, setting the saw fence for a perfect cut.

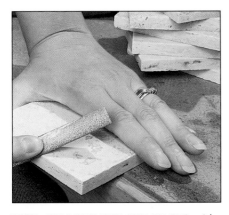

3 **SMOOTH THE CUT EDGES** with the abrasive stone; a rotary grinder is even better and faster, if you have one.

4 **CUT SQUARES OF FELT** ⅛ inch to ½ inch smaller than the tile squares so that the felt is recessed from the edges of the coaster.

5 **SPREAD JUST ENOUGH SEALANT** on the backs of the tiles to wet the felt. Apply the felt squares.

TILING A TABLETOP

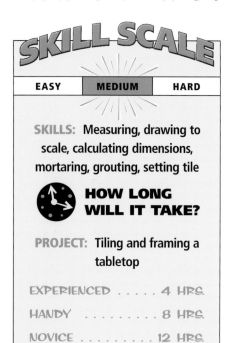

SKILL SCALE

EASY	MEDIUM	HARD

SKILLS: Measuring, drawing to scale, calculating dimensions, mortaring, grouting, setting tile

HOW LONG WILL IT TAKE?

PROJECT: Tiling and framing a tabletop

EXPERIENCED . . . . . 4 HRS.

HANDY . . . . 8 HRS.

NOVICE . . . . 12 HRS.

✓ STUFF YOU'LL NEED

TOOLS: Tape measure, framing square, combination square, felt-tip pen, miter saw, C-clamps, notched trowel, grout float, safety glasses

MATERIALS: ¾-inch AC plywood, 1⁵⁄₁₆-inch corner guard trim, colored silicone caulk, thin-set mortar, tile spacers, wood glue, dyed grout, tile, masking tape

A FEW IDEAS

A tiled tabletop can serve as the focal point of a room and serve as a horizontal work of art. Create a dramatic tabletop or an elegantly simple surface.

If you have particular tiles in mind, make your tile design first; then look for the table. If you already have the table, subtract 3 inches from its width and length, and sketch a tile layout to fill that space.

Since you will cover up the original tabletop, you can salvage a tag sale or discarded table. You need a solid base and legs to which you will fasten a new top of ¾-inch AC plywood, as shown in the drawing below.

Match the 1⁵⁄₁₆-inch, corner guard trim to the structure or design of the table. Determine the type of wood, and get a custom millwork shop to mill stock of the same species. See page 192 for information on contacting the manufacturer of the tables pictured at right.

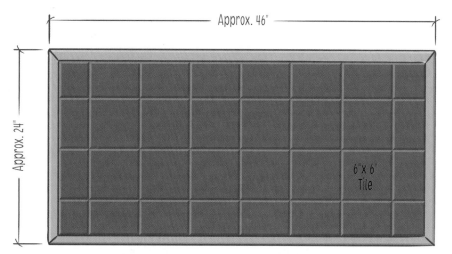

Approx. 46"

Approx. 24"

6" x 6" Tile

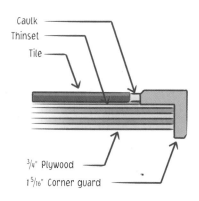

Caulk

Thinset

Tile

¾" Plywood

1⁵⁄₁₆" Corner guard

1 **USE A FRAMING SQUARE** to measure the four trim pieces; then cut them with a miter saw. With the tabletop upside down, measure and cut identical pairs of pieces so that the frame is ⅛ inch larger.

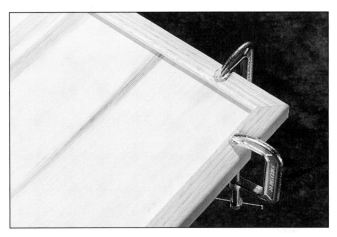

2 **APPLY GLUE** to the perimeter of the table and fit the trim pieces. Clamp the pieces loosely with C-clamps; make the final adjustments, then tighten the clamps securely.

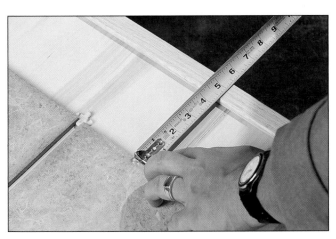

3 **DRY FIT THE FIELD (CENTER) TILES;** then adjust so the perimeter gaps are symmetrical. Measure the gaps to determine the width (allowing for joints) to cut the border tiles.

4 **MARK CUT LINES** using a combination square. Number cut tiles on the paper design and on the back of the tile to eliminate mistakes when setting tiles in the planned order.

5 **COMB THIN-SET** onto the tabletop inside the trim; then set tile from one corner inward. Use tile spacers instead of layout lines.

6 **GROUT THE JOINTS** after 24 hours. Protect the wood trim from the grout with masking tape. Remove excess grout, allow to cure 10 to 15 minutes, then clean up the grout haze, apply a penetrating tile and grout sealer.

MURAL BACKSPLASH

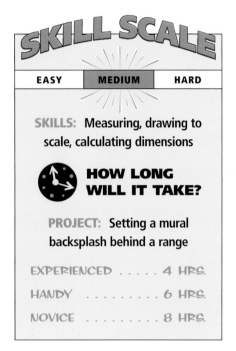

SKILL SCALE

EASY	MEDIUM	HARD

SKILLS: Measuring, drawing to scale, calculating dimensions

HOW LONG WILL IT TAKE?

PROJECT: Setting a mural backsplash behind a range

EXPERIENCED . . . . . 4 HRS.

HANDY . . . . 6 HRS.

NOVICE . . . . 8 HRS.

STUFF YOU'LL NEED

TOOLS: Carbide scorer, chalk line, drill with Phillips bit, framing square, felt-tip pen, wet saw, notched trowel, grout float, safety glasses

MATERIALS: Cement backerboard, field tile, mural tiles, listellos (optional), thin-set mortar, grout, Phillips backerboard screws, fiberglass reinforcing tape, sealant

The alcove above a kitchen range or stovetop begs for a window, or at least something different than an expanse of plain wall. A window is out of the question because of the amount of grease that gets splattered there. In fact, the prime requirements are that the surface be heat resistant, unaffected by grease, and easy to wipe down.

What could be better than a mural in tile? A tile mural can depict a scene one might see out a window, a cooking theme, or something dear to the heart of the cook.

Most tile stores display murals in a variety of motifs; catalogs picture hundreds more. If you don't find exactly what you want, take a sketch or photograph to a tile artisan to make one for you.

Mural techniques are the same as for tiling a wall (see Chapter 3, page 73). Lay the mural out on a table, cut listellos to frame and set it off (optional), and measure the total width. Determine the center of the space between the wall cabinets, and draw a pair of vertical lines equidistant from the center to mark left and right mural edges. After setting the bottom row of field tiles, set the mural between the vertical reference lines. After the mural is in place, cut and fit the rest of the field tile around it.

Seal the grout and tile against cooking splashes.

1 **APPLY CEMENT BACKERBOARD** as a base for the backsplash to protect it from steam and cooking, which can soften drywall. Wear safety glasses when drilling.

2 **SET THE MURAL FRAME** after the bottom row of field tile is in place. Use the bottom tiles as the straightedge for setting the listellos (optional) of the frame.

3 **SET THE MURAL** tiles tightly together and centered between the vertical lines. (It is more important that the mural be centered on the frame than on the lines.)

4 **SET THE REMAINING FIELD TILES.** Most of the cuts will be straight; use a wet saw to make the L-shape cuts in the top corners.

MURAL SAMPLES See page 192 for information on contacting manufacturers of the tiles pictured on these pages.

WINDOW TREATMENT

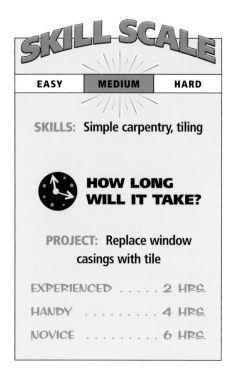

SKILL SCALE

| EASY | MEDIUM | HARD |

SKILLS: Simple carpentry, tiling

HOW LONG WILL IT TAKE?

PROJECT: Replace window casings with tile

EXPERIENCED . . . . . 2 HRS.

HANDY . . . . 4 HRS.

NOVICE . . . . 6 HRS.

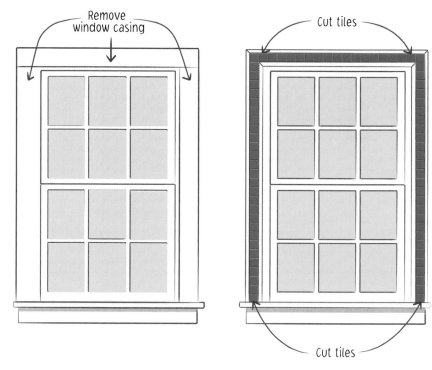

Remove window casing

Cut tiles

Cut tiles

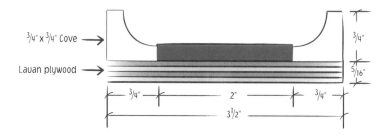

3/4" x 3/4" Cove

Lauan plywood

3/4"

5/16"

3/4"   2"   3/4"

3 1/2"

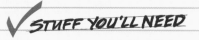
STUFF YOU'LL NEED

TOOLS: Hammer, pin driver or thin nailset, drill with Phillips bit, miter saw, tape measure, safety glasses

MATERIALS: Lauan plywood, 3/4" × 3/4" cove molding, 1⅝-inch Phillips drywall screws, 6d finish nails, 2-inch square tile, silicone sealant

Tile window casings enhance and complement kitchen or bathroom tile. Wall paint or wallpaper touch-up is not required when a new casing is at least as wide as the one it replaces. New casing should not project beyond the existing window sill that it abuts.

Remove the old casing, using a pin driver if you wish to salvage the wood. Replace the casing with strips of 5/16-inch lauan plywood. It's thin, but strong enough as a stable base for the tile and a nailer for the trim.

To hide the plywood edges and to avoid having to cut in the casing or wall joint, prime and paint the edges of the strips first.

Install the outside lengths of molding; use tiles as spacers to guarantee a perfect fit as you install the inside molding.

Paint or stain the molding before installing the tile. Install vertical columns first placing the tiles that need to be cut to fit at the bottom as shown above. Center the row of tiles across the top so tiles needing to be cut to fit fall at both ends of the row.

146

1 USE A PIN DRIVER OR THIN NAILSET to drive the finish nails most of the way through the window casing to allow salvage of the casings without damage.

2 REMOVE THE CASINGS. Cut through the paint with a utility knife where the casing and wall meet to avoid lifting the face of the drywall or wallpaper.

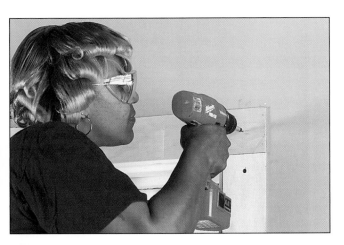

3 FASTEN STRIPS OF ⁵⁄₁₆-INCH LAUAN PLYWOOD in place of the wood casing with 1⁵⁄₈-inch drywall screws driven into the framing around the window.

4 MITER CUT THE COVE MOLDING. Purchase long lengths of molding. Cut, measure, and cut—each cut produces both an inside and an outside corner.

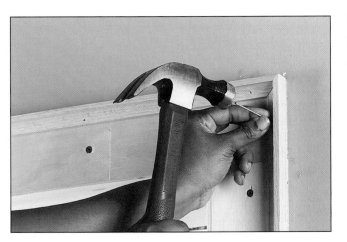

5 FASTEN THE MOLDING with 6d finish nails. Install the outside molding first. Use tiles as spacers to position the inside molding. Paint or stain the trim before installing the tiles.

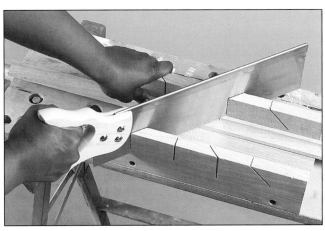

6 SET THE TILE with clear silicone sealant. Smear the silicone on the back of the tile, using only enough to achieve the bond so excess sealant won't squeeze out.

DOOR CASING ROSETTES

STUFF YOU'LL NEED

TOOLS: Tape measure, pencil, combination square, miter saw, backsaw, hammer, drill with Phillips bit, safety glasses

MATERIALS: Lauan plywood, ¾-inch square cove molding, brads, drywall screws, silicone sealant, two 3-inch-square decorative tiles

Install tile rosettes to decorate your door or window casings.

The design above uses 3-inch square tiles; use the size and design that fits your casings.

Prefinish the plywood edges to avoid having to cut in later when painting or staining.

Saw off the ends of the top door casing with a backsaw, using the inside edges of the side casings as a guide. If the remaining top casing is loose after removing the ends, drive 6d or 8d finish nails into the framing header.

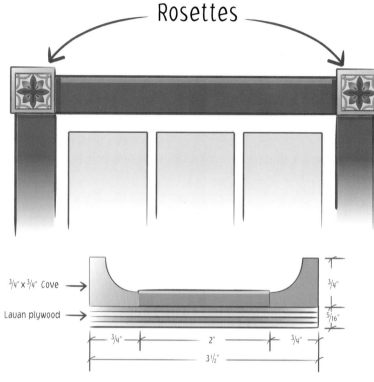

Rosettes

¾" x ¾" Cove

Lauan plywood

¾"

5/16"

¾" 2" ¾"

3½"

1 MARK and remove the ends of the top casing with a backsaw, using the side casings as a guide.

2 FASTEN COVE MOLDING to squares of lauan plywood to fashion frames; prefinish the frames.

3 ATTACH the frames to the framing beneath the drywall or plaster with several 1⅝-inch drywall screws.

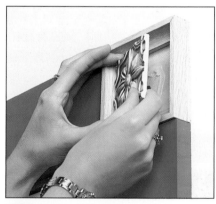

4 AFFIX THE TILE to the plywood with clear silicone, spread sparingly on the back of the tile.

MORE TILING PROJECTS

CHAIR RAIL

Pencil a line around the room at a height of 36 inches. Lightly sand the wall surface with 220-grit sandpaper. Starting at an inside corner, miter the corner pieces and affix them to the wall with ceramic tile mastic. Support each tile with masking tape for at least an hour.

If the wall is new, you can add blocking between the studs, backerboard, and a wood chair rail to protect the tile, as shown at right.

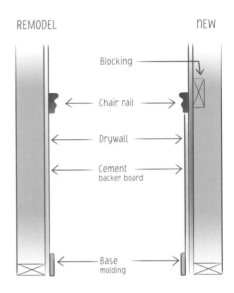

REMODEL NEW

Blocking

Chair rail

Drywall

Cement backer board

Base molding

1 **USE A 4-FOOT LEVEL** (or a laser level) to lightly pencil a horizontal line around the wall 36 inches above the floor.

2 **LIGHTLY SAND** the strip of wall above the pencil line with 220-grit sandpaper. Be careful not to raise the nap of the paper or to break through paint.

3 **MITER THE ENDS** of two inside-corner pieces of tile with a wet saw. Bevel a piece of wood at 45 degrees on a table saw for a tile-cutting jig.

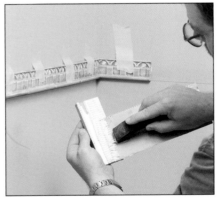

4 **APPLY CERAMIC TILE MASTIC** to the backs of the tiles and set them along the pencil line. Support the tile with strips of masking tape.

5 **IN NEW CONSTRUCTION** back the chair rail with blocking, and install backerboard under both drywall and tile, as shown. Wear safety glasses.

FRAMED MIRROR

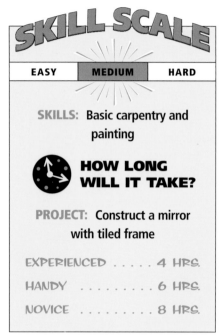

SKILL SCALE

EASY	MEDIUM	HARD

SKILLS: Basic carpentry and painting

HOW LONG WILL IT TAKE?

PROJECT: Construct a mirror with tiled frame

EXPERIENCED . . . . . 4 HRS.

HANDY . . . . 6 HRS.

NOVICE . . . . 8 HRS.

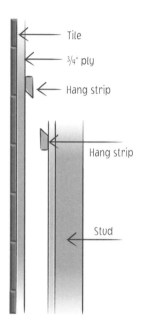

Tile

3/4" ply

Hang strip

Hang strip

Stud

✓ STUFF YOU'LL NEED

TOOLS: Tape measure, table saw, wet saw, drill with Phillips bit, caulk gun, paintbrush, pencil, safety glasses

MATERIALS: Assorted tile, ¾-inch plywood, two 1"×4" hardwood strips, beveled mirror, primer, silicone adhesive, Phillips drywall screws

MORE TILING PROJECTS

Select tile to frame any size mirror. Use the example above as a guide.

Lay out a beveled mirror and tile in modular sizes on the floor. Cut ¾-inch plywood as a base. Bevel a strip of hardwood at a 45 degree angle and attach it to the plywood and wall as a hanging strip. (If you want the mirror to hang vertically, attach a second strip to the bottom of the mirror.) Prime the plywood. Attach the mirror and tile with silicone.

1 **BEVEL-CUT TWO 1×4 STRIPS** of hardwood. Attach one piece to the back of the plywood base and the matching piece to wall studs.

2 **PRIME** the face and edges of the plywood. Arrange the mirror and tiles on the plywood. Trace the exact location of the mirror with a pencil.

3 **APPLY SILICONE ADHESIVE** in a serpentine pattern inside the mirror outline. While the silicone is wet, place the mirror within the lines.

4 **DRY LAY THE TILES;** then apply silicone to the back, one at a time. Press them into place. Grout the tile points if you desire a grouted finish.

150

STAIRCASE RISERS

Tiling stair risers originating at a tiled floor ties the tiled floor to the rest of the room. Choose tiles and colors for the stair treads to complement the floor tile.

You may need to trim the height of the tile and the widths of the two end pieces (make the two end cuts symmetrical). Since the height cut will be narrow, the cuts will have to be made with a wet saw (see page 33 for a description of its use).

You could also tile the surfaces of the treads. If you do so, however, the specifications will be more demanding:

■ the tread tile must be rated as a floor tile
■ the tile's coefficient of friction must be 0.6 or greater
■ the base should consist of at least ³/₄-inch underlayment plywood
■ the tile should be set in epoxy with no caulked joints

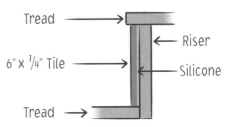

Tread → ← Riser

6" x ¼" Tile → ← Silicone

Tread →

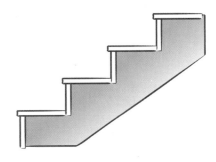

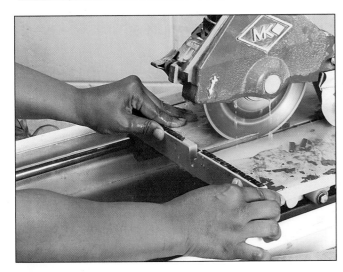

1 **CUT THE TILE TO HEIGHT** using a wet saw (see page 33). Before cutting, measure each riser to make sure they are all the same height. Lay a row of cut tile on a stair; shift until the ends are symmetrical. Mark the end cuts.

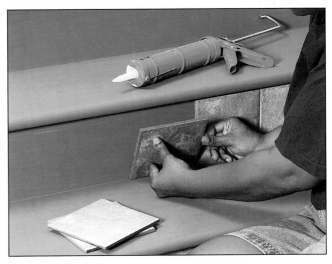

2 **APPLY SILICONE CAULK** to the back of each tile and press it into place. Apply sparingly to avoid squeezing out caulk. Use a damp rag to clean up any caulk immediately. Use the caulk gun carefully to avoid excess.

FIREPLACE SURROUND

SKILL SCALE

EASY	MEDIUM	HARD

SKILLS: Drawing to scale, cutting and setting tile and backerboard

HOW LONG WILL IT TAKE?

PROJECT: Installing a tile fireplace surround

EXPERIENCED . . . . . . 1 DAY

HANDY . . . . 1.5 DAYS

NOVICE . . . . 2 DAYS

✓ STUFF YOU'LL NEED

TOOLS: Tape measure, framing square, carbide scorer, wet saw, notched trowel, grout float, chalk line, felt-tip pen, safety glasses, dust respirator

MATERIALS: Tile, cement backerboard, thin-set mortar, unsanded grout, masking tape, 6d finish nails

ile dresses up a plain brick fireplace and can be substituted for brick in new construction at little or no additional cost.

After you form an idea of what you want to do, check local codes. Codes specify approved materials and the proximity of the fireplace opening to the mantel, trim, and other projections.

Make structural changes to the fireplace before you plan your tile design. You may wish to install a fireplace insert to increase heating efficiency. New tile can cover gaps between the insert and the old fireplace. Visit tile suppliers for inspiration. Ask them to show you what other customers have done.

Once you have the design on paper, lay the tiles out on the floor in front of the fireplace to determine how they will look and what cuts you will need to make. When you are ready, follow the steps in the photos.

See page 192 for information on how to contact the manufacturers of the tiles pictured on these pages.

1 **APPLY BACKERBOARD** to the face of the fireplace as a flat base for the tile. Use thin-set mortar without any latex additive as the adhesive.

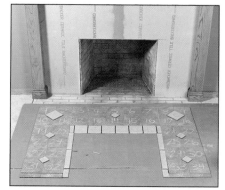

2 **LAY OUT** tile pieces on the floor to make sure the design will fit. When you are satisfied, number the back of each tile and note its position on the sketch.

3 **USE THE INSET TILES** as templates to mark the cut lines on the field tiles to fit the tile insets exactly.

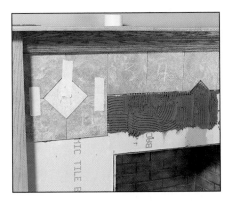

4 **SET THE TOP TILES** in thin-set, supporting the tiles with 6d finish nails driven into the backerboard. Support tiles below with strips of masking tape.

5 **USE BULLNOSE TRIM TILES** to finish the edges of the fireplace opening. The alternative is to bevel the exposed edges of the opening tiles.

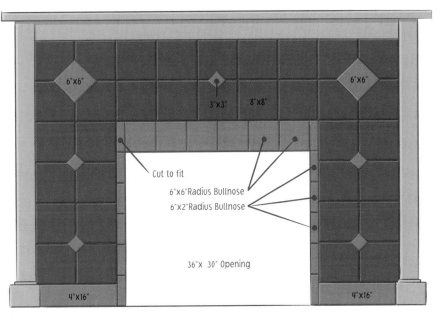

6"X6"   3"X3"   8"X8"   6"X6"

Cut to fit
6"x6" Radius Bullnose
6"x2" Radius Bullnose

36"x 30" Opening

4"X16"   4"X16"

FIREPLACE INSPIRATION

FIREPLACE HEARTH

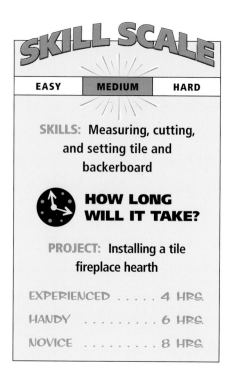

SKILL SCALE

EASY	MEDIUM	HARD

SKILLS: Measuring, cutting, and setting tile and backerboard

HOW LONG WILL IT TAKE?

PROJECT: Installing a tile fireplace hearth

EXPERIENCED	. . . . . 4 HRS.
HANDY	. . . . 6 HRS.
NOVICE	. . . . 8 HRS.

✔ STUFF YOU'LL NEED

TOOLS: Tape measure, framing square, carbide scorer, wet saw or circular saw with a masonry blade, ½"×½" square-notched trowel, ¼"×¼" trowel, grout float, chalk line, felt-tip pen, safety glasses, dust respirator

MATERIALS: Tile, cement backerboard, thin-set mortar, unsanded grout, sanded texture polyblend ceramic tile caulk, hardwood, 8d finish nails, sealer

Once you've tiled the surround, you may want to redo the hearth in the same or, perhaps, a complementary tile.

Consult with your local codes official for fire code regulations. Two areas of concern are the required dimensions of the hearth to the front and sides of the fireplace opening and the required thickness of the noncombustible hearth and its base. The safety alert at right lists the most common requirements, but check locally to make sure.

As with the fireplace surround, the hearth shown illustrates the principles involved rather than a code-approved design.

The design uses a double layer of ½-inch backerboard base. The double layer, mortared to the bricks beneath and to each other, adds fire resistance and stiffness to the base.

Before applying the first mortar bed, scrub the hearth to remove all traces of soot and ash. Apply and comb a thick layer of plain (latex additive would make the mortar less heat- and fire-resistant) thin-set mortar to the hearth with a ½"×½" squared-notch trowel. Let the first layer of backerboard set for several hours before setting the second layer in a thinner mortar bed.

Frame the backerboard with prefinished hardwood strips. If you have trouble finding hardwood strips to match the existing flooring, look in the Yellow Pages for a hardwood flooring installer, and see if he has any scrap tongue-and-groove strips of the same species. Rip the ¾-inch scrap into the desired dimensions and prefinish it to match your floor.

To prevent staining by soot, select floor tile with a smooth, nonporous finish. Set the tile in plain thin-set with no spaces. Wait 24 hours; apply plain unsanded grout. Use penetrating sealer to make cleaning the hearth easier.

1 CUT TWO STRIPS OF BACKERBOARD with a carbide scoring tool. The corner notches will have to be cut with a wet saw or a circular saw with a masonry blade.

UP TO CODE

CODES ARE SPECIFIC

Before you start tiling, you'd better make sure your hearth will meet the local code. Most codes require that the tile is distinguishable from the floor. Codes also specify the thickness of the noncombustible material of the hearth and how far the hearth must extend away from the fireplace opening.

Remember, codes exist to make sure you put in a safe hearth that provides a safe distance between the fire and combustible materials. Check with your local government building office to find the codes that are specific to your area.

2 USE MORTAR WITHOUT ADDITIVE to set both layers of backerboard. Apply the first layer with a ½"×½" square-notched trowel; the second with a ¼"×¼" trowel.

3 CUT AND MITER STRIPS OF HARDWOOD to frame the hearth. Match the species and finish if the surrounding floor is wood. Fasten the strips to the floor with 8d finish nails.

4 SET THE TILE in a bed on thin-set without additive. Fit the tile tightly to eliminate gaps, and caulk the joint between tile and wood strips with sanded-texture caulk.

5 APPLY UNSANDED GROUT WITHOUT ADDITIVE to prevent sparks from falling between the cracks. Remove excess grout, allow to cure 10 to 15 minutes, and clean away haze. Apply penetrating sealer liberally to keep the hearth clean.

MORE TILING PROJECTS

155

STOVE BASE

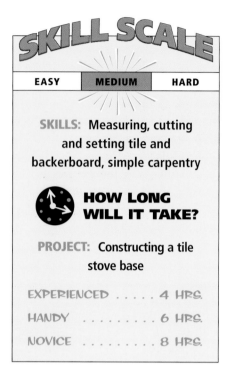

Tile is a popular material for stove bases because it is noncombustible, attractive, and easy to keep clean. Consult your local codes official before proceeding, however. If the official considers a stove base to be the same as a fireplace hearth, then the noncombustible base must be at least 4 inches thick. The exception would be for a stove with a heat shield attached to the bottom. Many stove manufacturers offer a shield as an option.

Cast-iron wood and coal stoves commonly weigh between 200 and 500 pounds. Because the immense weight is concentrated on four small feet, it is imperative that the selected tile be tough and that it be fully supported beneath with mortar and a stiff base.

The combination of ¾-inch plywood and ½-inch backerboard, mortared together with thin-set, provides the support and stiffness. Setting the base on strips of strapping lends the base the appearance of thickness, while creating a dead-air layer to retard downward heat flow. (The dead-air effect can be enhanced by stapling aluminum foil to the plywood.)

Don't let our choice of neutral gray tile intimidate you. This is your canvas! See what you can find at the tile store.

Although we used spacers between the quarry tile to emphasize the pattern, you may choose to eliminate the spaces, as is common in tiled hearths.

Finally, seal the tile and grout with a penetrating sealer so that they won't pick up soot and ash.

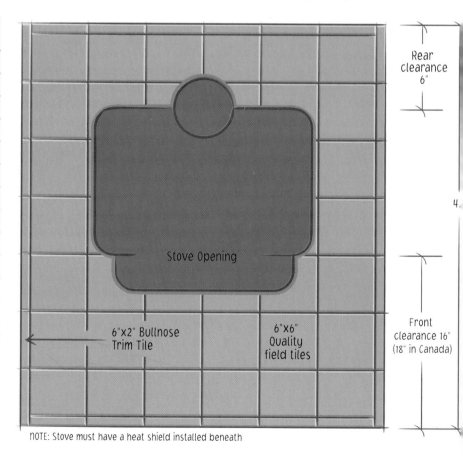

Rear clearance 6"

Stove Opening

6"x2" Bullnose Trim Tile

6"x6" Quality field tiles

Front clearance 16" (18" in Canada)

NOTE: Stove must have a heat shield installed beneath

1 **DRY-FIT** tiles and spacers on a sheet of ¾-inch plywood. Make the edges of tile and plywood flush; trace the other edges on the panel.

2 **FASTEN STRIPS** of strapping to the underside of the plywood with drywall screws. Space the strips 16 inches on-center and around the perimeter.

3 **CUT A MATCHING PANEL** of ½-inch backerboard, place it over the plywood, and snap chalk lines on its face along the wood strip centers.

4 **REMOVE THE BACKERBOARD.** Apply thin-set mortar without latex additive to the plywood using a ¼"×¼" square-notched trowel.

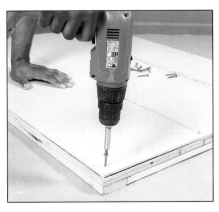

5 **PLACE THE BACKERBOARD** on the mortared plywood. Fasten with backerboard screws every 6 inches along the chalk lines.

6 **NAIL STRAPPING STRIPS** around the edges of the base as a temporary guide for setting the tile flush with the edges.

7 **SET THE TILE** in a layer of unmodified thin-set. Work from one corner outward, with the tiles flush against the wood strips.

8 **REMOVE THE STRIPS** after 24 hours and set back-buttered bullnose trim to the edges. Grout the joints and seal both tile and grout.

MORE TILING PROJECTS

GAS STOVE ALCOVE

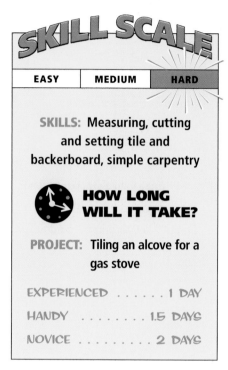

✓ STUFF YOU'LL NEED

TOOLS: Tape measure, framing square, carbide scorer, wet saw, drill with Phillips bit, notched trowel, grout float, chalk line, felt-tip pen, safety glasses, dust respirator

MATERIALS: Tile, cement backerboard, thin-set mortar, sanded grout, ¾-inch plywood, drywall screws, masking tape, tile spacers, finishing nails

Freestanding stoves, due to clearance requirements, take up a lot of floor space. If you don't want a stove to dominate the room and force the arrangement of furniture, a stove alcove might be the answer. The alcove shown is for gas stoves. An alcove for a wood stove would be similar, but would require the use of metal framing instead of wood. In either case, check local codes before proceeding.

Two things set this application apart from the tiling of a tub or shower enclosure (pages 94-97). First, a heat-resistant adhesive (thin-set mortar without latex additive) is used; second is the way tile is set on a ceiling.

The project assumes you have already constructed an alcove, sized to the stove and its clearance requirements, and built with conventional framing and drywall.

Begin by installing a panel of ¾-inch plywood overhead to provide a surface to accept the screws supporting the heavy ceiling tile panel.

Next construct a pre-tiled ceiling panel on the floor. Note that the spacing between tiles must be ¼ inch or greater to clear the heads of the support screws (drywall screws). After the tile has set, drill clearance holes for the shanks of the support screws at the four-way intersections of tiles. With help from an assistant, prop the panel in place overhead and screw it to the plywood.

The remaining operations are standard wall tile procedures.

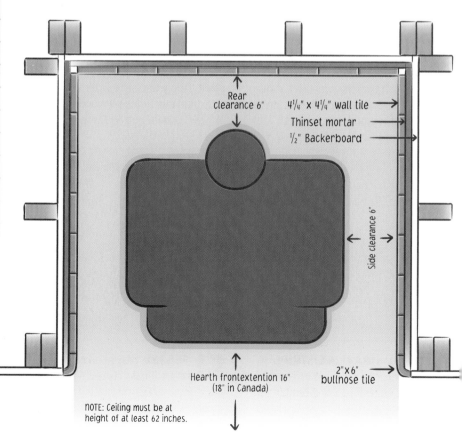

Rear clearance 6"

4¼" x 4¼" wall tile

Thinset mortar

½" Backerboard

Side clearance 6"

Hearth frontextention 16" (18" in Canada)

2" x 6" bullnose tile

NOTE: Ceiling must be at height of at least 62 inches.

1 **SCREW THE PLYWOOD** top panel to the ceiling joists of the alcove after sheathing the alcove walls with ½-inch drywall.

2 **CUT A BACKERBOARD PANEL** to match; lay out ceiling tiles with ¼-inch spacers, place the backerboard on top, and draw the tile trim lines.

3 **SPREAD AND COMB** unmodified thin-set mortar onto the backerboard panel with a ¼"×¼" square-notched trowel.

4 **SET THE CEILING TILES** on the mortared backerboard panel with the spacers. Make sure none of the tiles extend beyond the edges of the panel.

5 **DRILL ⅛-INCH HOLES** through the panel at the tile intersections nearest the panel corners and 8 inches on-center over the interior.

6 **PROP THE TILED PANEL** against the ceiling plywood, and fasten it to the plywood with 1¼-inch drywall screws through the drilled holes.

7 **APPLY ½-INCH BACKERBOARD** over the walls. Fasten with backerboard screws every 4 inches around the edges and 8 inches along the studs.

8 **SET THE WALL TILE** with spacers, starting at the top. Support the top row with finish nails and subsequent rows with masking tape.

9 **GROUT THE TILE JOINTS** with plain sanded grout, remove excess, allow to cure 10 to 15 minutes, and clean away grout haze. After removing the grout haze, damp-cure the grout for three days; apply penetrating sealer.

MORE TILING PROJECTS

159

STOVE HEAT SHIELD

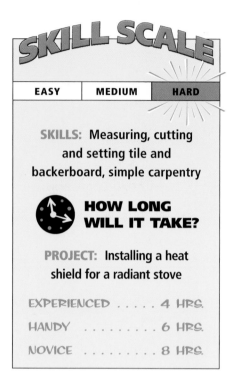

EASY	MEDIUM	HARD

SKILLS: Measuring, cutting and setting tile and backerboard, simple carpentry

HOW LONG WILL IT TAKE?

PROJECT: Installing a heat shield for a radiant stove

EXPERIENCED . . . . . 4 HRS.

HANDY . . . . 6 HRS.

NOVICE . . . . 8 HRS.

✓ STUFF YOU'LL NEED

TOOLS: Tape measure, 4-foot level, carbide scorer, wet saw, drill with Phillips bit, notched trowel, grout float, chalk line, felt-tip pen, hacksaw, safety glasses

MATERIALS: Tile, thin-set mortar, cement backerboard, sanded grout, hat channel or U-channel, strapping, drywall screws, self-tapping screws, 2×4 shim, tile spacers

A heat shield can reduce the required clearance of a radiant stove from the wall. All wood and gas stoves have designated clearances—with and without heat shields. Consult a stove dealer and local codes before designing a heat shield.

Key heat shield requirements are:
- noncombustible shield materials
- noncombustible shield supports
- specified free air space between the shield and the wall
- clearance at top and bottom of the shield to allow free air circulation

Begin your project by cutting a ½-inch panel of backerboard to the required size of the heat shield. Lay out tiles and spacers on the floor and lay the shield over them to mark the tile cut lines. Also cut three lengths of metal hat channel to the height of the panel.

Next, find and mark the centers of the studs in the wall behind the shield. Place a 2×4 shim at the base of the wall, and fasten the shimmed hat channel to the studs. Fasten the backerboard to the hat channel with wafer-head self-tapping screws.

Set the tile to the panel using heat-resistant (no latex) thin-set. Remove the shim and grout the joints.

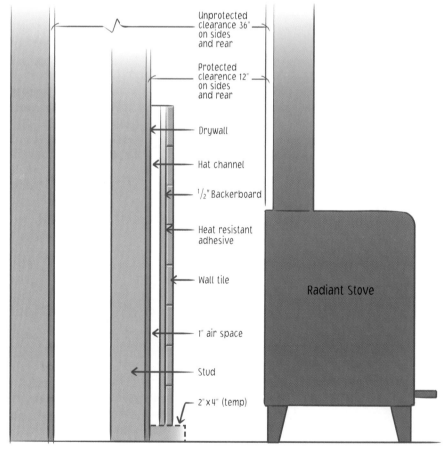

1 PLACE THE SIZED ½-INCH BACKERBOARD over a field of tiles and spacers on the floor. Trace the edges of the panel onto the tiles for cut lines.

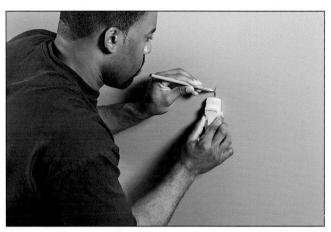

2 LOCATE THE CENTERS OF WALL STUDS in the area to mount the heat shield. Use a 4-foot level to draw a pencil line along the stud centers.

3 CUT THREE LENGTHS OF METAL HAT CHANNEL (or U-channel) with a hacksaw; stand on end on a 2×4 shim, and fasten to the studs with 2-inch drywall screws. Wear safety glasses when drilling.

4 SET THE BACKERBOARD ON THE 2×4 SHIM and use the 4-foot level to draw the centerlines of the hat channels on the face of the panel.

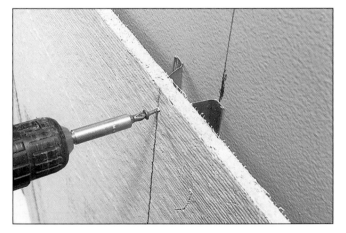

5 FASTEN THE ¼-INCH BACKERBOARD to the hat channel with wafer-head, self-tapping screws spaced every 4 inches. Drive the screw heads flush with the surface.

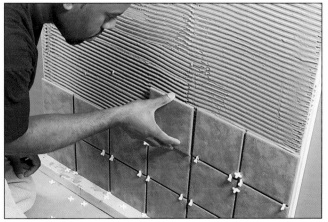

6 SET THE TILE in heat-resistant adhesive (unmodified thin-set mortar). After 24 hours remove the 2×4 shim and spacers, and grout the joints with unmodified sanded grout.

PLANT POT

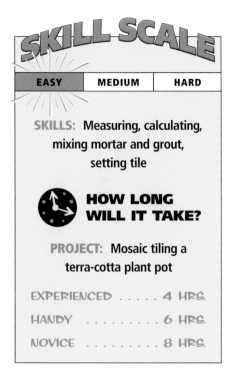

SKILL SCALE

EASY	MEDIUM	HARD

SKILLS: Measuring, calculating, mixing mortar and grout, setting tile

HOW LONG WILL IT TAKE?

PROJECT: Mosaic tiling a terra-cotta plant pot

EXPERIENCED . . . . . 4 HRS.

HANDY . . . . 6 HRS.

NOVICE . . . . 8 HRS.

✓ STUFF YOU'LL NEED

TOOLS: Tape measure, rubber or wooden mallet, tile nippers, V-notch trowel, margin trowel or putty knife, burlap bag, scrub pad, safety glasses

MATERIALS: Assorted glazed tile, 1"×2" surface bullnose trim tile, thin-set mortar, sanded grout with latex additive, terra-cotta pot

Making your own mosaic tile is fun, and applying the tile to the outside of a plain terra-cotta plant pot is the perfect use for it. The technique can provide hours of creative activity for parent and child, and it can convert a garden-variety planter into a piece of tile sculpture that complements your decorating scheme.

Select a terra-cotta pot. Although there is no minimum size for this project, choose a pot large enough to accommodate the growth of your plant so you won't have to repot right after you finish tiling.

Making mosaic tile yields about 50 percent waste and you will need about three times the surface area of the pot. Measure the height and the circumference of the pot top and bottom. Add the circumferences of the top and bottom together and multiply that figure times the height, then divide by two to get the surface area. (See formula at right.)

Check the sizes of the fragments you're making in step 2 below periodically until they average 10 percent of the bottom diameter. (A bottom diameter of six inches would require fragments approximately ½ inch in size.

Round the sharp points of the fragments with tile nippers, and lay out the pieces randomly to measure the area they will cover.

When you have enough, start tiling. Place the pot upside down and set unbroken bullnose tile the appropriate size around the rim. Next, set the mosaic tile over one quarter of the pot at a time.

Terra-cotta is porous, and soil is wet, so use latex additive in the mortar and the grout to make the pot more water-resistant.

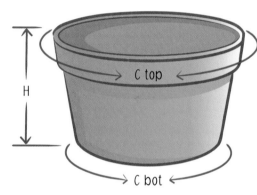

$$AREA = \frac{H(C_{top} + C_{bot})}{2}$$

1 **OBTAIN A TERRA-COTTA POT.** The pot can be any size—the larger, the simpler the project.

2 **PLACE WALL TILES** three times the area of the pot's exterior (see formula above) in a burlap bag.

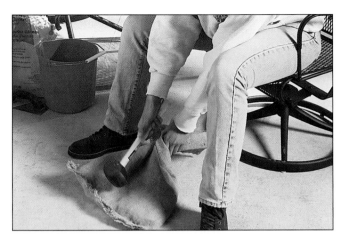

3 **POUND THE TILE** with a rubber or wooden mallet until the tile fragments are the desired size. Make the fragment diameter 10 percent of the pot diameter.

4 **ROUND THE SHARP POINTS** of the fragments using tile nippers. The mosaic will be most pleasing when the pieces are rounded like beach pebbles.

5 **TURN THE POT UPSIDE DOWN** and apply 1×2-inch surface bullnose trim tiles to the rim of the pot. Use a margin trowel or putty knife to back-butter the tiles.

6 **APPLY LATEX-MODIFIED THIN-SET MORTAR** with a $^3/_{16}$"×$^5/_{32}$" V-Notch trowel to no more than one quarter of the pot at a time.

7 **SET THE MOSAIC TILES** in the mortar. Lift the first few pieces to make sure the mortar is wetting both the pot and the tile. If not, scrape off the mortar and mix a wetter batch.

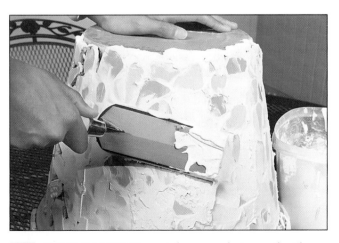

8 **AFTER 24 HOURS** grout the spaces between the tiles using a margin trowel or a 6-inch knife. Let the grout cure for 10 to 15 minutes then clean the tile surfaces with a plastic scrub pad and a soft cloth.

BIRDBATH

MORE TILING PROJECTS

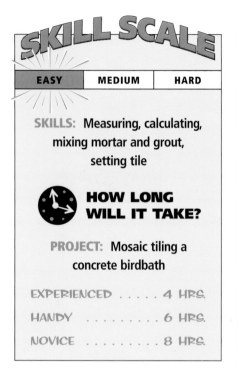

SKILL SCALE

EASY	MEDIUM	HARD

SKILLS: Measuring, calculating, mixing mortar and grout, setting tile

HOW LONG WILL IT TAKE?

PROJECT: Mosaic tiling a concrete birdbath

EXPERIENCED . . . . . 4 HRS.

HANDY . . . . 6 HRS.

NOVICE . . . . 8 HRS.

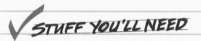

STUFF YOU'LL NEED

TOOLS: Tape measure, rubber mallet, tile nippers, putty knife, notched spreader, margin trowel or rubber spatula, burlap bag, scrub pad, safety glasses

MATERIALS: Assorted glazed tile, 1-inch-square bead tile, one art tile, latex-modified thin-set mortar, latex-modified grout, sealer

Birds will love this mosaic-tiled birdbath. Purchase a plain cast-concrete birdbath at a home center or garden supply store. Search local tile stores for decorative tiles to set in the bottom of the bath. After you have found the centerpiece, look for plain glazed wall tiles and 1-inch-square bead trim tiles to complement the decorative tile.

Calculate the area to be covered with mosaic pieces using the formula at right. Making mosaics results in about 50 percent waste, so purchase three times the area in plain tile. Make the mosaic pieces as shown on page 162.

Set the rim first. Back-butter 1-inch-square bead tiles with a putty knife and set them around the inside circumference.

Next back-butter the center tile heavily and press it into the bottom of the bowl.

Spread thin-set over half of the remaining area at a time with a plastic notched spreader, and set the mosaics. After 24 hours, grout the spaces using a rubber spatula. After the grout hardens, remove it from the tile with a scrub pad and seal the bowl.

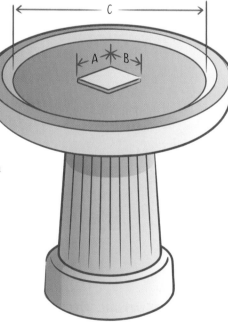

AREA = C×C − A×B

1 **MEASURE** the 1"×1" bead and the circumference of the rim. Mark the rim to take evenly-spaced pieces. Back-butter each piece with thin-set and set between marks.

2 **SELECT AN ART TILE** as a centerpiece—such as this entertaining frog. Back-butter the tile heavily and set it into the bottom. Remove excess mortar.

3 **MAKE A BATCH OF MOSAIC PIECES** by smashing glazed tile in a burlap bag (see page 162). Round the sharp points with tile nippers.

4 **APPLY AND COMB OUT LATEX-MODIFIED THIN-SET** with a plastic notched spreader. Cut down the spreader if necessary to conform to the curve of the bowl.

5 **SET THE MOSAIC PIECES** as tightly as you can while maintaining a random color pattern. Work quickly so the mortar doesn't stiffen before you finish.

6 **SPREAD LATEX-MODIFIED GROUT** in the joints with a margin trowel or a rubber kitchen spatula. Remove excess, allow the grout to cure 10 to 15 minutes then clean the haze away with a plastic scrub pad and soft cloth.

GARDEN BENCH

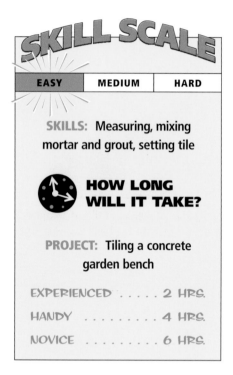

SKILL SCALE

| EASY | MEDIUM | HARD |

SKILLS: Measuring, mixing mortar and grout, setting tile

HOW LONG WILL IT TAKE?

PROJECT: Tiling a concrete garden bench

EXPERIENCED . . . . . 2 HRS.

HANDY . . . . 4 HRS.

NOVICE . . . . 6 HRS.

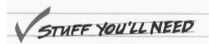

STUFF YOU'LL NEED

TOOLS: Tape measure, rubber mallet, combination square, wet saw, notched spreader, grout float, chalk line, pencil or felt-tip pen, scrub pad, soft cloths or rags, safety glasses

MATERIALS: Field tile, surface bullnose tile, surface bullnose down-angle tile (4), latex-modified thin-set mortar and sanded grout, 2×4 leveling board

G arden benches are widely available in cast concrete, and the flat surfaces beg for a personal touch!

The key to keeping the job simple is the availability of surface bullnose and surface bullnose down-angle trim tiles, which save smoothing edges.

Dry-fit perimeter tiles to determine which straight cuts you have to make to one or more interior rows. Once all the tiles fit, draw layout lines for the center field of tiles.

Set the center field within the layout lines first, using latex-modified thin-set mortar. Then set the perimeter tiles, aligning them with the previously set tile. Back-buttering the perimeter tiles saves cleaning excess mortar from the edges of the bench.

After 24 hours, fill the joints with latex-modified grout using a grout float. After the grout stiffens, clean the tile with a scrub pad and clean, damp rags. Apply a penetrating sealer to tile and grout.

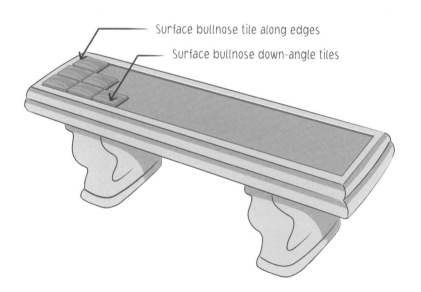

Surface bullnose tile along edges

Surface bullnose down-angle tiles

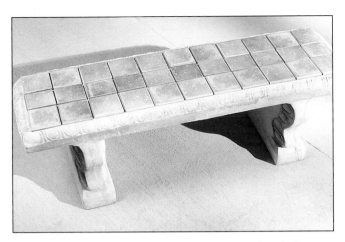

1 **DRY FIT** the tile to the bench top. Use surface bullnose tile along the edges and surface bullnose down-angle tile at the four corners. Cut interior tiles as needed.

2 **MARK THE LOCATIONS** of the dry-fit tiles with a pencil or pen. The only tiles you have to mark fully are the tiles along the center row.

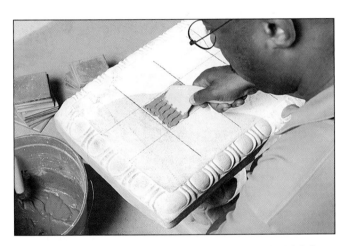

3 **SPREAD LATEX-MODIFIED THIN-SET MORTAR** for the center row of tile using a notched spreader.

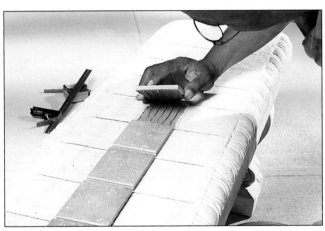

4 **SET THE TILE.** Place it straight down, twist it back and forth slightly, and align it with the marks. Place a short 2×4 board over the tiles and tap with a mallet to level the row.

5 **BACK-BUTTER THE REMAINING TILE** and set them with joints aligned with the center row joints. As you set, tap tiles level with the center row.

6 **SPREAD LATEX-MODIFIED GROUT** with a rubber grout float. When the grout is thumbnail hard (10 to 15 minutes), clean the tile with a plastic scrub pad and soft cloth, then apply sealer.

TILE NAME SIGN

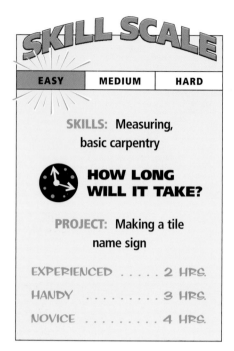

SKILL SCALE

EASY	MEDIUM	HARD

SKILLS: Measuring, basic carpentry

HOW LONG WILL IT TAKE?

PROJECT: Making a tile name sign

EXPERIENCED	. . . . . 2 HRS.
HANDY	. . . . 3 HRS.
NOVICE	. . . . 4 HRS.

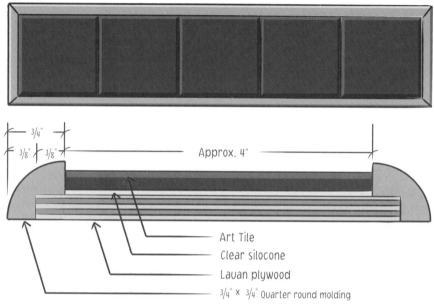

Approx. 4"

3/4"
3/8" 3/8"

Art Tile
Clear silicone
Lauan plywood
³/₄" x ³/₄" Quarter round molding

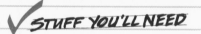

✓ STUFF YOU'LL NEED

TOOLS: Tape measure, table saw, paint brush, C-clamps or nails, pencil, safety glasses, dust respirator, ear plugs

MATERIALS: Animal alphabet tiles, lauan plywood, ¾-inch quarter round molding, carpenter's glue, silicone sealant, wood stain, polyurethane finish

The family name on a mailbox, a child's name on a bedroom door, or a piece of hanging art—all are made simple with animal alphabet tile. The project becomes a family affair when, under the family banner, you hang each child's name. Make each sign as shown, and string them together with pairs of screw eyes.

Start by laying out the name in animal characters. Fit the tiles tightly, using a straightedge to keep them aligned, and measure the total length and width.

Make a frame, as shown above, of ¾-inch quarter round molding glued to a backing of lauan plywood. Adjust the 4-inch dimension of the drawing above to fit the actual tile.

Prestain and finish the frame to prevent having to mask the tile later.

The tiles are attached with clear silicone sealant applied to the back of the tile.

THE ANIMAL ALPHABET

1 **LINE UP THE TILE** on a piece of lauan plywood with the tile flush with two panel edges; then hold a trim piece against the tile and draw the cut lines.

2 **CUT THE LAUAN PANEL** on a table saw. Make the panel ⅛ inch larger than the first marks. You can always trim it, but you can never make it larger.

3 **CUT THE ⅛"×⅛" RABBET** in the ¾-inch quarter round molding stock. Then miter the four corners to make the four sides of the frame.

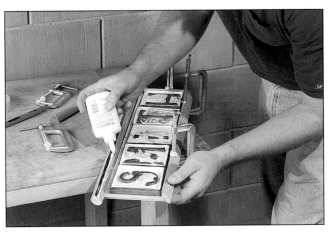

4 **GLUE AND CLAMP THE FRAME** to the lauan backing. Use carpenter's glue and C-clamps. If you don't have clamps, nail the trim from the back of the panel.

5 **FINISH THE FRAME** before setting the tile so you don't have to mask or clean up. For interior use, just stain; for exterior use, apply stain and water-based polyurethane.

6 **SET THE TILE** by applying clear silicone to the backs of the tiles and pressing into place. You can change the name later if you use contact cement instead.

WIND CHIMES

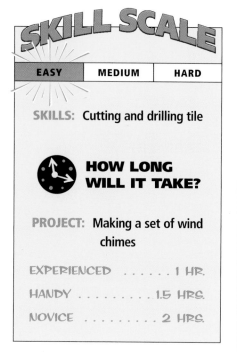
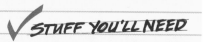

STUFF YOU'LL NEED

TOOLS: Wet saw, variable-speed drill, tape measure, masonry bit, 1¹/₂-inch foam brush, scissors, safety glasses, dust respirator

MATERIALS: Six 12-inch listellos, terra-cotta flowerpot, heavy-duty poly twine, large button, tube of superglue or silicone sealant, penetrating tile sealer, washer

Wind chimes are a simple rainy-day project for parent and child. All of the required materials are easily obtained. The only tool you may not have is an inexpensive masonry bit for drilling the holes.

This project used a 4-inch terra-cotta pot, available at any gardening supply outlet. These pots come in all diameters, from 2 to 24 inches. They also come in colorful glazes. Select the size and color pot which seems to fit your location.

We used five chimes, spaced every 2¹/₂ inches around the pot's perimeter. With a larger diameter pot, you would need to use more chimes because the chime spacing needs to be small enough for the wind to knock them together. Another combination that works is a 5-inch pot and 7 chimes spaced every 2¹/₄ inches.

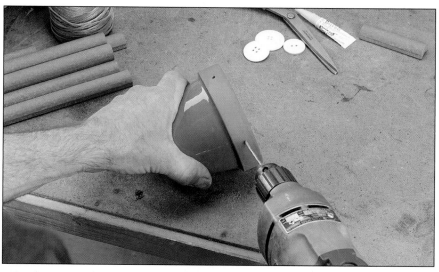

1 **MARK THE HOLE LOCATIONS** every 2¹/₂ inches (spacing depends on the size of the pot) around the rim of the pot and drill holes with a ¹/₈-inch masonry bit.

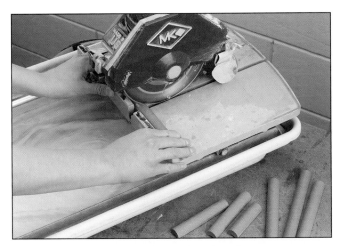

2 **CUT THE LISTELLOS** to various lengths on a wet saw. The lengths don't really matter because the chimes emit more of a clunk than a pure tone.

3 **DRILL HOLES** $1/2$-inch from one end of each of the listellos with the same $1/8$-inch masonry bit. Drill slowly so you don't break the listello.

4 **COAT UNGLAZED CHIMES** with a penetrating tile sealer to give them a sheen. We used unglazed listellos because a glaze will chip over time.

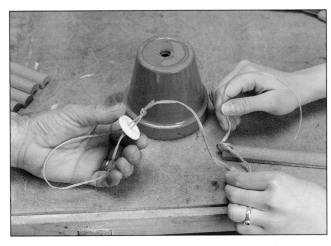

5 **TIE A BOWLINE** (ask any boater or Boy Scout) in one end of a cord and pass the loop through a button. Tie the free end to the center chime.

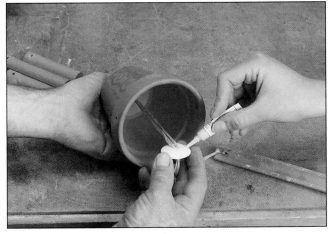

6 **THREAD THE LOOP** through the hole in the bottom of the pot; then apply glue or sealant to the face of the button and press a washer into place over the hole.

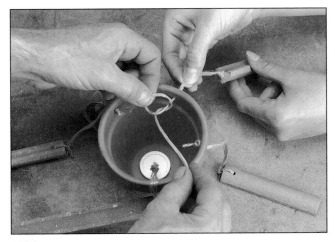

7 **STRING THE REST OF THE CHIMES** around the perimeter. Tie the overhand or figure-eight knots at the top so that the cords are all of the same length.

171

OUTDOOR CHECKERBOARD

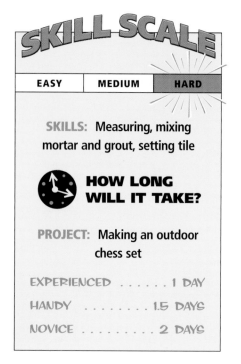

EASY | MEDIUM | HARD

SKILLS: Measuring, mixing mortar and grout, setting tile

HOW LONG WILL IT TAKE?

PROJECT: Making an outdoor chess set

EXPERIENCED . . . . . . 1 DAY

HANDY . . . . 1.5 DAYS

NOVICE . . . . 2 DAYS

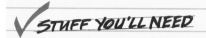

STUFF YOU'LL NEED

TOOLS: Tape measure, wet saw, carpenter's squares (2), straight-edge and clamps, notched trowel, margin trowel, scrub pad, rags, safety glasses, dust respirator

MATERIALS: 12"×12"-square marble tiles (1 black, 1 white), round precast concrete table or concrete mix, latex-modified thin-set, masking tape, bullnose tiles

If you like playing checkers under a shade tree in the summer, you will love this project. Don't be surprised if you get requests from your friends and neighbors to make one for them, too.

To find a round, cast-concrete table, look under "precast concrete" in the Yellow Pages, or pour your own from concrete mix.

Black and white 12"×12"-square tiles are used in the project above. For a subtle effect, pick nonstandard colors, such as brown and green.

Marble squares don't have to be exact dimensions. Judge the overall size of a checkerboard that would look best on the round tabletop, and set the wet saw at a straight edge to cut strips of one-eighth that size.

For the checkers, ask your tile

supplier to find 1-inch hexagonal mosaic tiles in red and black. Chances are they won't find red, in which case you'll have two choices: substitute another color, or paint 12 white tiles red.

1 **CLAMP A STRAIGHTEDGE** to the wet-saw table at the approximate dimension of the checkerboard squares from the blade.

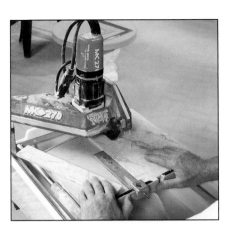

2 **CUT TILE STRIPS** using the clamped straightedge as a guide. Cut strips from half of the tile; turn the tile 180 degrees and cut the rest.

3 **CUT THE SQUARES** by passing the strips through the wet saw at 90 degrees. If the straightedge hasn't moved, the pieces will be squares.

4 **FIT THE SQUARES TOGETHER** using two framing squares to hold them in place. Cover the assembly with masking tape.

5 **MEASURE THE ASSEMBLY** and draw layout lines on the tabletop. Spread thin-set inside the lines with a $^3/_{16}$" $\times$ $^5/_{32}$" V-notch trowel.

6 **SLIDE THE TILE ASSEMBLY** from a thin panel onto the mortar. Press the tiles into the mortar with a flat object. Remove the tape after 24 hours.

7 **DRY-FIT SMALL SURFACE BULLNOSE TILES** around the table edge. When they are evenly spaced, mark the point where the joints fall.

8 **BACK-BUTTER THE EDGE TILES** and set them between the pencil marks. Edge tiles can also be a single color to make the table less busy.

9 **FILL THE GAP** between the checkerboard and the edge with latex-modified thin-set. Screed the mortar, then polish the surface with a steel trowel.

10 **AFTER THE MORTAR STIFFENS,** clean the tiles with a plastic scrub pad and clean, damp rags. After three days, apply penetrating sealer to the top.

ile is relatively permanent as building materials go, but it is not automatically permanently beautiful. To keep heavily used floor tile looking like new, you will have to periodically clean it and seal it. This may come as a surprise if you are a first-time tile owner.

Unless you have chosen a particular tile because it was natural and maintenance free and expect it to develop its own patina as it ages, you will need to do some periodic maintenance to keep your floor looking its best.

TILE NEEDS TLC, TOO

Grout is typically more porous than tile and so has an even greater need for sealing. Even if you don't seal your tile, do seal your grout as soon as it has cured. Being of uniform color, and usually light in color, it will immediately show stains and appear mottled.

With sealers you get what you pay for. Don't waste your money and time on surface coatings.

Go straight for a penetrating sealer which will soak down into the pores of the tile and grout and form a repository of protective armor.

Even a penetrating sealer will eventually evaporate, but the best (and most expensive) will require resealing once a year at most; the least expensive sealers will require resealing every few months, depending on traffic.

KEEP YOUR LEFTOVERS

If you have set your tile on a proper base, it will be fully supported from beneath. In all likelihood, however, someone will eventually drop a 400-pound cast iron stove and crack a tile. Make sure you have a few leftover full tiles stored away because there's no guarantee you will be able to match the tile a few years down the line. Equally important, save a little of the original dry grout in an empty paint can or a sealed glass jar so that you can match the grout when you repair or replace it.

CHAPTER SEVEN CONTENTS

176 **Maintenance**	*180* **Replacing Expansion Joint Materials**
176 Resealing	*181* **Diagnosing Cracks**
176 Removing Grout Haze	*181* **Isolating Cracks**
177 Removing Stains	*182* **Removing Ceramic Tile**
177 Removing Efflorescence	*183* **Replacing a Tile**
178 **Replacing Grout**	

MAINTENANCE

Some tile installations have been in place for a thousand years or more so it's safe to say that durability isn't an issue when it comes to choosing tile as a surface treatment for your home. However, that doesn't mean that a tiled surface is completely maintenance free. Sooner or later, you will have to remove a stain or replace, or reseal the grout. Following is an overview of basic problems that appear as the installation ages and solutions that will keep your surfaces in tip top shape.

RESEALING

Eventually floors and walls will have to be resealed to prevent moisture and stains from damaging the tile. Follow the tile manufacturer's recommendations for when to reseal. Tile suppliers offer a host of specialized products for sealing tile and grout. Topical sealers seal only the surface and can be worn away, leaving no protection. Impregnators penetrate the body of the tile and grout and can never be entirely worn away, although periodic reapplication is recommended.

A good penetrating sealer does not alter the appearance of tile or grout, yet forms an invisible barrier that repels water and stains. In spite of its water-repellent characteristic, however, it passes water vapor and will not trap moisture inside the body of the tile or grout where it might freeze and cause spalling.

Oil-based and epoxy sealers are the purview of professionals and are generally used only in high-traffic commercial applications. For residential use, apply at least three coats of a water-based penetrating sealer as soon as the grout cures.

REMOVING GROUT HAZE

If the haze is not bonded to the surface, it should come off with vigorous wiping with a clean cotton terry cloth (toweling). If that fails, try a commercial grout and concrete film remover. These products generally contain phosphoric acid, which dissolves the grout, so be sure to wear rubber gloves and eye protection. Remember that acids attack marble and limestone, so never use them on polished surfaces.

REMOVING STAINS

Don't let stains set or build up. Stains such as red wine act as dyes and are almost impossible to remove after they dry. **Never use bleach or strong cleaners on colored grout.** If the grout is stained, apply a stain-removing covering. For natural stone tile, apply a covering of plaster of paris with a mild hydrogen-peroxide solution and cover with plastic for 24 hours.

Many commercial tile and grout cleaners are safe for all grouts and tiles, including natural stones. Others contain acid, however, and will etch polished marble or limestone. Make sure your tile supplier knows what type of tile you are cleaning when you ask for guidance.

Follow these recommended practices to keep tile and grout looking like new:

■ wipe up food and spills immediately
■ keep the floor free of grit
■ reseal tile and grout as soon as you notice that water no longer beads on the surface
■ when attacking tough grout stains, apply the cleaner with a plastic scrub pad; let the cleaner act for 10 minutes, then scrub the grout with a stiff-bristled nylon brush. Rinse with clean water

REMOVING EFFLORESCENCE

Efflorescence is a surface deposit of mineral salts that has wicked up through the grout and appears as a powdery white deposit. To avoid having grout effloresce, mix it only with water that has a low mineral content. Also make sure the grout has fully cured—for a minimum of three days—before sealing.

To remove efflorescence:

■ wire brush the grout to remove loose deposits
■ saturate the area with clean water and let it soak for 15 minutes
■ mix 1 cup of sulfamic acid crystals in 1 gallon of hot water
■ wipe excess water from the grout and liberally apply the hot acid solution
■ scrub the grout with a stiff nylon toothbrush, let sit for 10 minutes; scrub again
■ wipe up the excess acid solution, then rinse with clean water
■ neutralize the remaining acid with a solution of ¼ cup of ammonia in 1 gallon of water
■ let the treated grout dry for 24 hours before sealing it with a penetrating sealer

REPLACING GROUT

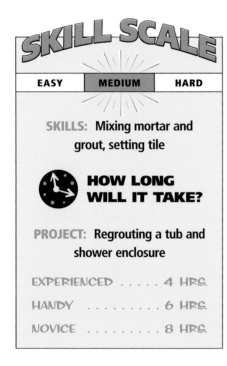

If grout begins to fall out, it means that the grout was improperly mixed or applied. Even worse, it could be that the wall behind the tile is moving, necessitating the removal of the tile and fixing the problem. In the former case, follow these steps.

If there is just a little grout to remove, use a utility knife or a grout saw, which is designed for the purpose. If you have a whole wall of grout to remove, see if you can get a rotary grinder with a diamond wheel. Do not use a screwdriver blade—the wedge-shape blade might dislodge a tile.

Clean out the debris with a toothbrush and wash down the surface to remove all dust. Let the wall dry completely before regrouting.

If the grout was colored, save some of the old chips and dust to try to match them to the colored grout samples at the tile dealer.

Mix dry grout with latex additive to make it stick better and be more water-resistant. Mix it with a margin trowel in a plastic container.

Apply the grout with a rubber grout float, forcing the grout into the joints. Remove the excess grout immediately by sweeping the edge of the float diagonally across the joints. When the grout resists denting with your thumbnail, scrub the grout from the tile with a damp sponge. Wipe the remaining haze from the tile with clean, damp cotton rags. Mist the grout several times a day for three days, then seal the tile and grout with a penetrating sealer.

1 **USE A GROUT SAW** to remove small amounts. Remove the grout to a depth equal to the width of the joint. Be careful not to scratch the tile face.

2 **A DIAMOND WHEEL** on a rotary grinding tool makes fast work of removing large amounts of grout.

3 **WASH OUT JOINTS** with water, let dry a minimum of 24 hours, then mix the grout in a plastic container using a margin trowel.

4 **APPLY GROUT** to the joints with a rubber grout float. Hold the float at a 45-degree angle to the surface of the tile, and press the grout into the joints.

5 **REMOVE EXCESS GROUT** with the same grout float. This time, hold the float at a 90-degree angle to the surface of the tile, and sweep it diagonally to the joints.

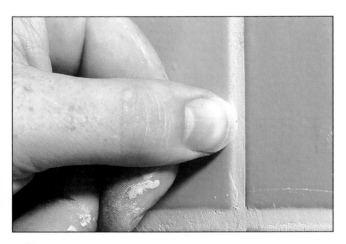

6 **APPLY THE THUMBNAIL TEST.** Wait 10 to 15 minutes (or follow manufacturer's instructions) until your thumbnail makes no impression in the grout before attempting to clean the surface of the tile.

7 **CLEAN THE TILE** using short strokes with a damp sponge. Avoid a wet sponge; too much water may change the color and strength of the grout.

8 **RINSE, RINSE, RINSE.** Keep the sponge as clean as possible. The water should be clean enough to drink; otherwise you are simply moving the grout around on the tile.

9 **REMOVE HAZE** with clean, soft rags. When the tile is clean, cure the grout by misting twice daily for three days. Seal the grout following the manufacturer's directions.

REPLACING EXPANSION JOINT MATERIALS

Expansion joints allow rigid masonry, such as concrete slabs, to be sectioned into smaller parts. Masonry cannot bend and, unless supported uniformly from beneath, will crack randomly. Expansion joints force (or at least encourage) the crack to occur in an ordered pattern. For slabs, place an expansion joint every 8 to 12 feet in both directions.

Another location for expansion joints is where tile meets wood.

1 **PULL OLD CAULK** and backer rod (if any) with needlenose pliers. Don't use a screwdriver because of the danger of unintentionally lifting the tile.

2 **INSERT FOAM BACKER ROD** into the joint with a putty knife. Select a diameter slightly greater than the crack, and press it below the surface.

Since wood shrinks and swells seasonally, an exposed joint between wood and tile floors allows the wood to shrink without opening a gap.

The obvious material to bridge and seal an expansion joint is silicone caulk. But caulk can stretch only if it is in a thin layer, not the full depth of the joint. The answer to this requirement is backer rod—a soft foam rope that fills most of the joint and backs up the thin layer of caulk.

When a caulk seal fails, it is best to replace the inexpensive, but critical, backer rod too. Pull up all of the caulk and backer rod with needlenose pliers. Never attempt to dig out the caulk with a screwdriver because the wedge-shape tip can exert tremendous pressure on the tile and break it free.

After blowing or vacuuming the joint free of debris, force new backer rod to a depth equal to the joint width with a putty knife, and apply fresh caulk. Apply only enough to fill the joint, and smooth it with a wet finger.

3 **CAULK** over the backer rod with silicone caulk. Use just enough caulk to fill the joint. Smooth the silicone with a wet finger.

DIAGNOSING CRACKS

Most concrete slabs have at least a few hairline cracks due to shrinkage as the slab cures and pose no problem. The cracks which cause failures of tiled floors are the cracks which are moving due to heaving or settling of the ground. If tile adheres to the concrete on both sides of the crack and the concrete moves, something has to give: either the bond on one side breaks, or the tile cracks.

There is a simple test to determine the nature of a crack: If the displacement of the two sides of a crack is strictly horizontal, it is a harmless shrinkage crack. If there is vertical displacement, it is an active crack.

Shrinkage cracks are going nowhere; ignore them and tile over them as if they didn't exist. Active—vertical displacement—cracks will continue to move after they are tiled. You must somehow

prevent the tile from bonding to the concrete on both sides of an active crack. The way you do this is by covering the concrete with an isolation membrane.

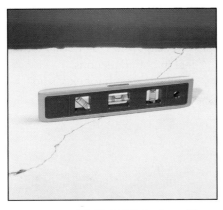

A SHRINKAGE CRACK is indicated by no vertical displacement across the crack. This crack probably occurred during the first year, as the slab cured.

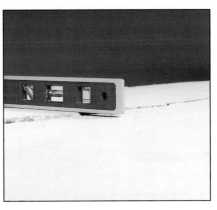

AN ACTIVE CRACK is indicated by vertical displacement across the crack. The cause is movement of the soil beneath, which will probably continue.

ISOLATING CRACKS

If the substrate beneath a tile floor shifts and cracks the tile above will crack as well. Unless you know the crack is stable (see "Diagnosing Cracks" above), tiling over it is not a good idea. You should find and repair what's causing the substrate to shift before you do any repairs or install a new floor. If the crack is reasonably stable, you can often isolate it with some form of bridging material which will relieve the stress on the tile.

ISOLATING MATERIAL FLOATS THE TILE

Materials are sold specifically as isolation membranes, although 15-lb. roofing felt (common tar paper) serves as well. Cut strips of felt about the same width as the tile, and center the strips over the crack. Use as many strips as necessary to follow the course of the crack.

Tile over the slab and felt strips. **Spread and comb thin-set over but not under the felt**. Set the tile as usual. When you grout the tile joints, however, fill the joints on both sides of the crack with silicone caulk. This way the tile over the crack is free to float, attached elastically to the tiles on both sides, but not to the slab beneath.

15-POUND ROOFING FELT (tar paper) is often used to isolate tile from active cracks in a concrete slab. Strips are centered over the length of the crack to prevent the thin-set from bonding the tile to the concrete and will prevent the tile from cracking.

REMOVING CERAMIC TILE

SKILL SCALE

EASY	MEDIUM	HARD

SKILLS: Hammering a chisel

HOW LONG WILL IT TAKE?

PROJECT: Removing a ceramic floor tile

EXPERIENCED . . . . . . 1 HR.

HANDY . . . . 1.5 HRS.

NOVICE . . . . 2 HRS.

You dropped your bowling ball on the kitchen floor and cracked a tile. Now what do you do? If you saved a few full tiles when you set the floor, you can replace the broken tile. Remove all of the grout with a grout saw. Then score the tile from corner to corner with a carbide scoring tool. Break up the tile with a hammer and cold chisel, and remove the adhesive. Then it's just a matter of buttering up a replacement, setting it in place, and regrouting.

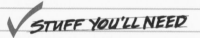

✓ STUFF YOU'LL NEED

TOOLS: Grout saw or rotary grinding tool, straightedge, carbide scorer, point punch, cold chisel, bricklayer's chisel, hammer, safety glasses

MATERIALS: None

1 **REMOVE THE GROUT** from around the tile using a grout saw or rotary tool. Score the tile diagonally with a carbide scoring tool and a straightedge. Repeat passes until the score is at least 1/16 inch deep.

2 **STRIKE THE CENTER** of the tile at the intersection of the score lines with a point punch. Wear protective goggles.

TOOL TIP

CHISELS WITH SAFETY GRIPS
You can buy cold chisels that come with plastic safety handles. It's not a bad idea. They will protect your hand from misplaced hammer blows.

3 **BREAK UP THE TILE** with a cold chisel and hammer. Strike all along the scored lines, which are zones of weakness.

4 **REMOVE THE ADHESIVE** with a bricklayer's chisel. You don't have to remove all adhesive, but enough to make room for the new thin-set.

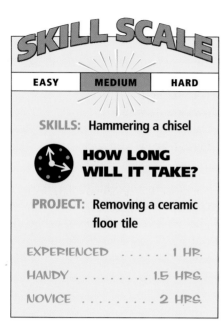

REPLACING A TILE

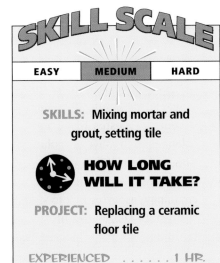

SKILL SCALE

EASY	MEDIUM	HARD

SKILLS: Mixing mortar and grout, setting tile

HOW LONG WILL IT TAKE?

PROJECT: Replacing a ceramic floor tile

EXPERIENCED ...... 1 HR.

HANDY .... 1.5 HRS.

NOVICE .... 2 HRS.

✔ STUFF YOU'LL NEED

TOOLS: Margin trowel, notched trowel, mallet and flat board, scrub pad, grout float, plastic container, mister, safety glasses, dust respirator

MATERIALS: Latex-modified sanded grout, replacement tile, penetrating sealer, thin-set mortar

After you remove the broken tile and all but traces of the adhesive, set the new tile. Make sure adhesive remnants are low enough so that the new tile is flush with adjoining tiles.

Mix a small amount of thin-set with latex additive in a small container. Let the thin-set rest for 10 minutes, then remix. Apply the mortar with the appropriate notched trowel (see page 36). Back-butter the replacement tile with the same trowel, and set the tile directly into the open space. Twist the tile back and forth as much as the space will allow; then align its edges and press down uniformly. Place a flat board over the tile and tap it with a mallet until it lies evenly and squarely with the surrounding tiles.

Remove excess mortar from the joints and let the mortar set for 24 hours. Grout the joints, clean the tile with a plastic scrub pad and dry rags, mist the grout for three days, then seal the grout with a penetrating sealer.

1 **MIX A SMALL AMOUNT** of thin-set with latex additive in a plastic container, using a margin trowel.

2 **SPREAD AND COMB** thin-set on the floor. Use the minimum amount required to wet the floor and comb with a ¼"×¼" square-notch trowel.

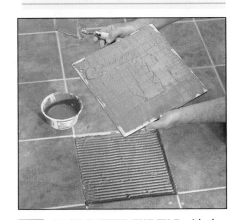

3 **BACK-BUTTER THE TILE** with the minimum amount of mortar required to wet the surface. Too much mortar will prevent the tile from lying flat.

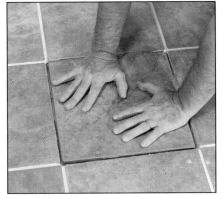

4 **SET THE TILE** in place and twist it back and forth. Tap it down with a flat board and mallet. Remove the excess mortar that squeezes into the joints.

5 **GROUT THE JOINTS.** After 15 minutes, clean the tile with a scrub pad. Mist the grout for three days. Apply penetrating sealer to the tile and grout.

MAINTENANCE AND REPAIR

183

GLOSSARY

Additive: chemical addition to mortar or concrete during the mixing process. Additives improve elasticity and aid in water and frost resistance.

ANSI (American National Standards Institute): Organization that provides information on safety in design and engineering.

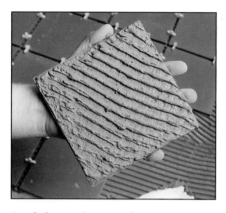

Back-buttering: applying mortar or adhesive to the back of a tile in order to increase the thickness of the setting bed.

Backerboard: *see cement backerboard.*

Back-mounted tile: a set of tiles connected on their back to facilitate setting in a uniform spacing.

Beating block: a flat board used with a mallet to set tiles at uniform height and to increase the adhesion between the tile and mortar.

Bisque: body of a clay-based tile.

Bond strength: the force required to separate tile and setting bed after curing.

Brick veneer tile: either real brick or concrete made in the shape of tile, but made to look like real brick when set.

Caulk: waterproof material applied as a viscous liquid, and turning into an elastic solid after curing, with the purpose of sealing a moving joint.

Cement backerboard: a rigid panel made of cement and sand and reinforced with fiberglass scrim. It is the ideal substrate for setting tile.

Cement-bodied tile: tile made of mortar instead of clay.

Ceramic tile: any tile made of clay or other nonmetallic minerals and fired at above 1,800 degrees F.

Chlorinated polyethylene (CPE) membrane: a heavy waterproof sheet material used under the mortar of a tile setting bed to either waterproof or isolate from movement.

Cleft stone: stone tile that is made by splitting natural stone, rather than extruding or sawing. The resulting stone is quite variable in thickness.

Coefficient of friction: the horizontal force required to slide an object horizontally across a surface, expressed as a fraction of the object's weight. A measure of slip resistance.

Control joint: a slot cut or cast into a concrete slab with the purpose of forcing the locations of any cracking.

Cove trim: trim tile formed with a concave face transitioning from floor or countertop to wall.

CTI: Ceramic Tile Institute of America.

Dot-mounted tile: tile in sheet form that is held together with dots of plastic or rubber between the tiles.

Down angle: trim tile with two rounded edges that form an outside corner of a countertop or other horizontal surface.

Efflorescence: a whitish surface deposit of minerals originating in mortar. The minerals in the mortar are dissolved and wicked to the surface where they are deposited when the water evaporates.

Expansion joint: a joint built into a tile or masonry surface to allow movement of the setting base without damaging the tile.

Extruded tile: tile formed by pressing clay (or other bisque) through a die.

Face-mounted tile: tile spaced and held together with paper attached to the face of the tile.

Field tile: tile that forms the main portion of an installation.

Freeze/thaw stability: the quality of being able to repeatedly freeze and thaw without deterioration. Vitreous tiles, which have virtually no pores to absorb water, are very freeze and thaw stable.

Frost resistance: one of six tile ratings appearing on cartons of floor tiles; a snowflake icon shows the tile is frost-resistant and is suitable for use in exterior freeze and thaw applications.

Gauged stone: stone tile cut to uniform stated dimensions.

Glaze: a decorative coating of silicates or metals and pigment fused to the face of a tile.

Glazed tile: a tile with a glazed face and often edges.

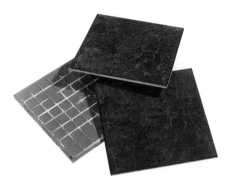

Grade: one of the six tile ratings appearing on cartons of floor tiles. There are three Grades: #1—Standard, suitable for most applications. #2—Second, structurally similar to #1, but with minor glaze or size imperfections. #3—Decorative, thin wall tile, suitable only for wall applications.

Green bisque: the material forming the body of a tile before firing.

Grip: *see bond strength.*

Grit: size of the particles in an abrasive; 100 grit would pass through a sieve of $1/100$ of an inch spacing.

Grout: a cement-based dry powder, mixed with water or other liquid, to fill the joints between tile.

Hang: the ability of uncured mortar or other adhesive to hold a tile in place on a vertical surface.

Impervious tile: tile that contains less than 0.5 percent voids. Such a tile is nearly waterproof and is highly resistant to freeze and thaw damage.

Inside corner: a corner where the angle between the intersecting surfaces is less than 180 degrees.

Isolation membrane: a sheet material or liquid used to separate a tile from its base to allow movement in the base without damage to the tile.

Latex-modified thin-set: thin-set mortar mixed with latex additive to increase flexibility, resistance to water, and adhesion.

Layout lines: lines drawn or snapped on a base as guidelines for tile placement.

Level: at right angles to the force of gravity. (A liquid will flow until it is level.) Also, a device to indicate when a surface is level.

Listello: tile meant to form borders around field tile. Listellos are usually long and narrow.

Margin: the perimeter of a tile installation.

Mil: one $1/1000$ of an inch. A common vapor barrier material is 4-mil polyethylene.

Mortar: a mixture of sand, cement, and water (or other liquid) used as a setting bed and adhesive to fasten tile to floor or wall.

Mosaic tile: tiles that are 2 inches square or smaller, usually packaged in sheets to facilitate spacing and installation.

Mud: jargon for mortar.

Nonvitreous tile: a soft, porous tile resulting from low-temperature firing. Since it absorbs at least 7 percent of its volume in water, it is not suitable for freeze and thaw conditions.

Open time: the predicted time after being spread before an adhesive forms a skin, and thus loses adhesion.

Organic mastic: a tilesetting adhesive based on petroleum products or latex. It is not as strong as mortar, but it does not require mixing.

Orthogonal: at a right angle.

Outside corner: a corner where the angle between the intersecting surfaces is greater than 180 degrees.

Paver tile: thick, low-fired tiles made for floors. Most are made in Mexico, Spain, or Italy.

PEI: Porcelain Enamel Institute. Also PEI Wear Rating—one of six tile ratings appearing on cartons of floor tiles. Wear Rating: 1, 2—not suitable for floors (walls only), 3—all residential, 4—residential and light commercial (restaurants, etc.), 4+—commercial and heavy traffic (airports, etc.)

GLOSSARY (CONTINUED)

Penetrating sealer: a sealer that penetrates tile and grout to form a long-lasting water and stain repellent.

Perimeter joint: an expansion joint around the edge of a floor, allowing for expansion of the floor without damage to the tiles.

Permeability: ability to transmit water vapor, measured in perms. A vapor barrier is any surface having a permeability of 1 perm or less.

pH: measure of acidity on a scale of 0 to 14. A pH of 7 indicates neutrality.
Plumb: vertical or perpendicular to a level surface.

Poly: common builder's term for polyethylene sheeting, often used to create a water or vapor barrier.

Polymer-modified grout or mortar: a grout or mortar mixed with latex or acrylic additive. The additive is sometimes in dry form in the bag of grout or mortar, or it may be a liquid to be added when mixing.

Porcelain tile: a ¼-inch-thick, high-density vitreous tile ideal for high traffic areas. Usually unglazed. Dye permeates the body of the tile.

Quarry tile: a ½- to ¾-inch thick tile ideal for high traffic areas. Originally natural stone that was quarried, quarry tile is now mostly extruded and fired clay in earth tones.

Radius trim (radius bullnose): a trim tile whose edge turns down and extends ¼ inch below the plane of the setting bed. It is ideal for trimming a field set on ¼-inch cement backerboard.

Reference lines: the two lines at 90 degrees that form the base for the grid of layout lines used in setting tile.

Retarder: chemical added to grout or mortar to retard the evaporation of liquid, slowing the curing process and increasing the strength.

Ridge-backed tile: tile with ridges on the back. The ridges increase the surface area and increase the strength of the adhesive bond.

Sanded grout: grout containing sand, which increases strength and decreases thermal expansion and contraction of the joint. It is used to fill tile joints over ⅛ inch wide.

Saltillo tile: terra-cotta tiles from Mexico having a distinctive rustic appearance. They are generally ¾ inch thick, yellowish brown, and sometimes contain animal tracks.

Screed: a straightedge seesawed across a pair of guide or form strips to remove excess mortar or concrete. Also, the act of using a screed to remove excess.

Sealant: elastic material used to fill cracks and joints, yet remain flexible. Similar to caulk, except generally more elastic and long-lasting.

Semivitreous tile: a tile that will absorb 3 to 7 percent of its weight in water. Because of the high absorption, such tile is not suitable for use in freeze and thaw environments.

Setting bed: a surface on which tile is set.

Set-up time: the time before an adhesive, grout, or mortar begins hardening after being spread on a surface.

Shower and tub pan: a heavy (usually 40-mil) waterproofing membrane installed below the mortar setting bed of a shower stall.

Sistering: adding a second element in parallel. To sister a joist is to fasten a second joist to the first, essentially doubling the size and strength of the first joist.

Slake: to allow grout or mortar to set after initial mixing. Slaking gives the liquid time (usually 10 to 15 minutes) to thoroughly penetrate the dry material before final mixing.

Spacer: *see tile spacer.*

Spacing lugs: projections on the edges of tile that result in a uniform, minimum joint width.

GLOSSARY

186

Square: forming a 90-degree corner. A square has four sides and four corners, each measuring 90 degrees.

Subfloor: the first layer of floor over the floor joists. When tiling, generally an additional underlayment is installed before setting the tile.

Surface trim (surface bullnose): a trim tile whose edge turns down to the plane of the tile body. *See also radius trim (radius bullnose).*

TCA (Tile Council of America): offers standardized information on specifications and installation of tile in the United States.

Terra-cotta: low-density tile made of unrefined natural clay baked at very low temperatures. Most are produced in Mexico and are used for flooring.

Thick-bed installation: tile set on a floated bed of mortar, rather than on thin-set mortar.

Thin-set adhesive: dry cement-based adhesives that are mixed with liquid before use. Thin-sets are stronger, more water-resistant and heat-resistant, and more flexible (if mixed with latex additive) than organic mastics.

Thin-set mortar: any mortar-based adhesive.

Three-four-five triangle: a triangle, the length of whose sides is in the proportion 3:4:5. Such a triangle always contains one 90-degree angle.

Tile spacer: a plastic cross shape, sold in a range of sizes as an aid in making uniform tile joints. Placed flat, the spacer controls the spacing of a four-tile intersection. Most tile setters use four spacers placed on end to achieve the same purpose, allowing the spacers to be removed easily.

Tone: one of six tile ratings appearing on cartons of floor tiles. A multishaded icon shows the tile has variations in tone. This is true of most tile, except for those of pure color, such as white or black. No tone variation is shown by all squares being the same shade.

Top coat sealer: a sealer that does not penetrate tile or grout, but rests on the surface. Also known as a topical sealer.

Trim tile: wall tile in a variety of shapes designed to trim the main field tile.

Trowel-applied membrane: a waterproofing membrane consisting of two layers of liquid latex with a layer of reinforcing fabric between.

TSP: Trisodium phosphate. A solution used to clean surfaces to prep them for painting or for mortar.

Tumbled stone: a natural stone tile with a rustic or antique look and rounded edges, usually marble sometimes slate, that is tumbled with an abrasive and often finished in an acid bath.

Underlayment: a solid, smooth surface nailed, screwed, or glued over a subfloor, on which tile is set.

Unsanded grout (also non-sanded): *see grout.* Used to fill tile joints less than ⅛ inch wide.

Up angle: trim tile with one corner that turns down. Used at the intersection in an inside corner.

V-cap trim: V- or L-shape tile used to finish the front edge of a tiled countertop. The tile edge is slightly raised to prevent water from running onto the floor.

Vitreous tile: dense, nonporous tile fired at high temperature. Vitreous tile is glasslike and contains only 0.5 percent to 3 percent air space. Because it absorbs little water, it can be used in freeze/thaw environments.

Waterproofing membrane: a waterproof layer under tile to protect the subfloor and framing from water damage.

INDEX

A

Adhesives. See also mortar; thin-set
  for countertops, 104
  for floors, 39
  mixing and spreading, 47, 62
  for patios, 122
  removing, 182
  for small projects, 138
  for walls, 80
Alcove, gas stove, 158–159
Alphabet tiles, 22, 168–169
Animal and bird motifs, 22
Aquatic motifs, 23
Art tiles. See decorative tile
Asbestos tile, removing, 45

B

Back-buttering, 29, 118, 184
Backerboard, cement, 184
  for countertops, 104, 108–111
  on drywall, 82
  fasteners for, 38, 110
  for floors, 38, 41, 46–49
  presetting screws in, 85
  scoring and cutting, 47, 84, 139
  for small projects, 139
  for walls, 80, 82–85, 95
Backer rods, 129, 180
Backsplashes, 106, 109, 144–145
Bathrooms
  children's, 22
  laying out tile floors in, 55
  safety bars in, 95
  shower and tub surrounds, 88–97
  shower pans, 66–71
  tile sizes in, 9
Benches, garden, 166–167
Birdbaths, 19, 164–165
Bird motifs, 22
Bisque, 8, 184
Bonding mortar, 80
Border Gallery, 17
Borders, 14, 21, 55
Brick, cement-bodied, 27, 119

C

Calibration of sizes, 9
Carbide tools, 30, 32, 35
Ceiling tiles, 158–159
Cement backerboard. See backerboard, cement
Cement-bodied tiles
  for floors, 27
  for patios, 119
  for small projects, 136
  for walls, 74
Ceramic tile, 184
  features, 28
  for floors, 26
  removing and replacing, 182–183
  sizes, 9, 28
  for small projects, 136
Ceramic tile mastic, 80
Chair rails, 149
Checkerboard tabletops, 172–173
Children
  motifs for, 22
  projects for, 162–163, 168–171
Cleaning tile and grout, 176, 177
Cleanup tools, 30, 37
Coasters, tile, 141
Codes, for fireplaces and stoves, 152, 154, 155, 156, 158
Coefficient of Friction Rating, 8, 12, 184
Color, designing with, 10–11, 63
Concrete slabs
  cracks in, 43, 123, 181
  joints in, 123, 125, 129, 180
  tiling over, 43–44, 123–125
Concrete walls, tiling over, 83
Control joints, in concrete slabs, 123, 125, 129, 180, 184
Corners, wall, 87, 95
Countertop tile
  base preparation, 106, 108–111
  grouting, 114, 115
  over laminate, 106
  laying out, 107
  marking and cutting, 112
  materials, 104
  project planning, 105
  sealing, 114, 115
  setting, 113
  trim, 100
  types, 100–101
Cracks, in concrete slabs, 43, 123, 181
Curves
  cutting, 34, 60
  mosaic tile for, 9
Cutting boards, in countertops, 100
Cutting tile
  countertops, 112
  curves, 34, 60
  floors, 59-60
  glass cutters for, 89
  holes, 34, 35, 60, 79, 89
  marks for, 57-58, 88–89, 112
  notches, 33, 59-60
  for small projects, 140
  tools for, 30, 32–35, 76, 78–79
  triangles, 13
  walls, 89

D

Decorative tile, 18–23, 74, 136
Decorative Tile Gallery, 20–23
Design elements, 7
  color, 10–11, 63
  layout, 50–56
  pattern, 7, 14–17, 53–54
  size, 9
  texture and shape, 12–13
Diagonal patterns, laying out, 53-54
Door casing rosettes, 148
Drywall, fastening backerboard to, 82
Dye lots, 10

E

Efflorescence, removing, 176, 184
Expansion joints, in concrete, 123, 125, 129, 180, 184

F

Fasteners, for backerboard, 38, 110
Field tile, 18, 184
Fireplace hearths, 154–155
Fireplace surrounds, 152–153
Flexible thin-set mortar, 80, 104, 122
Floors
  concrete, 43–44
  previously tiled, 45
  resilient, 45
  squeaky, 42
  wood, 41
  wood-framed, 42
  subfloors, 41
Floor tile
  base preparation, 41–49
  in bathrooms, 55, 66–71
  colors, 10–11
  over concrete slab, 43
  grouting and sealing, 63-64, 65
  guidelines, 29
  height transitions and, 40
  Home Depot ratings, 8
  in kitchens, 40, 51-52, 55, 56
  laying out, 50–56
  listellos, 14, 21
  materials, 38–39

INDEX

murals, 20
project planning, 40
ratings, 8, 28, 29
setting, 61-62, 71
in shower pans, 71
textures, 12
trowel size guide for, 36
types, 26–27
over wood frames, 42
Frost Resistance Rating, 8, 184

G

Gas stove alcove, 158–159
Glass cutters, 89, 184
Glaze, 8
Glazed tile, 184
for countertops, 100, 101
for floors, 26
sizes, 9
for small projects, 136
for walls, 74
Gloss finish, 12
Grade Rating, 8, 184
Granite, 13, 27
Grinding tools, rotary, 30, 32
Grout, 185
cement-based, 39
cleaning, 176, 177
colors, 10, 63, 114
contrasting, 9, 10, 11
for countertop tile, 104, 114–115
curing, 64, 93, 115, 131
discoloration, 177
estimating amount needed, 130
for floor tile, 39, 63-64, 65
haze, removing, 176
mixing, 64, 65, 97, 114
for natural stone, 27
for patio tile, 122, 129–131
removing and replacing, 178–179, 182
sealing, 39, 64, 65, 93, 97, 114, 115
for small projects, 138, 140
spreading, 65, 92, 97
stains, removing, 115, 176
tools for, 30, 36
types, 39, 80
for wall tile, 92, 97

H

Handmade tiles, 13
Hearths, 154–155
Heat shields, 160–161

Height considerations, for tile floors, 40
Holes in tile
cutting, 34, 35, 60, 89
marking, 58, 89
House name signs, 22, 168–169

I

Insets, marking cuts for, 96

J

Joint alignment, 14
Joints, in concrete slabs, 123, 125, 129, 180

K

Kitchens
countertop tile in, 100, 101, 105–115
decorative tile in, 19
floor tile in, 40, 51-52, 55, 56
mural backsplash in, 144–145
tile stove base in, 156–157

L

Latex additive, 80, 104, 122
Layout Gallery, 55-56
Layouts
countertops, 107
diagonal patterns, 53-54
floors, 50–56
patios, 124–125
planning, 50
small projects, 139
tools for, 30, 31
walls, 86–87, 95
Listellos, 14, 21, 185

M

Marble, 13, 27
Marking tile for cutting
countertops, 112
floors, 57-58
patios, 126
small projects, 140
walls, 88–89
Masonry walls, tiling over, 83
Mastics, 39
Matte finish, 12
Measurements
for floor tile, 50–53
for patio tile, 124, 125
tools for, 30, 31
for wall tile, 87, 95

Membranes, waterproof
seaming, 68
for shower and tub surrounds, 94
for shower pans, 67–69
types, 38
Mirror frames, 150
Mortar, 185
for floor tile, 47, 62
mixing and spreading, 47, 62, 90–91, 127, 128, 140
for patio tile, 127, 128
patterns, 29, 36
self-leveling, 44
setting of, 122
for small projects, 140
surface preparation, 43, 44
for wall tile, 90–91
Mosaic tile, 185
for birdbaths, 164–165
for curved surfaces, 9
features, 28
listellos, 21
for plant pots, 162–163
random, 138
in shower pans, 71
sizes, 9, 28
for small projects, 136, 138
trowel size guide for, 36, 77
Murals, 19, 20, 144–145

N

Name signs, 22, 168–169
Nippers. See tile nippers
Non-sanded grout, 80, 104, 122
Notches
cutting, 33, 59-60
marking, 58

O

Orthogonal, 185
Orthogonal lines, 52, 53, 56, 124, 125, 139
Outdoors, tile for, 26, 29, 118–119. See also patio tile

P

Patio tile
base preparation, 123, 125
cleft stone, 132–133
laying out, 124–125
marking and cutting, 126
materials, 122
project planning, 122

ratings, 118
sealing, 122, 129, 131
setting and grouting, 127–131
tools, 120–121
types, 119
Pattern Gallery, 15–17
Patterns
  as design elements, 7, 14
  diagonal, 53-54
Paver tile, 9, 185
PEI (Porcelain Enamel Institute) Wear
  Rating, 8, 185
Permeability, 185
Permeability to Water Rating, 8
Plant pots, 162–163
Plaster walls, tiling over, 83
Plywood
  as countertop base, 106, 108
  tiling over, 41
Pool surrounds, 19
Porcelain Enamel Institute (PEI) wear
  Rating, 8, 185
Porcelain tile, 185
  for countertops, 100, 101
  for floors, 26
  sizes, 9
  for small projects, 136
  through-body, 26
  for walls, 74
Primer, latex, 44
Project planning
  countertops, 105
  floors, 40
  patios, 122
  small projects, 138
  walls, 81

Q
Quarry tile, 186
  for countertops, 100, 101
  for floors, 26
  for patios, 119
  sizes, 9
  for small projects, 136
  for walls, 74

R
Ratings, tile
  for floors, 8, 28, 29
  Home Depot, 8
  for patios, 118
  for walls, 75

Reference lines, 186
  countertops, 107
  floors, 51, 52, 53, 55, 56
  patios, 124, 125
  small projects, 139
  walls, 87, 95, 96
Relief, raised, 21, 23
Removing tile
  asbestos, precautions for, 45
  from floors, 182
  tools for, 30, 37
Repeat, in patterns, 14
Replacing tile, 183
Rod saws, 30, 32
Rosettes, tile, 148
Rotary grinding and cutting tool,
  30, 32, 60, 76, 78, 103, 121, 137
Rough-textured tile, 12, 29

S
Safety
  asbestos tile and, 45
  tools, 30, 33, 37
Safety bars, in bathrooms, 95
Saltillo tiles, 12, 13, 36, 186
Sanded grout, 80, 104, 122
Saws
  hole, 32, 35
  rod, 30, 32
  wet, 30, 32, 33–34, 137
Sealers and sealing
  countertops, 104, 114, 115
  floors, 39, 63, 64
  patios, 122, 129, 131, 132
  small projects, 138
  types, 176
  walls, 80, 93, 97
Setting tile
  countertops, 113
  floors, 61-62
  small projects, 140
  tools for, 30, 36
  walls, 91, 96
Shapes of tiles, 12–13
Shaping tools, 30, 32
Shower pans, custom, 66–71
Shower surrounds, 90–97
Sink cutouts, 107, 108, 109
Sizes of tiles, 9
Slabs, concrete
  cracks in, 43, 123, 181
  joints in, 123, 125, 129, 180
  tiling over, 43–44, 123–125

Slate, 27
Snap cutters
  for countertop tile, 102, 103
  for floor tile, 30, 32, 35, 60
  for patio tile, 120
  for small projects, 140
  for wall tile, 76, 78, 79, 88, 89
Spacers, 62, 128, 129, 186
Spiral cutter, 32, 76, 78, 103, 121, 137
Stains, removing, 115, 176
Stair risers, 151
Stone, natural
  cleft, 132–133, 184
  for countertops, 100, 101
  for floors, 27
  honed, 13, 27
  installation tips, 29
  for patios, 119, 132–133
  polished, 13, 27
  for small projects, 136
  trowel size, guide for, 36, 121
  tumbled, 13, 27, 65
  for walls, 74
Stove alcoves, 158–159
Stove bases, 156–157
Stove heat shields, 160–161
Subfloors, 41, 186

T
Tabletops, 142–143, 172–173
Terra-cotta tiles, 186
  back-buttering, 29
  designing with, 13
  for floors, 27
  for patios, 119
  for small projects, 136
  for walls, 74
Texture of tiles, 12–13
Thin-set, 186
  for concrete slabs, 43
  for countertops, 109, 111
  described, 39
  latex-modified, 39
  mixing, 62, 90, 109, 111
  for patios, 122, 127
  for resilient floors, 45
  for small projects, 138
  for walls, 90–91
Thin-set mortar, 80, 104, 122
Tile grades, 8
Tile nippers
  for countertop tile, 102, 103
  for floor tile, 30, 32, 35, 60

for mosaic tile, 138
for patio tile, 120
for small projects, 137
for wall tile, 76, 78, 79
Tone Rating, 8, 187
Tools
    cleaning, 49
    for cleanups, 30, 37
    for cutting and shaping, 30, 32–35,
        76, 78–79
    for grouting, 30, 36
    maintaining, 30
    for measuring and laying out, 30, 31
    for removing tile, 30, 37
    safety with, 30, 33, 37
    for setting tile, 30, 36
Triangles
    cutting, 13
    reference lines and, 51
Trim, countertop, 100
Trivets, 18
Trowels
    for countertops, 102, 103

for floors, 30
for patios, 120, 121
size guides, 36, 76, 121
for small projects, 137
for wall tile, 76, 77
Tub surrounds, 90–97
Tumbled stone, 13, 27, 65

Underlayment, 151, 187

Vapor barriers, 85

W

Wallpaper, removing, 82
Wall tile
    base preparation, 82–83
    grouting, 92, 97
    insets in, 96
    laying out, 86–87, 95
    listellos, 14, 21

materials, 80
murals, 19, 20, 144–145
project planning, 81
ratings, 75
setting, 91, 96
in shower and tub surrounds, 90–97
trowel size guide for, 77
types, 74
Water Absorption Ratings, 8, 187
waterproof membranes
    seaming, 68
    for shower and tub surrounds, 94
    for shower pans, 67–69
    types, 38
Wet saws, 30, 32, 33–34, 137
Wind chimes, 170–171
Window casings, 146–147
Wood floors, tiling over, 41

METRIC CONVERSIONS

U.S. Units to Metric Equivalents			Metric Units to U.S. Equivalents		
To Convert From	Multiply By	To Get	To Convert From	Multiply By	To Get
Inches	25.4	Millimeters	Millimeters	0.0394	Inches
Inches	2.54	Centimeters	Centimeters	0.3937	Inches
Feet	30.48	Centimeters	Centimeters	0.0328	Feet
Feet	0.3048	Meters	Meters	3.2808	Feet
Yards	0.9144	Meters	Meters	1.0936	Yards
Square inches	6.4516	Square centimeters	Square centimeters	0.1550	Square inches
Square feet	0.0929	Square meters	Square meters	10.764	Square feet
Square yards	0.8361	Square meters	Square meters	1.1960	Square yards
Acres	0.4047	Hectares	Hectares	2.4711	Acres
Cubic inches	16.387	Cubic centimeters	Cubic centimeters	0.0610	Cubic inches
Cubic feet	0.0283	Cubic meters	Cubic meters	35.315	Cubic feet
Cubic feet	28.316	Liters	Liters	0.0353	Cubic feet
Cubic yards	0.7646	Cubic meters	Cubic meters	1.308	Cubic yards
Cubic yards	764.55	Liters	Liters	0.0013	Cubic yards

To convert from degrees Fahrenheit (F) to degrees Celsius (C), first subtract 32, then multiply by $\frac{5}{9}$.

To convert from degrees Celsius to degrees Fahrenheit, multiply by $\frac{9}{5}$, then add 32.

ACKNOWLEDGMENTS

T = Top, C = Center, B = Bottom,
L = Left, R = Right

Azuvi (International, Spain)
Phone: 34-964-50-9100
www.azuvi.com
21CL

Coastal Tile and Stone Co.
Phone: 207-230-0585
22CL, 22TR

Custom Building Products
Phone: 562-598-8808
www.custombuildingproducts.com
Tile and stone installation products
39, 80BR, 104BR, 122TR, 138BL, 174

Daltile
www.daltile.com
21CR

Elon Tile Stone and Bath
13 Main Street
Mt. Kisco, NY 10549
Phone: 914-242-8434
21TR

Foxhill Tile
Phone: 207-688-2245
20TL

Gray Birch Craftworks
Phone: 603-692-8301
142TR, 142CR, 142BR

Heirloom Tileworks
Phone: 207-729-9283
www.heirloomtileworks.com
*not all tiles are featured on the
website, contact them for more
tile information
18TR, 18BL, 18BR, 19TL, 19TR, 19BL,
19BR, 23TR, 23CL, 23CR, 150TC,
153BC, 153BR

Live Tile
www.livetile.cz
23BL

M&S Imports
Phone: 847-439-1995
21BL, 21BR

Shep Brown Associates
Phone: 617-935-8080
20TR

Surving Studios
Phone: 845-355-1430
www.surving.com
22BR

Swede Inc., dba Banan Appeal
Phone: 678-837-4551
65TL, 65BC, 65TR, 65BR

The Stem of Things
Phone: 920-380-0636
74TR, 144TR, 152, 153CC, 153CR

Tile Art Studio
Phone: 800-949-0170
145BR

Tile Craft
Phone: 843-856-0077
22BL, 23BR

Tilearts
Phone: 866-642-5760
www.tileartsinc.com
20BL, 20BR, 21TR, 145BC

Decided on a Project?

Start it <u>today</u> using The Home Depot® Consumer Credit Card.

GET INSTANT CREDIT*

The application only takes a few minutes and can be processed while you shop.

BUY NOW, PAY LATER**

Special defered billing offers throughout the year.

AFFORDABLE, CONVENIENT PAYMENT OPTIONS

Enjoy low monthly payments and the convenience of making your payments in any Home Depot store.

EXCLUSIVE TO CARDHOLDERS

Receive advance notice of special buys, promotions, and events.

BUY MORE, SAVE MORE

Special interest rate for all purchases over $2,000.

* Subject to credit approval.
** Interest may accrue.